VERBAL ABUSE

ABUSE

SURVIVORS

SPEAKOUT

On relationship and recovery

VERBAL ABUSE

ABUSE

SURVIVORS

SPEAKOUT

On relationship and recovery

Patricia Evans

ADAMS MEDIA CORPORATION
Holbrook, Massachusetts

Published by Adams Media Corporation
260 Center Street, Holbrook, MA 02343

ISBN: 1-55850-304-8

Printed in the United States of America

F   G   H   I   J

The names of correspondents and interviewees used in this book are not the names
of the actual persons. These names are fictitious.

This publication is designed to provide accurate and authoritative information with
regard to the subject matter covered. It is sold with the understanding that the publisher is not engaged in rendering legal, accounting, or other professional advice. If
legal advice or other expert assistance is required, the services of a qualified professional person should be sought.
     — From a *Declaration of Principles* jointly adopted by a Committee of the
American Bar Association and a Committee of Publishers and Associations.

COVER DESIGN: Peter Gouck.
REAR COVER PHOTO: Ruth Kadlec.

This book is available at quantity discounts for bulk purchases.
For information, call 1-800-872-5627 (in Massachusetts, 781-767-8100).

Visit our home page at http://www.adamsmedia.com

Table of Contents

Preface

The complexity of the problems facing us on both a personal and a global scale requires that we draw upon all of our resources and all of our potentials to bring increased balance and well-being to our planet. We might begin by assessing our own relationships. Certainly, the adult couple relationship presents us with an opportunity to develop the mutuality, cooperation, and balance of power required of peoples and nations to survive, not to mention the survival of our relationships, our families, and our institutions.

The desire of all of us to give our children a better, safer world cannot be fulfilled in an oppressive atmosphere, and yet the oppression of verbal abuse seems to have become rampant in our civilization. This oppression is maintained by demeaning, disparaging, and coercive verbal abuse. It is sometimes backed up by the threat of physical force and is so deeply woven into the fabric of our society it often goes unnoticed.

Oppression is mandated by a Power Over Life approach to life that moves against the thrust of life itself. Since life is expansive, changing, creative, and mutually supportive, moving against life is ultimately defeating. Alternatively, moving with the expansive, changing, creative, mutually supportive flow of life gives rise to Personal Power.

— *Patricia Evans*

Acknowledgments

I am grateful to all who supported me in writing this book. If women from all over this continent and from as far away as Peru and The People's Republic of China had not, with overwhelming candor and courage, told their stories and spoken their truth in letter after letter after letter, this book would not have been written.

To all who responded to the survey in *The Verbally Abusive Relationship, How to Recognize it and How to Respond*, (Adams Media Corporation, 1992), to all who sent notes, letters and journal excerpts, and to all who shared their knowledge of verbal abuse with others, I thank you very much. Please regard this book as my response to all of you.

I am indebted to my sister, Beverly Amori, for her support and research and I thank Robert Brownbridge, L.C.S.W., for his insights and his time as consultant to this work.

Lisa Fisher and Alina Stankiewicz, my publicists with Bob Adams, Inc., offered continuous encouragement and were outstanding in their dedication to bringing the issue of verbal abuse to the attention of the public. Many thanks also to Kate Layzer and Brandon Toropov, my editors, and Helen McGrath my agent and advocate.

Finally, I am especially grateful to my children for their enthusiastic support.

— *Patricia Evans*

Introduction

I receive between one hundred and two hundred letters and notes a month from the survivors of verbally abusive relationships. I read every single one. Some survivors had been so devalued and undermined that they have even requested *permission* to send their thoughts and feelings on this subject. Some letters are more than twenty pages long. As I read these letters, I am often overwhelmed by the suffering they express. Never would I have dreamt that there were so many, in so much pain, so silently enduring. I am moved by the spirit of their quest for understanding and freedom from abuse and I am grateful and touched that they have taken their time to tell me their stories. Often they do so, as they say, ". . . in case it may help someone else." It is my hope that the changes that they are making in their lives and the increased awareness that they are bringing to the problem of verbal abuse will create a healthier, more balanced society.

In *The Verbally Abusive Relationship: How to Recognize it and How to Respond* (Bob Adams, Inc., 1992), I discussed the categories of verbal abuse, the patterns of behavior that show up in a verbally abusive relationship, and the experience of the victims of verbal abuse. That book was based upon the experience of forty verbally abused women, and it brought forth a resounding cry from people all over this continent: "At last there is a name for the relationship I had never understood!"

Since 99 percent of the people writing to tell me of their experiences of being verbally abused have been heterosexual women, this book is about their experience. But even if you are in the minority of respondents, if you are a male, a homosexual, an elder, or a child living in the pain, anguish, and fear of a verbally abusive relationship, you may well recognize yourself in some of these stories. If you are on an emotional roller coaster, being put down, feeling confused, hurt, thrown off balance, experiencing frequent small shocks, feeling stunned, wondering how you could be hearing what you are hearing, wondering what you could have said or done, feeling isolated, being called names, disparaged or subtly cut to the quick, and you have sought to nurture and understand the relationship—if your experience was negated, the experiences of the women in this book will resonate with you. You have encountered a verbal abuser.

If you are or have been in any abusive relationship, you will understand the women who have written to speak out against the abuse they have suffered. Their experiences may validate you and their courage may hearten you. You may hear your own cry in the cries of those who tell their stories and shed their tears, sometimes in secret and sometimes in hiding.

Women have taken the time to write at length about how verbal abuse had circumscribed their lives within the narrow boundaries of self-doubt and paralyzing pain. The impact of hundreds of letters arriving every month is truly tremendous. Women write on flowered note paper, sheets of binder paper, yellow tablets; they type on little note pads and print out pages from computers, send pages of journals and pictures of family and even maps of where they live in hope of finding help near by. Almost all say, "I never knew anyone anywhere had a relationship like mine."

They offer their feelings, their lost hopes and their hopes renewed, their despair and their dreams, their pain and their joy, their questions and their answers, their confusion and their clarity. They offer volumes of documentation and express their desire to assist and the hope to be assisted. Many say, as in the words of one woman,

If I can be of help, if you need further information, if you need some more dreams—I have some good ones; if there is anything I can do, if you want to look at my journals, if it will help someone else, if you can use this idea, if others would benefit, if even one other person is saved from this nightmare, if you want me to expand on this, if you can use this, if you have a question, I pray I will make some difference. Don't hesitate to call or write.

— E.M., PALATINE, IL

Though they apologize for taking my time, I am grateful they gave me theirs. I can only share with the world what they have shared with me, sorting through it, looking for meaning, for patterns, and for purpose. I receive with gratitude their blessings and encouragement and much heart-felt support. In many ways this book is my response, that each may know the other on every page, that their words may strike a chord in every reader whether victim, witness, or perpetrator.

My first purpose is to offer the survivors, as well as those who are just now recognizing verbal abuse in their relationship, an opportunity to hear from many others who have had similar experiences. I hope that anyone reading this book who has suffered from verbal abuse in a relationship will recognize many kindred spirits. There are thousands of women who have recognized verbal abuse for what it is. In the unity of this time they have spoken out and they have begun the long hard process of gaining their freedom from the often subtle yet wholly pervasive oppression under which they have lived—some for fifty years or more. Many have taken a strong stand, some have left, some are preparing to leave, and some, with motivated and caring spouses, are seeing change for the better.

Women who have not seen good will and the intention to change on the part of their mates have begun taking steps toward either surviving more healthily within the relationship, at least for a time, or developing their resources in order to leave the abusive atmosphere. The effort of ending verbal abuse now by refusing to accept it, insisting on the abuser's accountability, and fine-tuning the antenna of awareness is bringing about what looks to be a significant change.

Here, excerpts from hundreds of letters present the reader with the experiential reality of the verbally abusive relationship, as well as giving witness to women's ways of coping, standing strong, moving out, and moving on. Furthermore, in order to bring into focus the specific categories of verbal abuse, I present these categories in an overview from the standpoint of *control*, showing that verbal abuse is, in fact, an attempt to control, to have Power Over, the other.

This book also reveals the results of a survey on the verbally abusive relationship, answering such questions as, "What are the most commonly experienced categories of verbal abuse in a verbally abusive relationship?" and "What percent of women in verbally abusive relationships are afraid of their mates?"

Finally a composite of women's insights for healing and recovery is presented. The recommendations and suggestions are designed to further the survivor's movement from survivor to creator, from wounded to healed, from part to whole, from disintegration to integration.

I wish you well on this journey, and hope this book will support and inform all those whose lives have been touched by verbal abuse.

Part 1

THE CHAPTERS THAT FOLLOW describe the typical survivor of a verbally abusive relationship and tell what she has to say about her experience, her relationship, her determination, and her resolution. The focus here will be on the issues of control that lie at the heart of every kind of verbal abuse. The objectives of abusers are discussed, and a method of analyzing and understanding control and abuse in a relationship is revealed through the analysis of an abusive interchange in a woman's journal.

Throughout, real women speak out about their increasing awareness and about the way they have been affected by this covert method of control. In letter after letter, survivors tell their stories. We learn how the survivor's integrity is threatened, resulting in self-doubt and lost confidence. We also learn more about how the survivors have come to terms with their experiences and how, with their new awareness, many are refusing to be blamed for the abuse that they suffer. We find many who feel trapped in their relationships, many who want better relationships, many who feel that their spirit is dying, and many who are making their plans for freedom from the abuse either by seeing changes in their relationship or by leaving it.

Chapter 1

The Survivors

It's very sad because I loved him very much. He's destroyed both my love of him and my trust in him.

— A Survivor

Deep within the human psyche, evolved over millions of years, are the eternally true, ever-present needs, drives, and desires that propel us through life's experiences. Because of this universality within the diversity of human experience, the suffering that abuse generates is both the unique experience of the victim and a universally felt pain. The differences between the kinds of abuse the partners of verbal abusers have suffered are chiefly differences in detail.

Every person who has shared her experience here has in many ways shared a common experience. The voices of the survivors seem to echo and merge in one voice seeking truth, understanding, and validation. Most alarming is the seemingly epidemic proportions of verbally abusive relationships, the significance of which has so far managed to escape public attention. There may be hundreds of thousands of women who suffer from, or have suffered from, verbally abusive relationships. A constant stream of letters, some fifteen to twenty pages long, from women from all over the United States and Canada gives evidence of this phenomena. These women, and *all* who recognize verbal abuse for what it is, are survivors of or witnesses to the oppression of verbal abuse.

Surely the creative and intellectual potential of each one of us can thrive best when there are no emotionally debilitating obstacles thrown in our path—obstacles such as verbally abusive diminishment and invalidation.

A woman who recognized the debilitating effects of verbal abuse wrote,

> *Like nearly every verbally abused woman, I don't want to leave, I just want him to stop abusing me. But I fear it will probably never happen because he believes he deserves the power and prestige he thinks he has.*
> — L.S., OAKLAND, CA

This writer touches on many issues. Women everywhere are confronting the dilemmas of not *wanting* to leave while facing the possibility of *needing* to leave to put an end to mental and emotional anguish; of wanting him to *stop* while realizing he may prefer his Power Over approach to the relationship. Unfortunately, there is the possibility that his will to control her, to have Power Over her, to dominate her, will override the prospect of *mutuality* in a loving relationship. If so, he is choosing to remain apart from her in a "place" where dominance and control over others reign and where one is either overpowering the other or being overpowered by the other. There is no mutuality in this "place." I call this "place" *Reality I*. Let me explain further.

Psychologically speaking, dominance and mutuality are worlds apart—so far apart, in fact, that those who seek to dominate or control another through the exercise of Power Over another might be said to be living in a different reality, Reality I. If you took a giant step up from Reality I, you would move into *another* reality, *Reality II*, where mutuality and cooperation prevail.

It is amazing how much projection (attributing one's own actions or attributes onto another) goes on in a verbally abusive relationship. One woman whose husband was cruelly abusive said that he called her not only a "nothing," a "zero," but also a "minus."

A woman of great courage and intellect, who had tried everything to bring harmony into her relationship, now faces the realization that *all* she had hoped for, *all* that she imagined might be there "if only she could find it," was not there. What was this *all* that was so ineffable, elusive, and long-sought? It was a kind and mutually nourishing relationship. Even without this she might have gone on if only the abuse had ended. She tells us with sadness and strength that,

> *After 50 years of verbal abuse it is almost impossible for me to determine which kinds of verbal abuse I have experienced the most—withholding, accusing, blaming, name calling, abusive anger, etc.*
> *I have been away for some weeks but am sure there will be a call "ordering" my return. I pray that I will have the courage to say "No."*

I just now am becoming able to discuss my abuse, but if there is anything I could do, or say, to anyone to prevent or to help, I am willing to come forward and speak.

— J.N., ATLANTA, GA

As painful as it was to realize what was wrong in her relationship, this woman like countless others, felt relieved to know that what had been unnamed was indeed real and had a name. The source of her pain was verbal abuse. Not only do the young, falling out of love and into the reality of abuse, find that they must leave their relationships; many mature women, some over sixty-five, are making this discovery.

The survivors write of their new-found clarity and increased self-esteem arising from their new understanding of what had been happening to them. They had lived in a world in which the abuse they suffered was not only unnamed and denied but was also subtly increasing, strangely intense, and usually unpredictable. These women suffered small shocks, confusing incidents, and frightening outbursts while the perpetrators said, in so many words, "What's wrong with you—making a big deal out of nothing." In this way their connection to the world about them, their *integration* with their environment, was shattered, leaving them with feelings of powerlessness and futility.

The gradually increasing intensity of verbal abuse was referred to by a man who wrote,

As painful as it is to say—I know and now realize that my two previous wives did the right thing by divorcing me. The water had been very warm for a long time before they finally crawled out too weak to jump.

— G.D., FORT WAYNE, IN

This man's former wives had gradually become accustomed to the increasing abuse, like a frog in the experiment in which the temperature increases so gradually the frog doesn't even realize it, and so boils to death. In this case, fortunately, they did become aware in time, and although it was very difficult, "crawled out too weak to jump." They saved themselves.

The following story from a survivor of a verbally abusive relationship reveals how verbal abuse can subtly, but with increasing consequences, undermine a woman's self-confidence and self-esteem *almost without her knowing it*. It also stands as a remarkably clear illustration of the similarity between verbal and physical abuse—both are attempts by the abuser to control his mate and both are devastating to the abused partner, not to mention the relationship itself. In this story all names and identifying circumstances are changed. The overall pattern of this story is so typical of the experience of the partner of a verbal abuser as to be nearly universal.

Story of Disintegration

It started out harmlessly enough. He said I had beautiful eyes and why didn't I wear a little eye shadow? And that skin! Look how the sun dries it out! A little moisturizer, maybe? He bought me some. He loved me in hats and long skirts and bare feet rather than the shorts and topsiders I was accustomed to; and once, after a dinner party, he scolded me for being too quiet. "You can be so charming when you want to be."

I admit it bothered me when he asked me why I didn't get the little mole on my shoulder removed and if it was too late—at thirty-five—to get braces to correct that crooked eye tooth. I protested meekly. "I don't think it looks that bad." I thought he was a little overly solicitous and possessive because he loved me—oh, perhaps a bit critical, but nothing I couldn't live with. He was so handsome and romantic. Devoted to me.

The first time he yelled at me, I "deserved it." An inveterate athlete, I was always on my way to a workout or just finishing up. He said I wore my running clothes to get attention. Short shorts, T-shirts, lycra biking pants. Didn't I see how men looked at me? I "flirted" with the gas station attendant. In fact, my very manner was "flirtatious." I was "too flip," too. My language was "unladylike." Why did I "persist" in talking with old boyfriends? "They're my friends," I said feebly. "They've been my friends for fifteen years."

"You're obsessed with them. You can't let go," he announced too loudly.

I was ashamed. Perhaps I was unconsciously flaunting myself. Self-consciously, I thought, "Me, in my late-30s hanging onto old boyfriends and flirting with teenagers in the supermarket. How embarrassing." I could feel the tears starting, as he continued to make his point, finally demanding that I be honest with myself, I was "obsessed with sex." And he left the house, slamming the door behind him. I vowed to behave better in the future. I felt dreadful.

We were on vacation in the islands when he lost his temper. We were at a club. He'd gone to get us drinks and a tall Rastaferian-looking native offered to show me the steps to a dance everyone was doing. When Bert returned to the dance floor, the native dancer and I were laughing at my clumsiness. What happened then made my head spin.

Bert stormed onto the dance floor, took my hand and pulled me out of the club, yelling at me. What did I think I was doing? What kind of behavior was that? Hadn't we been all over this before? He poked his finger in my face, backing me up against the wall of the building. He called me a whore. He said I was sick. Out of the corner of my eye, I saw people watching us.

He yelled at me all the way back to the hotel in the taxi, and when we got there, the driver opened the door for me. "If you need help," he whispered to me, "I will help you. You don't have to go in there with him."

I was sure he would calm down. He was jealous, that's all. But he didn't calm down. He ranted for hours. When I locked myself in the bathroom, he left and didn't come back till morning.

I had never been treated that way before. I came from a family who never yelled. My parents punished me by making me go to my room or sit in a chair by myself for five whole minutes. I had never been shouted at. Never. Not even during the ending of an early unhappy relationship.

I refused to see Bert after that. I even refused to sit next to him on the plane going home. But he was mortified and sorry. He sent flowers. He said "I beg of you. Come back." He said, "I love you." And I gave in. Six months later I married him.

Why is it that I like many others was blind? Is it only human to ignore things we don't want to see? Love is blind and all that. Then you add to "all that" the indoctrination of centuries: Try to understand the other person. Look at things from his point of view. He means well. Examine yourself. What are your shortcomings? Remember, "To err is human. To forgive is divine." I began accepting the unacceptable. After all, anyone who lost his temper so quickly and so violently must be a very unhappy person indeed. All I had to do was love him and understand him. He would soften.

He continued to be critical. In one week alone, I was told: I was "anal" about laundry, I had a "sycophantic" relationship with my son, I was "bossy," "impatient," "coarse" and "flip." I was a "pseudo-intellectual," I "made things up." I was "over-sexed," "rude" and "oversensitive." I had a "bad temper," I was "hysterical," "impossible to talk to," and "played the victim" to make others "feel guilty." And, because I ended up sleeping sprawled out on the bed I had "no respect" for his sleep. I was a "sucker" when it came to my friends. That was so painful—to hear that my friends didn't really like me because I was the one doing favors.

"No one ever does favors for you. You should examine that." he said.

"Why don't your friends really like you?" he pressed.

I didn't know.

Furthermore, didn't I have the "good taste to keep private conversations private?" I "whined" to my friends and ran "our dirty laundry out for the world to see" and made our private lives "the subject of gossip." So I quit talking to my girlfriends.

I was trying to adjust to living with another adult, I told myself. I'd been happily alone for ten years, and marriage was a big change. That must be the reason for my jumpiness. I was easily startled, quick to tears and frequently defensive. I tried to pay attention to Bert's needs and to listen to his suggestions about how I could improve myself. I took aspirin and Pepto Bismol at night, to calm my stomach so I could sleep. If I could just be sweeter, more devoted, more wifely.

Bert called several times a day, and when I wasn't at home or at the office, he asked where had I been? What did I buy? What time was that? When I asked him why he wanted to know, he said, "Just curious." But I started to postpone my errands until he came home from work so we could go together. When I had to go to the grocery store during the day, I often called him to let him know I was going, and he called me shortly after I got home. Finally, I recognized the feeling that was upsetting my stomach. It was guilt.

I recognized the jumpiness, that startled, apologetic manner. I'd seen it before, nearly ten years ago.

A woman who worked for me was a battered wife, but no one knew. She was small and thin. She never wore make-up or bright colors, always some dun-colored skirt and a blouse a little too big for her. She never looked at me. Usually I stopped and looked over her shoulder to say good morning and to ask how she was doing. She always nodded politely, but she never turned nor did she look up from her desk. Sometimes she smiled.

The quality of her work was fine, but her bad attendance and lateness affected her productivity. I had spoken to her several times, and each time, there was some extenuating circumstance—usually an accident or a sick child. Then she returned from a three-day absence and sat at her desk hiding the side of her face with an open hand.

I called her into my office. She moved slowly, looking at her feet, clearly ashamed and embarrassed. "Ella," I said, and gently pulled her hand away from her face, revealing bruises and cuts. She looked away.

"I fell down again."

She hadn't fallen. Someone had beaten her. It made me shiver. I closed the door, stood behind her and felt the indignation and rage as though it had been me. Who could have been brutish enough to strike Ella? She barely weighed one hundred pounds. While I tried to decide what to say to her, she covered her face with her hands and began to cry. "I just fell down again."

"No. You didn't." I touched her—left my hand on her shoulder. "Who beat you up?"

It took an hour to get the truth. She made me lock the door. She made me call the baby sitter to check on the children. She made me promise not to tell anyone.

For more than four years—and I checked the attendance records for absences and lateness—her husband had been beating her and threatening her. And she had taken it. Apologized for it. Felt ashamed of it.

It took me a week to get her to pack up and move to a shelter with her children. She pressed charges and successfully escaped her abuser. I was the only person she had ever told. She said it had felt as though she had been living in a dungeon all alone with a tormentor, and for some reason, it was all her fault.

I never really understood Ella. I didn't understand why she had stayed for so long, or why she hadn't told anyone, why she felt it had to be a secret, and why she hadn't stood up for herself.

I remembered all this late one night while I was standing in the kitchen drinking Pepto Bismol out of the bottle. This was a nightly trip to the kitchen. I'd become used to it. Out of nowhere, I'd remembered Ella.

The only difference between us was that her abuse was physical. I was college-educated, athletic, attractive and kind. So why was I sneaking out to drink antacid in the dark? Why did I allow my husband to back me up against the kitchen counter and scream at me?

Ella started a new life and in the absence of her abuser, she developed a personality and gained weight. She bloomed.

As for me, I finally said "no." I was not ever going to be yelled at again. He had to leave and he couldn't come back until he got help. He is getting help and he is back but the progress is slow. He is convinced he can just stop. Actually he has gone a few days without being really nasty. However, it's like living on a fault line: I never know when or what will set him off. I have determined to leave if he doesn't change soon. I am much more protective of myself than I used to be when I was younger and, I thought, tougher. Now I know just how fragile people can be.

In this story we see the partner's gradual loss of autonomy and the gradual disintegration of her integrity as her relationship or connection to her world, her reality, her truth, was split asunder. The loss of autonomy and the disintegration of integrity ensuing from verbal abuse will be discussed in the coming chapters as we hear from more survivors.

A key phrase in the story that demonstrates the partner's lack of knowledge, her complete ignorance of her mate's reality, her trust in him and her own growing self-doubt, is "Perhaps I was *unconsciously* . . ." Many partners, before recognizing verbal abuse, might have thought, "Perhaps I was *unconsciously* . . ."

> sounding unkind.
> trying to pick a fight.
> saying the opposite of what I thought I had said.
> making a mess.
> being thoughtless.
> acting smart.
> being illogical.
> flirting.
> trying to be right.

The partner's integrity gradually disintegrates from the small shocks of verbal abuse. What are these small shocks? How do they happen? And why is it so difficult to recognize verbal abuse?

In order to "experience" the answers to these questions, imagine, if you will, taking part in this drama with a verbal abuser. The curtain opens. The drama begins. You and your mate have gone out for Sunday breakfast. Your children are staying over at a friend's for a birthday party. Or you don't have children, or they are grown, if that is easier to imagine. You are seated at a table drinking coffee.

Although this scene is brief, in a strange way it never really ends because different versions of the dialogue continue. This is what the partner must survive. In this drama you are Ann. Your mate is Zee. If you are a male, please go ahead and imagine that you are Ann.

Ann and Zee are finishing their coffee when Zee scowls, turning toward Ann, a frown creasing his forehead. Earnestly, leaning toward her, he asks, "What are you looking at?"

"That bike out there. Why?" Ann asks, wondering about the scowl.

"Nothing. Forget it." He turns away—his shoulder almost between them, a shade of exasperation in his tone.

Wondering what happened to the conversation she thought they were about to have, she quickly thinks of a new topic.

"Well, how did the company game go last night?" she asks brightly.

"What do you mean, 'How did it go?' If you're trying to say, 'Did we *win*?' then just come out and say it." His tone of exasperation, now magnified, borders on contempt.

"I meant . . ." Ann's need to clarify, her feeling of inadequacy, her desire to express her interest in the game, and her frustration at not being able to say it "right" all merge as she is interrupted with,

"Will you quit interrupting? Damn! You ask me something and then you won't let me finish."

"Go ahead," she says. Pain floats through her, coming to rest behind her eyes.

"Never mind," he says, standing. "We're leaving."

She rises, not quite finished—too off-balance to care. There seems no way out of this labyrinthine dialogue.

He picks up the tab, moves to the counter, and says, "You want some cookies to take home? We'll take a dozen of those," he says, not waiting for her answer.

In the car Ann takes a deep breath. "I'm really trying, hon. When I asked you how the game went I really thought . . ."

"Do you have to rehash everything?" he interrupts angrily. "The discussion is *ended*. Okay!"

The day passes with no conversation between them except an occasional exchange: "I'm going to the store. Back later."

"Okay."

That evening he watches TV. In the kitchen, she takes a minute to catch up on family news on the phone with her mother.

He yells, "Do you have to keep making all that racquet!"

"It's not me. It's next door," she replies. "They're still moving stuff."

She, too, had heard the doors slamming and people talking.

"You're always on the phone," he yells.

Feeling uncomfortable, she tells her mother she'll call back later and hangs up.

She walks in at the commercial saying, "Honey, I'm not always on the phone and I feel I have a right to a phone conversation." She's in pain. *I try so hard.*

With anger and exasperation he says, "I'm sick of your arguing and always trying to be right."

"But I'm not," she says, stunned.

He rises. Faces her, staring hard.

His jaws are clenched angrily while he tells her, "You've always got to have the last word. You're not happy unless you've got something to fight about. I've had it with you." He turns up the TV.

Imagine being alone, trying to sort this out. Most partners of verbal abusers end up isolated in some way and are both alone and lonely. Imagine trying to explain the "conversation" to someone.

He asked me what I was looking at then wouldn't answer why. He didn't think I was specific enough. I couldn't get him to understand I'm not always on the phone.

Ann has been a victim of verbal abuse. Now, as a survivor, she has just recognized that she is in a verbally abusive relationship, and as she thinks about the previous day's events, she writes in her journal.

What happened yesterday?
What kinds of abuse took place?

Ann wrote down a key word or phrase about what was happening when she felt hurt, confused or frustrated. This is list A. Then, after each key word or phrase, she wrote down the kind of abuse taking place.

Ann's Journal

This is what happened yesterday morning.

A	B
He turns away.	Withholding
Come out and say it.	Criticism/Ordering
His tone of contempt.	Undermining
You interrupt etc.	Accusing & Blaming
Never mind.	Blocking & Diverting
We're leaving.	Ordering & Demanding
You rehash everything.	Accusing and Blaming
Said angrily.	Abusive anger
The discussion is ended.	Withholding/Ordering

Yesterday Evening	
You're making a racket.	Accusing & Blaming
You argue.	Accusing & Blaming
You have to be right, etc.	Accusing & Blaming
Being yelled at.	Abusive anger
Turned up the TV.	Withholding

[Ann saw that she was abused more than a dozen times. She continued in her journal.]

I used to think I always was "saying things wrong"—like I didn't ask about the game right, or like I shouldn't have asked him why he wanted to know what I was looking at—even when he looked so worried and upset. And how come he thinks I'm trying to start a fight?

Just like a physically battered wife I always used to think it had something to do with me.

Through her pain and anger she wrote,

I'm setting limits starting today. I'm telling him outright, No more verbal battering is acceptable. And when he says he doesn't know what I'm talking about I'll tell him, "No problem, I'll let you know every time."

I know what I need to do. I need to blow the whistle and hold up the stop sign a whole lot more.

Have You Adapted to Verbal Abuse?

Sometimes we become so adapted to being diminished, blamed, and discounted, the spirit of life at our center gradually grows dim while we, unaware, keep trying to make life better. If you want to determine whether you are adapting to abuse in your relationship without realizing it, try the following exercise. Record in your journal or a notebook an incident or two with your mate. Any conversations or exchanges that come to mind from the past week or so will probably work. Then exchange roles in your imagination. Imagine yourself saying and acting his part and him saying and acting your part. Then ask yourself,

❏ Does the conversation sound like a conversation between two friends?

❏ Is it easy for you to imagine talking *like* him? (Not necessarily *about* the same things. For example, you might substitute "a movie" for "a ballgame" if you have different interests.)

❏ Is it easy for you to imagine him talking like you?

❏ Does each of you show good will and an effort to understand the other?

❏ Is there any ordering or blaming going on?

Although verbal abuse is so prevalent that I cannot imagine that anyone has lived to adulthood without experiencing it, the *frequency* of verbal abuse in a verbally abusive relationship is astonishing. Furthermore, the devastating effects of verbal abuse in a relationship are so great that survivors often need extensive support and much time to recover. Overall, the survivor is engaged in a long, hard struggle to obtain freedom from oppression.

Strangely, considering the extreme pain and "reality warping" that verbal abuse engenders, it is in part culturally mandated by "might makes right" beliefs as well as discriminatory attitudes against women and various minorities. Even some men (certainly not all) who adamantly state that they believe in the equality of women still feel compelled to take a superior stance in relation to women, particularly to their mates. Abusive men stop at nothing to squelch, put down, correct, criticize, belittle, trivialize, ignore, snub, sneer at, and, when all else fails, put on displays of rage in order to dominate and control their mates. As one survivor wrote,

> I had four children and raised them almost alone to be strong, contributing citizens, two boys and two girls. I was like a "super mom" doing everything and I held down a job most of the time—My husband who was a financial success and was gone most of the time said, "As for work, you haven't done anything."
>
> — L.B., MEDFORD, NJ

Be assured that not all men are cultured to control, and that numbers of men stand strongly for the ideals of cooperation, equality, and mutuality. From such a man I received the following.

"The objective of verbal abuse is to destroy your partner in three ways: by diminishing her (making her less than she is), "thingifying" her (making a thing out of her) and threatening her." (From the List of Controlling Behaviors compiled by women of The Marin Abused Women's Services and by men in the Men Allied Nationally Against Living in Violent Environments [MANALIVE] Program.)

William J. Sherman, Director/Facilitator of the Napa, California, men's program furnished me with the MANALIVE List of Controlling Behaviors, which I will explore in future chapters. He pointed out that *"Had it not been for the courageous women in these types of programs* [abused women's services] *men would not begin to address their violence."*

His point is well taken. Verbal abuse is a form of violence and verbally abusive relationships appear to be very common. Across America, at all socioeconomic levels, this oppressive behavior seems to be passed on through the culture. Men, and women in some instances, may actually believe that they have a right to control and dominate and have Power Over others. This Power Over stance negates the basic meaning of human relationship.

The inequities in our society are only gradually being recognized and rectified. There is clearly an imbalance of power in our culture, and it appears to be reflected in personal relationships. The great number of women who have spoken out about their experiences as survivors of verbal abuse suggests that an unexpectedly large portion of our society has been living in an oppressive environment.

Inequity is the result of oppression, and so is abuse. Oppression originates with a desire to control another and is generally justified by a prejudice against the other. For example, the Native Americans were oppressed and called "savage." The Africans were enslaved and called "primitive." Women were kept out of many socioeconomic realms and called "irrational."

Few, until recently, have spoken out about oppression in relationships. For the most part, the victims of verbal abuse have lived in isolation—each thinking she was the only one who was suffering; consequently, each found it extremely difficult to define the cause of her suffering. The survivors have almost all been blamed for their suffering.

Now, with divorce rates so high and the incidence of domestic violence increasing, the entire question of *dominance, control,* and *oppression* requires particular scrutiny. At both a global and a personal level, dominance, control, and oppression create suffering.

When we address the issues of oppression, some primary losses come to mind: (1) the loss to the oppressed of human rights, among them the right to peace, the right to freedom, and the right to live free from harassment and fear; (2) the loss to all humanity of the human potential stifled by discriminatory practices; (3) the personal loss of self-confidence and self-esteem suffered by the victims of oppression; (4) the loss of autonomy; (5) the experiences of disintegration and loss of integration; (6) the loss to children of a stable home life.

Many of us may hold false beliefs about our abilities. We may have come to believe in unwarranted limitations because we learned limiting beliefs about ourselves in childhood. For example, most know the self-doubts that stop one from trying something new. These pale, however, in comparison to the limitations the abuser places upon his partner. Again and again survivors show us that the debilitating effects of verbal abuse are more painful and more limiting than any self-doubts they may have harbored from childhood.

Survivors tell us that verbal abuse always lowers self-esteem, no matter how much they may try to ignore it. *The survivors of verbal abuse consistently reported that they came to believe what they were hearing.* Eventually they believed that their goals and their activities were unimportant, or so very unremarkable that they could only serve as diversions, or were even somehow wrong, or certain to meet with defeat. Without realizing it, the survivors had "absorbed" limiting ideas and beliefs from their mates, adding these to the personal store of limitations they had "learned" in childhood long before the abusive mate entered the scene. Consequently, they frequently reported feeling trapped and powerless to act on their own behalf. Demonstrations of rage and anger on the part of the abusive mate added to their fear. To act for their own betterment and the realization of their potential became, for many, a kind of taboo.

A taboo is a prohibition, something proscribed by the society or culture, that carries with it an emotional sense of wrongdoing if it is broken—as well as the fear of dire consequences, such as being ostracized, condemned, or doomed. Some survivors felt powerless to take charge of their lives, almost as if they *knew* that they were not supposed to be in charge of their lives, that this too was a taboo. Some believed all along that they *were* in charge of their lives but that they just didn't have the energy or the confidence to undertake anything significant. Some lost the will or the motivation to proceed on their own behalf in their own best interests. And some nearly lost their will to live—all the time wondering what they were doing wrong.

Many of the survivors of verbally abusive relationships suffered not only the tremendous pain of verbally abusive rejection but also the frustration of being so confused by it that they were unable to give expression to their creativity, to make their way in the world and to become that which they were most capable of becoming. The survivor's personal loss is immeasurable. The loss to human society is unthinkable.

To live fully, creatively, and enthusiastically requires that the survivors of verbal abuse know fully what they have encountered and how many of them there are. With this knowledge they can break the taboos and bring about change.

Some survivors have developed satisfying careers and are fulfilling themselves in the world. However, within their relationships they have been unhappy, even despairing, and, until recently, unable to tell why.

Many who are, or who were, in verbally abusive relationships, could not talk about it because they did not realize what was wrong. Some were even asked by their counselors, "Why do you need a name for this?" Indeed, some survivors *are* counselors, saying, "Until now I did not know what was wrong in *my* relationship."

The women who share their experiences in this book are from every walk of life and every circumstance: women who grew up in happy homes, women who grew up in very difficult circumstances, women who enjoyed life, women who suffered much, women who achieved scholastically, women who barely got by, women who were well educated and women who were uninformed; of all these, none ever expected that the man who seemed to share her values, who said he loved her, who wanted to be with her, would act against her subtly, covertly, sometimes overtly, and always hurtfully.

These women are the survivors. Their awareness of their mate's hostile behavior was often clouded by the shadows of shock, confusion, and pain. With no context, no framework, no rack on which to hang their experience, it fluttered and folded and fell into an unclear and incomprehensible heap of words and feelings, foreign and frightening, not in keeping with and not fitting with reality as they knew it—*If you are kind, he'll be kind. If there is a problem, he'll want to talk it over with you. He is as happy for your achievements as you are for his. He'll always ask nicely if you do. He chose you because he loves you.*

In the next chapter, we will find that "I love you" may have meant "I want to get you and control you." In the verbally abusive relationship, *control* is the issue.

Chapter 2

Oppression and Control

I responded back with anger—the worse I felt the more satisfied he seemed!

— A SURVIVOR

This chapter discusses the manner in which a verbal abuser can dominate his partner by exercising control. Much of this information on control has come not only from the survivors of verbally abusive relationships but also from work done by women and men in programs that address domestic violence. Fourteen categories of verbal abuse are shown to be methods by which the abuser controls his partner in the relationship. Some survivors, familiar with these categories of abuse, have wondered "Why?—Why would he be sarcastic or critical? What exactly does that have to do with control? How do abuse and control fit together?" Let us take a look and hear from some survivors.

> *I began to wonder if the awful things he said were true. And I wondered why, if he had all bad things to say about me, we were still together after thirty-five years.*
>
> — L.R., DENVER, CO

> *It is so hard to accept that I am the kind of person who has allowed this to continue. What is it about me? I will take a stand. I will stop cringing. Then if he doesn't change, I'll walk away from it.*
>
> — S. L., MARIETTA, GA

These women are living in Reality II (seeking mutuality), and therefore find the abuse always shocking and incomprehensible. They, like many, tell us that this behavior drives a woman away, eventually, rather than "keeping" her in the relationship—eventually gives her the determination to leave. Abusers do not seem to be able to understand this or to change their behavior when their mates begin to protest. Generally they become more controlling and more abusive when their mates begin to protest.

By saying and doing everything possible to diminish her, the abuser seeks to feel superior to, and in control of, his mate, with the motivation that she become so downtrodden and powerless she would not be able to leave him—all the while remaining oblivious to the fact that his behavior may, over time, produce the opposite effect.

It is often with great difficulty that survivors have stood up to verbal abuse, because frequently they have become very, very downtrodden before realizing what has happened to them. They express their dismay and describe their experiences below.

> *I need to know more about how to think clearly in order to develop the self-esteem I need to go on with my life. I need to be stronger. I feel emotionally weak. I feel very hurt.*
>
> — A.V. LEVITTOWN, NY

> *I know I was verbally abused and I still think "but maybe I caused it!" At times I was reduced to almost a catatonic state when I could not think or function. This could last for several hours or occasionally up to a day.*
>
> — B.H. NORTH PALM BEACH, FL

> *How could he be so cold and cruel to me and so happy-go-lucky around others?*
>
> — S.B. DES MOINES, IA

> *My reading about abuse was done in hiding since I knew my husband would be explosive at seeing the title. He belittles all my self-help books and tries to undermine any beliefs I have.*
>
> — D.F. NAPERVILLE, IL

> *My verbal abuser has a high standing in government but when he sees something he doesn't like on TV or in the paper the slow rage would start, a comment or two, then he directs it towards me—the glare, the tenseness, the clenched jaw. Sometimes I think I see evil itself.*
>
> — L.D. VANCOUVER, WA

People who now recognize their own verbally abusive behavior have said that, until the moment they learned that disparagement of another, angry outbursts, ordering, and put-downs in general were abusive, they never for a moment realized that they were being abusive. They knew what they were saying but, like the rapist or the murderer, were unconcerned with the effects of their behavior. They almost always felt better after abusing.

Verbal abuse as a method of controlling another is found in every kind of relationship. Is there anyone who has not seen a parent verbally abusing a child with lost temper and feelings of being out of control? Is there anyone who has not seen or heard of bosses abusing employees, men abusing women, women abusing men, mothers abusing daughters, fathers abusing sons, and vice versa?

We are only beginning to learn about the dynamics of verbally abusive communications. However, with regard to female/male relationships we have already learned a great deal about the issue of control. Some abusers who are more overt abuse physically. Others, less overt and with different cultural/family backgrounds, abuse verbally. *Whether control is exercised verbally or physically, the dynamics are the same.*

> *Male role control works by physically, verbally or emotionally destroying your partner's physical and emotional integrity so that she will be afraid to be herself, will control herself and therefore be available to be controlled by you.*
> — (MANALIVE LIST OF CONTROLLING BEHAVIORS)

The survivors of verbal abuse have described verbally abusive mates who are very loud and explosive as well as verbally abusive mates who are so covertly controlling they seldom if ever raise their voice. One verbal abuser said, "I can cut her to the quick without even raising my voice." Although he was very verbally abusive to his wife, he said that he had "no clear idea as to why." He continued,

> *I have "written the book" on how one strategically tears down every ounce of self-worth in his wife. I'm pleased that I have not as yet lowered my sights on my child, and now that I recognize verbal abuse this may not occur. What I have become painfully aware of over the past few days—is how abusive I have been over the past ten years to my wife. It pains me to know how deep I have cut her over the years.*
> — W.O., WOODSTOCK, NY

Emotionally controlling behavior is implemented through verbal abuse, body language, and deprivation (withholding). These behaviors are "the way the abuser treats his partner." They are described to me by many survivors of verbal abuse, and these survivors describe ministers, laborers, corporate executives, therapists, lawyers, celebrities, business people, salespeople, the wealthy, and the poor.

Most verbal abusers seem to be unaware of the effects of their behavior, and generally, even when they are intellectually aware of the effects, they are unaware of *why* they are behaving abusively. The MANALIVE List of Controlling Behaviors, cited earlier, sheds light on this dark and unconscious realm. It states, *"The purpose of controlling behavior is to destroy your partner by depriving her of commonly held resources that are essential to her well-being and sense of integrity."*

The verbal abuser who controls one or more of these resources usually *combines words and actions.* Verbal abuse, then, becomes part of other controlling behaviors that are in general *undermining* to the partner. The methods of control that I discuss below are from the MANALIVE List of Controlling Behaviors.

Controlling Her Time

The abuser controls his partner's time by *usually* not showing up for appointments and by saying something like, "We never had an appointment," or by showing up, saying he's ready to talk or to do something, and then doing something else while his partner waits.

> *When I start to cry, or he knows I'm upset, he often snaps, "that will cost you five minutes more," and slows down.*
> — M.H., Greenwood, IN

The abuser may also control his partner's time by grandstanding, that is, monopolizing the conversation. If she tells him she is unhappy about the incident, he will usually deny it happened, discount her feelings, or accuse her of trying to start a fight. A survivor wrote,

> *I'd fix dinner. Then just before it would be time to eat he'd walk out the door—not a word and I'd have no idea when he was coming back. I could have made plans for the evening. If I asked him later why he hadn't talked to me or told me of his plans so I could have planned something for myself, he said, "Quit complaining, if I'd told you I was going out you probably wouldn't have wanted me to."*
> — G.C. Lansing, MI

This abuser was not willing to discuss or negotiate his plans. To do so would have been giving up total control.

Controlling Her Space

The abuser controls his partner's space by taking over shared space or intruding in her personal space. There are many ways to do this. Some examples follow.

- ❏ Controlling her social space by limiting her contacts with friends, for example, saying she's not home when she is, or by refusing to allow her to invite others over.

❑ Controlling her intellectual space by using elaborate arguments to wear her down in a discussion or by interrupting her.

❑ Invading her quiet time, for example, by talking to her when she wants to be alone.

❑ Invading her privacy, demanding details of her activities, or opening her mail or packages.

❑ Interrupting her sleep.

❑ Pressuring her to have sex.

The survivors refer to all of these issues frequently.

"He'd follow me from room to room yelling."

"He isolates me from relatives and friends by finding fault with them and ridicules me if I do see them."

Controlling Her Material Resources

The verbal abuser may control any one or all of his partner's material resources by *withholding* general information and financial information as well as by withholding money, or work which he has promised to do, often by "forgetting."

When I asked for the weekly household money, he'd usually give me part of it, claiming that he was momentarily short. I then had to ask a second time, and he'd get angry, that the timing is wrong, either he was busy with something else, or perhaps he just was relaxing with TV or newspaper and could it wait a little. I felt belittled.

— L.W. KIMBERLY, WI

Controlling with Body Language and Gesture

The verbal abuser uses body language to control his partner, just as he uses words. The words and gestures go together. In this way he uses *himself* to control his partner. Following are some hurtful and intimidating ways of controlling that are forms of *withholding* and *abusive anger*.

❑ Sulking

❑ Refusing to talk

❑ Withdrawing affection

❑ Strutting and posturing

❑ Stomping out

❑ Walking away

❑ Hitting something

❏ Kicking something

❏ Driving recklessly

Controlling by Defining Her Reality

When a verbal abuser exercises controlling tactics, he often attempts to shape his partner's reality. This form of control is very oppressive. When he tells his partner what reality is, he is playing God. Defining the partner's reality is a form of abuse that completely discounts the partner's experience by defining "What is true." Following are some examples.

That's not what you said.
That's not what you did.
That's not what happened.
That's not what you saw.
That's not what you felt.

Each one of these statements violates the partner's boundaries and is very verbally abusive. By defining the partner's reality, the abuser righteously declares that he knows more about his partner's experience than she knows herself. He is saying that he is right about what his partner said or did, or right about what happened, or right about what his partner saw, or right about what his partner felt. All he really knows is what he heard, saw, or felt; in other words, what he experienced.

By making himself right and her wrong, he has not only claimed Power Over her but also has violated her integrity by negating her experience.

We all perceive the world through all of our senses, and with the power of mind, we interpret these sensory perceptions. When the congruence between perception and interpretation are assaulted on almost a daily basis, the partner's sense of competence, integrity, and Personal Power are gradually eroded.

Just as she perceives in many ways, she also expresses herself in many ways. When her feelings, expressions, and thinking are denied validity, the assault on her integrity is unconscionable and destructive.

It is hard for many to imagine that anyone would attempt to tell someone else what they saw, felt, or said. One might expect to find this kind of abusive behavior only in a prisoner of war camp, where the perpetrators, in a depraved condition, have lost their sense of humanity and so perpetually attempt to brainwash their captives, telling them that they did not experience what they did experience.

Verbal abusers control, confuse, and throw their partners off-balance by

Reality Warping: I know I said it, but it's not true.

Demanding agreement: What I say is so.

Defining the truth: You don't know what you're talking about. (Only I know the truth.)

Controlling by Defining Her Motivations

When the verbal abuser defines his partner's motivations, he tells her why she has done what she's done as if he knew. Therefore he controls not only her perceptions, as we have seen earlier, but also her self-awareness. This is crazymaking behavior—behavior that can leave the partner feeling off-balance and confused. Tactics such as "You're just trying to be right," or "You're just looking for a fight" destroy the partner's integrity. In his "heart and soul," the abuser knows his partner is not trying to start a fight.

On the other hand, his partner believes that her mate is rational and that something she has done has caused him to believe that she isn't committed to understanding, indeed, isn't dedicated with all her being to understanding. Consequently, she wonders why she can't figure out why he thinks she wants to fight. *There is no correspondence between what she is communicating and what he is telling her she is communicating.*

A survivor of verbal abuse wrote about the experience of having her motivations defined by her mate.

> *He asked me to shop around for the best interest rate for a bank deposit that was maturing; I did. Later after dinner I stayed up to watch a TV program. He went to bed ahead of me. After a while he came downstairs raging that we could be out fifty dollars because I chose a bank for its proximity—not for the best rate. This was, of course, a lie.*
>
> *He shouted and yelled as usual but this time he foamed at the mouth. The foaming really scared me. He was like I have read about animals that go mad, and foam at the mouth. To this day the memory of these incidents preys on me. I do not seem able to erase them. There were many more, too many to list.*
>
> — M.A., ROCHESTER, NY

Controlling by Making Her Responsible

By telling his partner she is responsible for his behavior, the verbal abuser attempts to avoid all responsibility for his behavior. In other words, he avoids accountability for his behavior by *blaming* and thus stays in control. He doesn't have to change.

I did it because of you.

I did it because of what happened.

I said it because you made me mad.
I said it because of what happened.
You make me want to _____ you.

A more subtle way of making his partner responsible is pointing out something as if she were responsible for it by saying in an angry and accusatory way.

What's that doing there!
How did this happen!

In this way the abuser tries to coerce her into "fixing it" as if it were her fault. (Good responses are: "Beats me!" or "Haven't a clue!")

Controlling by Assigning Status

Putting her down, disparaging her, may in time lead her to doubt her competency in what she does best.

Putting her up, commending her, may lead her to believe that she's only fit to do certain things, and these may be what she has the least talent and inclination to do. This puts the abuser in control and diminishes the partner's independence and confidence. Following are some examples.

Putting her down: You're the worst mother. You're a lousy driver.
Putting her up: You're the expert at changing diapers.

Other methods include:

Sentencing: You are wrong/right to . . .
Categorizing: Women are all the same.
Characterizing: You're just like your mother.

Survivors write about the consequences to their self-esteem of having been told that what they do well is what they do worst.

I was a professional person beaten down emotionally to the point of not be-lieving I could get a job other than maybe cleaning a house or flipping a burger. Today I am director of marketing for the entire western region.
— R. F., SACRAMENTO, CA

I am really a very competent person. Yet my husband had me con-vinced otherwise. He belittled everything I did. Now, I'm vice president of a medium-sized company.
— D.L., COLUMBUS, OH

I could not imagine that anything I said was acceptable or in fact un-derstandable, something was "wrong" with almost every sentence out of my mouth. I'd spend hours trying to figure out how to say things right. Guess what! Five years later and I'm a professor and my students love what I have to say!

— G.C., FULLERTON, CA

The Abuser and Control

Earlier we read a letter from a woman whose husband berated her for learning a dance step from another man. He was obviously jealous and felt that he might lose her to this stranger. He wanted to keep her under control. If he had asked her to show him what she had learned, he would have drawn her to him. She would very likely have been filled with happiness that he respected her efforts and wanted her to teach him the steps. His behavior, however, drove her away, at least temporarily.

Why would he behave in such a way that he would drive her away when he wanted her closer? Because he felt powerless and wanted to fend off his feelings of powerlessness. Control and defense go hand in hand. When the abuser criticizes and berates his partner, his feelings of powerlessness are dispelled by his *display of superiority*. He denys his true feelings, and at the same time, if he believes he is superior, he feels more able to control the one he believes he is superior to.

Why in the world, one might ask, would a person feel more powerful when he is, for example, being critical? The verbal abuser feels more powerful because he *believes in his display* just as he believes in his ideal image, which is usually Mr. Nice Guy.

Criticism, for example, is a display of superiority—a display of "superior knowledge." The abuser wants to believe that he knows better than the one he is criticizing and is therefore superior or more powerful. As a result, he wards off, for the time being, the feelings of powerlessness and inferiority that haunt him.

When the abuser discounts his partner, he defends himself against her perception of the abuse by denying the impact of his behavior. For example, when he says, *"You're making a big thing out of nothing,"* he wants to believe that if he can get her to believe it, or at the very least, not object to it, then it is true! Of course, she may be too frightened of him to object or she may have heard it so often she's come to believe that he must be right. Even so, he is usually dead wrong. If anyone tries to see her mate's viewpoint and tolerates for too much in the way of irritable snaps, opposition, and put-downs, it is the partner of a verbal abuser.

How else does verbal abuse relate to control? Certainly it can seem strange that a person who wants to be in control, that is, have his partner do, be, say, and perform the way he wants at the time he wants it, would also be compelled to say abusive things to her. Wouldn't one ask nicely if one needed something or really wanted a favor?

The abuser isn't able to ask nicely. Why? Because he doesn't believe his mate should have the opportunity to say "No." If she said "No," he would not be in control. He therefore uses verbal abuse to lower his partner's self-esteem so that she will doubt herself and thus be more easily controlled and manipulated.

Another way to understand the abuser's behavior is to understand that one only feels confident and sure about controlling another person when one can in some way have authority over that person, as a policeman does over a driver, or can suppress that person, as a dictator suppresses the populace by limiting freedom of action and freedom of dissent.

The verbal abuser gains his sense of control by *invalidating his mate* to such an extent that she doubts herself or gives up trying to reason with him. Each time he gets her to "back down," that is, comply and give up trying to reason with him, he believes he has won. And the winner of a battle is in control, right? A nation that wins a war is generally in control of the other nation. (And remember, the conquered usually end up *serving* the conqueror.)

Anyone who verbally abuses another does so to maintain some form of control over the other and to keep his own feelings of powerlessness under control. The abuser is often so used to relating to his mate in an abusive way that it does not even occur to him that he is being abusive. Some men who are learning how to stop verbally abusing their mates have said that it seems as though disparaging or even cruel comments have become a routine, almost automatic way of behaving.

The verbal abuser is so accustomed to being in control that he rarely, if ever, questions his behavior; nor does he think of it as oppressive. One man wrote that his last wife told him she was divorcing him because he was verbally abusive. At the time he couldn't imagine why she would say such a thing. Later, after he read about verbal abuse, he wrote,

> *I'm a verbal abuser. I caused so much pain for myself and others and never realized it—I don't understand how I could have destroyed my life and not have known it.*
>
> — L.F., ASBURY PARK, NJ

The belief in the need and right to control another can be instilled in a person from the earliest years of childhood. If this is a person's experience, it may take some rather drastic and shocking emotional events over the course of a lifetime for him to seek change in himself.

The more we know about verbal abuse and the more we recognize it, name it, stand up to it, respond to it, speak up about it, and stop it or leave it, the sooner we will collectively bring about the awareness we need for good relationships at home, at work, or wherever people have the opportunity to relate to one another.

The following excerpt talks about control.

> *I knew but could not comprehend why he was capable of holding his temper outburst if he chose to. It could be to certain people who mattered. It could be office help that he depended upon. It could be in social situations when someone angered him, but it would have been inappropriate to explode. With me, he could hold his temper when people that mattered to him were around.*
>
> — M. K., LOS ANGELES, CA

The abuser is often so good at control that he can turn his intimidating displays on and off in order to continue to "look good" to the outside world. Many survivors describe this as Jekyll/Hyde behavior. Many, like the writer above, "could not comprehend" why their mates raged at them only when people who "mattered" were not around. Never did they suspect it was because when they were "chosen" they became the chosen scapegoat. Verbal abuse is a behavior originating with the abuser's intense need to control his mate as well as his own feelings of powerlessness. He does this by diminishing her and venting his feelings on her while blaming her for them.

The Categories of Verbal Abuse and the Issue of Control

1. *Withholding:* By withholding, the verbal abuser is saying, *I've got something you want and I can withhold it from you. Therefore, I am in control. Or, If I don't respond, if I refuse to answer, I can control the outcome, that is, I can maintain the status quo. I can be sure that there will be no change. I don't have to ask. I don't have to say "no." I don't have to say "yes." I don't have to be vulnerable. I can stay in control and therefore risk nothing.*

2. *Countering:* By countering his partner, the verbal abuser is saying, *I can think for both of us. What you think is wrong. What I think is right. If I can get you to doubt yourself, I can control you more easily.*

3. *Discounting:* By discounting his partner's perceptions, the verbal abuser is saying, *I can decree the worthlessness of your perceptions and actions. I am not accountable. I can stay in control.*

4. *Verbal abuse disguised as a joke:* By telling his partner that the

abuse is only a joke, the verbal abuser is saying, *I feel so up putting you down that I never want to give it up, so I decree that my comments are humorous—I'm in control. I can say what I want.*

5. *Blocking and diverting:* By thwarting his partner, the verbal abuser is saying, *I do not accept any responsibility to respond to you as a rational person, so I can change the conversation at will—I am in control.*

6. *Accusing and blaming:* By blaming his partner for his abuse of her, the verbal abuser is saying, *You are to blame for your pain and for everything I say or do to you and for everything that isn't the way I want it to be, so I do not have to stop my behavior. I'm in control.*

7. *Judging and criticizing:* By judging and criticizing his partner, the verbal abuser is saying, *When I tell you what is wrong with your thoughts and actions, I put myself in charge of you and therefore in control of you.*

8. *Trivializing:* By pretending that his partner, or her actions or perceptions or opinions or thoughts or concerns, are less than they are, the verbal abuser is saying, *When you see how insignificant you are, I will have more power to control you.*

9. *Undermining:* By undermining his partner, the verbal abuser is saying, *When I erode your confidence and lessen your determination, you are easier to control.*

10. *Threatening:* With this very obvious means of control, the verbal abuser is saying, *I have Power Over you. I am in control. Do as I say. If you don't, I'll . . ., or if you don't, you might get hurt—* implying physical harm by a fit of rage or by an unspoken threat like punching the wall.

11. *Name calling:* By calling names, the abuser is saying, *You do not exist. You are annihilated, you are now BLANK. Now that you are wiped out, I'm in control, just like in a war.*

12. *Forgetting:* When the abuser regularly forgets appointments, agreements and/or incidents, he is saying, *I'm in control of your time, energy or reality and I don't have to be accountable because I'm in control.*

13. *Ordering and demanding:* With these direct displays of control, the verbal abuser is saying, *I have a right to assert Power Over you in an overt act of control. If all the other intimidating behaviors achieved my goal, you will do as I demand.*

14. *Denial:* By denying all of his abusive behavior, the abuser is saying, *I can keep everything exactly as it is, with you under my control, and I will not be held accountable.*

15. *Abusive anger:* By being abusively angry, the abuser is saying, *As long as I am scary and threatening to you I can have my way.*

A great many women fear their mates at times, and not without reason. Often a display of rage, superior strength, raised fist, push, or other similar intimidating demonstration will have the impact of leaving the partner in fear of her mate for a long time to come. Of course, once this occurs, the relationship is definitely one of oppression. A survivor writes,

> *His angry outbursts have been worse during the past few weeks since I've been standing up to him—But, I am prepared to return to work outside of my home to escape the abuse.*
>
> — J.F., St. Paul, MN

It is the nature of abuse that it is never justified and that it is not about a conflict. It is, instead, about control. The following letter describes a very significant and prevalent attitude that confuses many survivors and sometimes counselors as well. This is that if there is verbal abuse in the relationship, it can be *resolved* because two adults should be able to work out their *conflicts*. Actually, in the verbally abusive relationship there is no conflict around the abuse. When one is ordered, one is abused; there is no justification and no conflict. When one is criticized, one is being abused; there is no justification for this abuse and certainly no conflict.

> *Now I see more clearly all the stages I went through in the past ten years: being stunned, depressed, confused and then finally angry, angry that I had to live my life being on guard and ready to stand up to each verbal assault. Before I didn't have the knowledge or confidence to respond appropriately for all our situations. Besides that, I thought that his behavior was "our conflicts" to be worked out somehow.*
>
> — R.P., Lubbock, TX

In the next chapter we will explore a key reason why women find it so difficult to walk away from verbally abusive relationships they know are getting worse, not better—relationships in which the abusive mate refuses to admit to the abuse and sometimes even claims that the victim is the abuser. This reason is the *destruction of integrity*.

I believe this issue is so important that it deserves some time and consideration, some thought, some imagination, some feeling of what it would be like to step into the shoes of the woman whose integrity is being violated—violated so ruthlessly that she can no longer act in her own best interests. If you are already in her shoes, then you, like thousands, may be able to plant your feet on the bedrock of reality, which until now seemed never to stop moving.

Chapter 3

Disintegration

As we have come to see, the need for Power Over another arises from a sense of Personal Powerlessness. In the late nineteenth century, the philosopher Nietzsche proposed that the primary force driving humanity was the will to power. I would propose that the first force, the primary force, is not the will to power but is instead the *Creative Force* which unfolds events and time, as well as life. It is only when one is disconnected from this creative force, adrift, unanchored, that one seeks to gain Power Over another.

The Creative Force is itself invisible and unseen, yet it has impelled the creation of music, art, poetry, literature, and dance—works that resonate in the souls of millions born after. These works ripple out into future time, changing and shaping and bringing to human experience that which had never been known before.

Knowing that what is possible, that what might be, is itself unknowable, we cannot condone the oppression of anyone. Oppression goes against the very thrust of life itself. Whenever possible, we must protect ourselves from it.

We thrive when we experience our Personal Power as the Creative Force. When we touch our creativity, practice our arts, and artfully live, we participate in the unfolding of the universe. This participation reveals a correspondence or integrity between ourselves and the universe.

Life from the Power Over perspective, on the other hand, is suppression and exploitation. According to this view, each one *acquires* power through Power Over another—as if the primary force *could* be acquired, were of one's own making, and could be stored in a vault in one's soul. Long-held beliefs in Power Over permeate our culture as if a toxic cloud had gradually gathered over the land.

And yet there is a new awareness in the wind that would dissipate the cloud. This is the awareness that life is an unfolding, a stream or force evolving out of itself. Through our connection to this force we come to realize, individually and collectively, that the domination of another is the attempt of life to go against itself. This is the core violation that verbal abuse enacts and that results in the *disintegration of integrity—the fragmentation of the thread of connection to the Creative Force—a violence to spirit that all victims of abuse in some way recognize.*

We might envision a time when the validation of every human being from infancy on might end the pain and chaos by strengthening each one's connection to the Creative Force. Feeling their Personal Power from within, none would seek to gain Power Over another.

The survivors of verbal abuse express a profound awareness of their need for freedom from domination and control—even as they weigh and face the possibilities of change—the cost and the pain. They are usually determined not to lose their connection to the core of life. Often they feel the fear, like the breaking of a taboo, that a move toward freedom from oppression can bring. Usually, however, they will not abandon themselves—they will not abandon the spirit of life itself.

As for the abuser, no matter how many times he may attempt to thwart life, to Over Power life, to take command and control, ultimately he will not succeed. Ultimately he must face himself and his personal loss of power—his own "disconnection." One loses one's power the moment one derives it from another. Power Over through dominance denies life and the fundamental force of the universe out of which we arise.

Living with integrity increases integration. The dictionary defines *integration* as behavior of an individual that is in harmony with the environment. By living in harmony, accordance, balance, and congruence with one's inner and outer environment, one becomes increasingly integrated.

Abuse brings about disintegration. When the correspondence between one's inner environment—that is, one's perception, experience, feelings, intuition, and intention or meaning—and one's external environment—what one sees, hears, or is told—is violated, one's integrity is assaulted. The ability to act in accordance with the dynamics of life unfolding within and without is impaired. This results in the *destruction of integrity.*

Something is integrated when everything that belongs to it is intact. Nothing is missing. A painting is integrated when there is nothing in the painting that doesn't belong in the painting. It is in balance and it is all of one style. When a person is integrated, everything about that person fits with that person. She doesn't say one thing and do another; nor does she take up activities that are in opposition to her goals. Her activities belong with her. Most aspects of the person, if not developed, are on some level available for development, and actions, words, thoughts, values, and goals are congruent. This congruence is an expression of her integration.

When a person experiences violation, such as by being constantly told that what she experiences isn't so or that the reason she is doing something isn't the real reason she is doing it, or that what she said isn't what she said, or that what she does well has no value, then her integrity is damaged. To her, what happens "in here" doesn't seem to correspond with what happens "out there." This represents a grave threat to survival. Without integration between ourselves and our environment, we cannot act in accordance with our values and intentions—even when we think we can and want to.

Why do we live in a world of Power Over, where so many diminish so many? Possibly because so many people have themselves been diminished, divided, abandoned, and shamed. The disintegrated are most often severed from their feeling self; they have lost their Personal Power and have sought to take the other's power by perpetual devaluing, communicated by such phrases as,

Who do you think you are?
What makes you think you know it all?
You're to be seen and not heard.
You've always got to put in your two cents.
Don't *you* think you're smart?
Nobody asked you.

Since verbal abuse diminishes and impairs our thinking, feeling, and perceptions, it disrupts our connection with the universe and clouds our instincts. One of the most debilitating forms of verbal abuse is when the abuser picks his mate's most noticeable or outstanding talent or ability and disparages it, in some cases more or less constantly. I met a painter who made some of the best portraits I have seen, in or out of a museum. Her husband sneered at her work and refused to let her hang a painting anywhere in her home. He disparaged her work in so many ways that it was hard for her to trust in her great talent until she was away from the relationship.

Another woman wrote wonderful children's stories, which she kept in a trunk at the foot of her bed. She felt impelled to write them, but she didn't think they would be well received: her abuser was often saying things like, "I can't believe you waste your time on that junk." No wonder she had so much difficulty recognizing her own abilities.

Unless one realizes that there are people who say things solely for the purpose of putting another person down, to be in control, one can easily be led to doubt oneself. A survivor writes,

> I am slowly getting used to the idea that my husband of more than twenty years is a serious abuser. I just wish I had realized it much earlier—and I wish I had followed my instinct not to associate with him. But he was so persistent and I gave in, not wanting to hurt him, but now I realize how much I hurt myself.
>
> — D.K. , LYNDEN, WA

A natural instinct may warn us of impending disintegration, but if our feelings are invalidated, we may use our energy to adjust to the other, to act against ourselves. The following writer says,

> When I was verbally abused at first I used to cry, then I tried harder to please him.
>
> — A.M., BOONE, IA

When we hear the opposite of the truth, or believe that another is telling the truth, we may become convinced of an untruth. In this way our connection to our own truth, our intuitive knowledge, is broken. Disintegration occurs.

The following letter excerpt tells one survivor's story of disintegration and recovery.

> He criticized my cooking and ironing. He said I was too easy with the children. He was stingy for me and for himself. I could never win. I was resigned to it. I was belittled in front of others and I felt very embarrassed and tried to save face whenever possible.
>
> He kept saying that I have to have everything my way, and after a while he convinced me, but now, in the perspective of time, I think it was not so.
>
> — M.A., TORONTO, ONTARIO

Since hundreds of thousands are, or have been, in verbally abusive relationships for many years, many wonder why partners of abusers remain in the relationship as long as they do. The survivors themselves wonder why they find it so difficult to leave. I have received many letters that ask in one way or another, "Why do I stay?"

or "Please tell me why I let this happen to me" or "Why can't I just walk away?"

I believe that being "convinced" by another's words, becoming "resigned," losing one's "instinct," gradually adapting and learning to doubt yourself, and believing that something is wrong with you are all symptoms of shattered integrity. This shattering and the ensuing confusion result in something like a paralysis of spirit. Even a battered mouse plays dead. Might not the spirit do likewise? A survivor wrote,

> *All of my feelings would overwhelm me, and I couldn't speak or act. What was happening? I didn't know.*
> — W.M., Providence, RI

It takes time to recover one's confidence. Another survivor speaks out about courage and self-doubt.

> *In spite of all that is past and all that is to come I am on the journey to a better life for myself and my daughter. Most of the time, I have faith in my future success. The years of abuse have their legacy though; there are moments and even days where I am overwhelmed by feelings of not being able to cope. I know that I was well-trained to doubt myself and my strengths.*
> — L.C., Grand Rapids, MI

A woman is often intuitive—aware of herself in relation to the universe around her. It is a great crisis for her to have this connection broken by constant criticism, blaming, trivializing, and so on. In the next letter excerpt, a woman speaks for many as she describes the confusion of having lived with verbal abuse.

> *I have never been able to explain to anyone the fact that he can turn his verbal, emotional rage on me one day, and the next day ask me if I'd like to go for a hike!! So much of my predicament is because I "accepted" as "normal behavior"—the jealousy, possessiveness, controlling and hot temper— for thirty-five years. What I really accepted was that there was something wrong about me. I do know I've got to figure a way out.*
> — D.O. Grapevine, TX

Without a witness to her wounding, without a sign from her culture, without a word that *this* is abuse, this woman accepted her mate's behavior as normal. In fact, within her culture, her community, he was deemed not just normal but exemplary!

Another woman spoke out about her need to find validation. This need is real, because all abuse is invalidating. She writes,

When I would tell someone, a friend, family member or just an acquaintance of something that would transpire between my husband and myself, they would say things like, "Well I believe you were right in saying this or that." I was always looking for validation.
— C. B., JERSEY CITY, NJ

Invalidation, possibly more than anything, shatters one's integrity.

After fifty-two years of abuse he still denies—saying my mind has to be twisted. Perhaps I would be better off if this was true, and would wake up one day to find it was all a very bad dream.
— H. G. FLINT, MI

Not finding validation, the writer looks back and sees her life as a very bad dream. It is a great tragedy that there are so many for whom she speaks. The survivor's sense of unreality is often a result of invalidation leading to the destruction of integrity ("dis-integration"). In the following letter excerpt a survivor eloquently describes the destruction of integrity. One might see her as out on a limb, whipped back and forth by the changing winds of her environment.

I have always been so thrown off center, then confused and numbed, then in a major depression, then stronger and sucked back into working hard to have a good, intimate, mutual relationship with someone who seemed to be just short of being understood and understanding, then thrown off center etc., etc. blah, blah, ad nauseam.
— M.F., BURLINGTON, VT

As survivors describe what they've gone through, we find that their experiences of verbal abuse are very similar. These samples reflect the feelings of thousands, if not millions, worldwide.

I thought I was crazy and somewhat dumb or empty-headed—not intelligent enough.
— S.L. SAN FRANCISCO, CA

In my support group we've decided we've all been involved with the "same man."
— D.H., ATLANTA, GA

I feel frustrated, helpless, defenseless, angry, frightened, crazy, indecisive, frozen.
— G.F., BROOKLYN, NY

I realize how well-conditioned I was to his voice. When he called my name, I involuntarily shuddered. Most of the time it would be for in-

different reasons or pleasant reasons, but the memory of the bad ones was so strongly imbedded that I shuddered at his voice. He harped on everything—My motto was "Peace at any Price"—I had lost much of my identity, but was not aware of it.

I was able to go away by myself for a few weeks from time to time, and that was my release valve. On returning, I kept thinking of the next getaway.

I was constantly pushed to do things against my will on a daily basis. Avoiding arguments but not agreeing with the issue. More pretending. He never admitted being wrong, never, ever, apologized.

It is still important to me to understand what happened in my past and to go on with my life.

— R.L., LOVELAND, CO

Can it be that for centuries people have lived with such emotional pain, struggling to identify the problem or, having identified it, finding they did not have the skills or means to be free of it? I believe that today holds out hope for change. Awareness and determination form the foundation for creating more healthful relationships, as described in the following letter.

Right now, I am angry. I think that as people realize (further down) that they can't get away with physical abuse, they will resort to controlling others with mental anguish and emotional dependence. Verbal abuse is much more subtle and harder to identify and in that way I think it's more damaging. If I had been hit I would have left. But instead I allowed myself to be threatened and my self-esteem torn down. For that I take responsibility but never again will I take responsibility for someone's rage and deranged way of thinking.

— K.N. OAKDALE, PA

How does verbal abuse shatter the correspondence between one's inner and outer environments? How does it undermine one's ability to act in accordance with the Creative Force that nourishes the spirit within? How is one impaired and how is the connection broken?

Let us look again at this idea of correspondence, which seems to be a function of integrity. The partner of a verbal abuser performs a task—washes the dishes, for example. Looking in from the outside (through her kitchen window, so to speak), there seems to be a correspondence between her intention to do, her action done, and the physical result: the clean dishes. However, this integration or correspondence between thought, action, and result may be shattered for her by verbal abuse. For example, if *criticism* is the abuser's method of control, she may hear that the dishes were washed

> the wrong way.
> at the wrong time.
> too noisily.
> with too much hot water.
> with not enough hot water.
> not carefully enough.
> with the wrong amount of soap.
> with the wrong soap altogether.

If *blaming* is the abuser's style she may hear,
> You knew the noise would bother me.
> You're trying to make me look bad.
> You did it so you could take my beer mug.

If other controlling tactics are used, she may hear,
> You haven't got anything better to do.
> You couldn't do anything more complicated than
>   dishwashing.
> You know I could have hired a cleaning lady if I
>   had wanted to see the dishes being washed.
> You like washing dishes because you're a woman.
> You are the expert at washing dishes.

The examples above show how, on a day-to-day basis, the integrity of the partner is shattered by verbal abuse. What the partner of the abuser thought was so *isn't so*, according to her mate. *This generates a feeling of helplessness*—especially if one doesn't know that this is abuse. This shattering of integrity will likely take place in any verbally abusive relationship, whether from one adult to another, from an adult to a child, or from one child to another.

> *I would like to know more about how I let another human being crawl under my skin and control and manipulate my mind!*
> — W.B., MOUNTAIN VIEW, CA

The writer asks how she let another manipulate her mind. I believe that she simply did not know that she was being lied to. When a woman marries or makes a relationship commitment to another, she includes the other in a feeling of kinship that usually dispels distrust. Trusting makes the partner of an abuser vulnerable to the destructive power of verbal abuse, which shatters the partner's perception of a correspondence between her thoughts, decisions, and actions, and their results. Partners who are verbally abused over a period of time experience this.

When there is little or no correspondence or integration between the environment and the self, one feels disoriented and unsure. Women report a "strangeness" about the communication in their relationship best described as an unreal feeling.

It is essential to our mental health and emotional well-being that we experience a correspondence between our inner and outer worlds. What we think, say, and do should to some degree correspond with what others perceive—especially in relationships. If we were in the hands of an enemy we would know there was little or no truth in what we heard; we would know we were being faced with opposition. In a verbally abusive relationship, however, a woman does not know she is being opposed for the sake of opposing. She will be likely to assume that "errors" arise and not because she has been mistaken.

The inner and the outer of us is connected, as if there were a thread of reality running through our thoughts and actions and their effects. Verbal abuse unravels this thread. It can, however be reintegrated—rewoven into something stronger, more sure, more to be counted upon, more dependable then ever before. This is the work of healing and recovery. Knowing how one got there and knowing what others have experienced speeds this process.

The survivors of verbal abuse represent every age and social group—from young high school dropouts to mature, accomplished people. Some are elders suffering from abuse from adult children. Some are suffering in work situations. Some are abused by parents.

The vast majority who have written to me are women who often wonder how they could have been in situations where they suffered verbal abuse. It seems that for many the unraveling of the thread of integration began in childhood. Subtle control of women such as "Sit like a lady," and "Don't speak unless you are spoken to," began the process of undermining confidence and self-esteem. Men heard "Don't show your feelings" and "Big boys don't cry," *words that for many didn't just start the thread unraveling but severed it all together.*

By adulthood, women's natural instincts and intuition were no longer their guide. "Try harder." "Be more accepting." "Be more understanding." "See the other's point of view." This invalidation, combined with inexperience, cultural pressures and their naive expectation of acceptance, have brought many women unawares into relationships they have no hope of comprehending.

Some women believe what their mates tell them because they have great trust and faith in them. Some especially respect their mates as the father of the family or as a man of the world.

At the same time, women who are strong are often seen as weak. The very strength a woman uses to try to understand, to set a good example, to express her feelings, to set aside personal goals for the sake of family and children, is seen as weakness and likely is rejected or ridiculed by her mate, if he is abusive.

If she "gives up" or "backs down" because she knows he would never apologize or allow her to explain, or because she thinks he's crazy, or because she feels sorry for him, or because she thinks he has fears or feelings of inferiority, or because some kind of "win" seems to be important to him—she does so because of her strength. She may even congratulate herself that she can "let it go" while he's "just trying to be a big shot."

Some come to fear their mate's anger and abuse, with good cause. The partner's fear or retreat or confusion leads the abuser to believe she is weak and that he is therefore stronger, more secure, more sure of his ability to be in control. For many women, a line is finally crossed: They can no longer "let it go." But in the meantime the thread has been unraveling. A woman wrote,

> I thought that if I tried hard enough, I could get him to understand and to change. How silly of me! Now, I understand that a person who has more power than you can find it easy to ignore any requests to give up that power.
>
> I told myself not to quibble about this or that. That is, if it was a matter of "male pride" with him that he was in charge or control of this or that—"it didn't matter." After all, he "loved me and I could live with it." But at what price?
>
> So, I conceded on this—and on that—and on this—and on that. And pretty soon, I realized that he was controlling me so much, that I had lost track of who I was, what I wanted, how I felt, etc. I'd argue. I'd really fight and nothing happened. He'd refuse to discuss it any longer. Instead, he'd want to discuss the problem of "How emotional I'd get."
>
> I thought I could change him through love: I'd be so warm and nurturing and loving—that eventually he'd no longer feel threatened and would realize he could relax and treat me with respect. So, this became my dream, my fantasy, my goal in life.
>
> I sought out counselors. But the counselors didn't seem to have the wisdom to say to us—"You two have conflicting beliefs as to what your relationship is. One believes in a dictatorship—the other, a partnership. You can't make your relationship work until you agree on one system."
>
> — W.H., JOPLIN, MO

The consequences of verbal abuse are many. Not only does the partner suffer; her children may also suffer from hearing angry outbursts or disparaging comments. How seriously the children are wounded depends on a great many factors. In some cases the relationship does not improve, and if it ends, the children also must cope with the disruption of their home life.

We take for granted that from grade school on, girls and boys will learn appropriate communication skills—and will also learn what is inappropriate. The very idea that an adult would diminish and try to control another can seem unthinkable in a society that values its freedom. Indeed, a young woman of intelligence, education, and talent may find it ludicrous that anyone would imagine they should be in charge of her. Such control is simply oppression; she knows that. Nonetheless, if she should find herself in such a relationship, she may find it difficult to convince her mate of this.

It is the "unthinkableness" of this kind of abuse that seems to baffle many women. Even when they "know," they ask, "Why would he do this to me?" The woman who wrote, "I thought I could change him through love" is typical of many. Over a period of many years, despite her desire to understand her mate, she could not identify the real issue in her relationship. He wanted not only to control her but also to vent his feelings with impunity. All the while, she believed that he only felt a bit insecure and needed to feel more loved.

Many survivors held the belief that if they were extra kind and giving, if they were extremely loving and generous and nourishing, their mates would feel loved, secure, and more confident, and would then be happier, kinder and warmer toward them—and certainly more appreciative. They reasoned that their mates would not feel the need to put them down to feel more important if they, the women, could make the mate feel important. This belief turns out to be false.

The writer we heard from earlier tells us that she came to that realization when she wrote, "Why would he give up power and control when he got all of his needs met by dominating and controlling me?" While she was treating her mate with extra kindness and still suffering his abuse, her integrity was assaulted. She felt powerless—unable to understand why this was happening. She "lost track" of who she was. The thread of connection between thought, deed, and result unraveled. When she thought he would be pleased, he was angry. When he said he loved her, his actions sent a different message. When she thought she would be complimented, she was disparaged. However, she never gave up hope that, even though he did not respect her as an equal and treat her kindly, somehow, some way, she would make sense of it all. She would *know* the meaning of it all. She would know so that never in this life or another would she live in the pain and confusion she had endured.

She shared many writings with me and inspired this poem.

> *Survivors speak out,*
> *Write in the night,*
> *Sometimes in hiding.*
> *The threads are unraveling*
> *The pieces are scattering*
> *The spirit is floundering.*
>
> *Retreating, reweaving*
> *Collecting themselves*
> *Writing in journals,*
> *Writing in letters,*
> *Survivors speak out:*
>
> *"Never again."*

Chapter 4

Awakening Awareness

I know with my mind what I've known with my heart all these years.

— A SURVIVOR

We are just beginning to awaken to the magnitude and depth, the pervasiveness and destructiveness of verbal abuse—a behavior and attitude that desecrate the sacred, the spirit, the center, the divine in whose image we are made. Women and men are waking to the realization that any one person's disparagement diminishes us all. One arrow loosed pierces the heart of generations; the effects ripple out like a toxic wave. A man wrote of his own awakening.

In my childhood I was constantly verbally attacked and told I was nothing and would amount to nothing. Now I recognize that I am verbally abusive.

— R.J., FLINT, MI

A child of eight years, knowing something was wrong, touched her own center—her Creative Force—and in a few moments unfolded a remarkable poem for her mother.

The Garden of Your Conscience
— by Mira

You are just a bird
A bird flying, flying
Sometimes over the sea of love.
The unbreakable currents
And waves and white foam

Flooding beaches where lovers sit
Drawn in
Pulled in
By the currents
To drown in the sea of love.

Your flight is not so easy

There is the pirate ocean with its
Alligators with red eyes,
Evil alligators of death.
This ocean is black.

Then there is the stream of good hope
There all necessary wishes come true.
This stream is pink.
Then sometimes there is a cloud
An orange cloud that half hides
Everything from view.
It is like a mist that covers your eyes,
A mist that you can see through.

Yet you can't.

It's like a brass cage that you can fly from

If you know how.

Then there is the red cloud
The cloud of blood, your blood
Then there is the white cloud
A snow carpet that you ride on
That carries you to the stream of good hope
And it takes you to the garden of your conscience
That helps guide you in right and wrong
In what or who to trust
Or not to trust

This is where you stop and rest.

   Reading that the "red eyed alligator," a reptile guided by a primitive reptilian brain, is "of death," I felt that the child who talks of "good hope" seems to have more awareness than most. She takes us to a garden where we are guided in what or whom to trust. I trust her a lot more than the red-eyed alligator! She embodies the good hope of which she speaks, because her thread is not unraveled, her connection is still clear, and she shows us where to rest.

Awakening to the realities of verbal abuse is not easy for anyone. One woman who, after much abuse, is awakening to the realization that what she is experiencing is abuse, wrote to me. In the excerpt of her letter that follows, she asks why she is with this abusive mate. Our child poet says the answer lies somewhere in the "garden of your conscience." In this garden, the ability to discriminate grows if it is well nurtured. We nurture it when we pay attention to it and when we can build the strength to withstand invalidation by verbal abuse. This calls for real faith in ourselves. Faith, indeed, may be one of the greatest gifts we can give ourselves.

The ability to discriminate, to know who is toxic and who is safe, is felt as an inner sense of what is right or wrong for us. This sense also impels us toward right action. This survivor is beginning to weigh what is right and wrong for her. She feels the pain of the abuse. She is aware, even if the world says, "Nothing happened." She writes,

> I wonder at the things I put up with—being in public and feeling the "invisible to other's dagger hit me"—and I just sit there shocked with my mouth open because only he and I know what happened. Why do I put up with it!?"
>
> — V.R., PITTSBURGH, PA

"Why do I put up with it?" There are many reasons women put up with abuse. Many survivors say that, because no one else in the universe can see the crime, to break up her "happy home" would seem to go against everyone. Another reason she may stay is that she seems to feel immobilized or paralyzed by the disintegration of integrity, of the correspondence between what is on the inside, her feelings, and what is on the outside, his response—with no one to validate its cruelty.

Awareness can bring change. With awareness as a starting point, you can begin to gain faith in your feelings. The pain of the "invisible dagger," for instance, is a sign that you are in fact being abused. One of the characteristics of the invisible dagger is that no one will ever find the weapon. The abuser's crimes often go undetected. Except, of course, by you.

The cutting remark, the invisible dagger, is something shocking. Even more shocking is the realization that what one is hearing *is* abuse and that one is actually being abused by the person one loves. Survivors say that they have come to feel that what no one else sees is not real.

A child of eleven heard me mention the "invisible dagger." She asked what that meant. I told her, "It's when someone says something hurtful but no one else knows." She said, "I know what that is."

I said, "Oh? Can you tell me about it?" I was wondering if she could grasp a concept like that.

She said, "Yes, well, you see, my dad knew about this story about a china doll that was really a murderer and went around killing people."

I could see that this was a pretty horrifying creature to contemplate.

"And my dad really knew. But when we're around other people he'll call me his china doll, and people think, 'Oh, isn't he sweeeet.'" She dragged it out for emphasis. "But he'll give me this look and I know he knows. But I can't say, 'Don't call me that,' cause then he'll be even worse and everyone will think I'm the one that's mean. That's the invisible dagger."

Awakening is a process by which parts of ourselves that were forgotten—that had gone to sleep—awaken. Have you ever experienced part of your body, a foot or an arm, going to sleep? When the "sleeping" part begins to recover, there's a tingling, waking feeling that one can sometimes hardly stand. It may really hurt. We rub it hard to get the circulation back. We pay attention to it. So it is with the awakening parts of our spirits.

When we stand and have to find and use a part of ourselves that was immobilized, we awaken it, we discover it. And sometimes it hurts. We must attend to it.

The survivors quoted in this book found themselves in relationships where what they said and thought and felt was "sat on," just as if it didn't exist. These parts slipped away from conscious awareness and seemed to go to sleep, leaving them feeling numb or paralyzed. That is the sad part. The happy part is that they can be awakened, brought to consciousness, discovered. When we discover ourselves actively and consciously, when we discover our own value, we awaken what was lost in the trauma or the abuse. What is discovered this way is deeply treasured.

Since verbal abuse in relationships has only recently surfaced as a pervasive problem, it is no wonder that the survivors of verbal abuse have had great difficulty in understanding their relationships. A great many today are still immersed, are still drowning, in the toxic atmosphere, with no way to reach safety or find rest. One way in which a woman can become aware is to live for a time—two, or three, or four years—meeting her needs in an environment in which there are *no* detractors or disparagers; in other words, in a nonabusive environment. Sometimes women have this opportunity when they first leave home or go off to college.

When a woman lives free from abuse for a time, she is usually more aware of it the next time. When she hears, "You're too sensitive," for example, she will be immediately outraged that anyone would attempt to violate her boundaries in this way. The violation stands out for her because she is able to see the abuse in contrast to the nonabusive environment in which she has been living. This contrast is a requirement for clarity. If we do not live in a healthy environment, how can we make the distinction? Like the child, we know something is wrong—something barely seen, elusive, and very damaging. But what? Often "nothing," according to those around us.

Sometimes a survivor is aware of her mate's predicament and feels sorry for him because she sees he has lost his connection to the Creative Force. Intuitively she senses his sad, almost pathetic, weakness: he is afraid of his own feelings. Intuitively she knows he is searching for something. Without knowing what to do with this knowledge, she believes that she can "be there" for him.

Many survivors of verbal abuse say they believed that if they were kind enough, their mate would have enough confidence to feel he did not have to "act superior." Women often say they see abusers as weak, while their abusers say that they believe they were doing nothing wrong and felt in fact that they were "real men."

We are aware now of the abuser's reality. He lives in the Power Over mode. He acts to have Power Over his partner, often by covert means: disparagement, undermining, blaming, diminishing, dictating, countering, manipulating, and, in some cases, physical force. He may act in an extremely covert way or he may fly into frightening rages or angry outbursts to accomplish his aim. Since his partner seeks mutuality and cooperation, she finds it extremely difficult to perceive her mate's reality. He has no perception of hers.

Some survivors, while feeling the constant shocks of verbal abuse, were even more shocked as they became more aware of their mate's reality. It was incomprehensible to them that any adult would believe he had the right to dominate another. Others did not even see themselves as oppressed but rather as being inadequate in some way. Many survivors spent lifetimes, as we shall see, trying to bring about a relationship. The survivors and abusers, metaphorically speaking, lived not only in different realities but also in different worlds.

Often the "Reality II types," as some survivors call themselves, have lived for years in the abusive atmosphere of Reality I, unaware of its toxicity while their self-esteem diminished and their self-doubt grew. Their lives became more and more confusing and less satisfying because their words, actions, and very beings were reflected back to them in the greatly distorted mirror of Reality I.

The two realities can be thought of in the following terms: To act within the context of Power Over serves one. To act within the context of mutuality sustains two or more. I believe that personal power expressed through mutuality is the most practical power, and might be thought of as good because it is not self-defeating or destructive or false, like Power Over.

If a person who seeks mutuality, a Reality II type, is with a mate who seeks to dominate and control others, his behavior may be extremely confusing. "Why would he be saying this to me?" the partner asks. "Is what he says true?" "Why does he object to everything I say?" and "Why won't he answer me?" Unable to grasp the incomprehensible, unaware of his Power Over reality, the partner often believes she is saying things wrong, is not smart enough, doesn't know how to express herself, just doesn't do things right, makes an inordinate number of mistakes, or isn't adequate in some way.

Without awareness, the partner often has no idea how to deal with this controlling, Reality I behavior. Sometimes advice has been given to her by people who are themselves unaware of the dynamics of communication in these relationships. A survivor writes,

> I was told I am crazy, detach from his behavior, not from him. I was confused because I thought if I could detach from him I could still be with him or if I separated the behavior from the person I could still "keep the family together." Both of these behaviors seemed to intensify his abuse.

> — J.S., RICHMOND, VA

It is wise to be aware that some Reality I, Power Over types believe that if their partner objects to their controlling tactics, she is being abusive. I once overheard a conversation between a man and his wife in which he dictated and planned her entire day. When she asked a question, he brushed it aside with, "This is how it's going to be." When she asked to negotiate something he had decided that was going to affect her life, her home, her time, and her energy, he went right on saying, "This is what *we're* doing." His verbal onslaught was so relentless, I felt as if I was listening to an aerial bombardment. The man *believed* he had a right to speak as he did. At last his partner became angry over his behavior and told him "I object to this!" He thought that she was abusive. He said, "I don't need to hear your attacks!"

The abuser seemed to have no awareness whatsoever of the dreadful impact of his verbal onslaught. This may seem like an extreme, even shocking, example, yet it is all too common when two people in two different realities are in a relationship.

A woman wrote that she had much difficulty dealing with verbal abuse because her husband of many years truly believed that he was "the good guy" in their relationship. Some abusers believe in their "good guy" image, and are unaware of the effects of their actions. They believe that they should be in charge of another, and that "put downs" in general are not abusive but just a part of being in control. Some believe that this behavior is expected of a "real man." All the while they deny the abuse and their weaknesses, their lack of personal power, their fear of being found out, and their need to have someone to control. This thinking or attitude permeates Reality I.

A survivor describes her experience of her mate's behavior and her awareness of his reality.

> *He definitely denies his anger but it hits me like a sledgehammer. I realize now that he is completely unaware of how much he has hurt me because it made him feel so good.*
>
> — JD, LANSING, IL

How strange this seems to those who are abused. To these survivors the essence and meaning of a relationship is encouragement, shared joy, separate and shared endeavors, mutual support, consideration, kindness, and respect. Consequently, many partners said that when they awakened to the fact that what they were hearing wasn't true, that nothing was wrong with them and that they *were* being abused, that awareness itself was shocking.

With her gradually awakening awareness, a woman wrote,

> *I had thought I'd done something he thought was wrong, or that he misunderstood me or maybe I was missing something, but most of all I have felt sad and hurt. Now as the problem is better defined I am feeling confusion and uncertainty about what this mess really means. I'm looking at it all with "new eyes."*
>
> — A.J., SAN DIEGO, CA

A man wrote,

> *I want to encourage you to continue helping women understand that they are often times not the problem.*
>
> — M.G. HARTFORD, CT

Becoming aware of what is and is not good for us is one of the most important lessons we can learn in the school of life. If we are here, we are worth protecting. Surely the consequences of unawareness are great, as the following letters testify.

> *The abuse began on our honeymoon. I was so shocked! I had married a stranger. I spent thirteen years trying to make it work because it was my second marriage, I don't believe in divorce and I was so ashamed! I finally came to my senses, left, moved away and have had no contact with him at all.*
>
> — R.H., ATLANTA, GA

Women write,

> *"How can I detect a verbal abuser in the early stages of courtship?"*

> *"I wish those abusive men came with a tag on their forehead."*

> *"I would like to know how I can best recognize a potential verbal abuser."*

> *"What way is there to avoid getting into relationships like this when people are so well-behaved before marriage and kids?"*

> *"I want to avoid destructive relationships. How?"*

> *"I don't want to spend my life fighting for my rights and feelings."*

> *"I want to be aware enough to spot a potential one."*

> *"I want to stay out of verbally abusive relationships."*

> *"How can I be sure in a new relationship?"*

> *"What should I watch for?"*

> *Had I known the abusive side of my husband I would never have married him two years ago. I had dated him for five years and did not see the anger for some reason. Marriage has put him in the mode of controlling and trying to manage me. I'm sick of it and want to be free. He's high up in the church and I've told on him. It's out of the closet.*
>
> — B.M., DAYTON, OH

So many women have faced these issues, they deserve to be addressed here. These questions are especially important because many abusive personalities don't show their abusive side before marriage.

The writer just quoted recounts that when she said, "You weren't this way before we were married," her partner said, "If you knew how I was, you wouldn't have married me." Of those who recognize that they are verbally abusive, most say, "She didn't see that side of me before we were married."

If a woman is with a controlling personality, in the beginning of a relationship he may put a lot of his energy into *getting* her. While he's making "progress" getting her he feels in control. To accomplish his aim, he will show her his best behavior. Therefore, it may be very difficult to recognize an abusive, controlling personality early in the relationship. During courtship he is, so to speak, casting a hook with a very alluring lure; then he reels in his catch and lands—her. Suddenly she is in a completely different reality. It's a lot drier and a lot rougher than she ever imagined. His attractions—the lure that attracted her—are now tossed aside.

Pursuing this analogy further: after he's "landed" her, the abuser continues his controlling behavior, but this time with a different intention: that of keeping her under control. What a good catch! It's unthinkable that he will tolerate her having an opinion different from his, acting as if she could slip away, as if she's not in his control. Sometimes, by instilling a little fear and intimidation or by causing her to doubt herself, he can "stop her from going against him." Sometimes just undermining her self-esteem will do it.

Assessing New Relationships

If you are considering a new relationship, watch out for extremes. Be aware. Beware of excessively razzle-dazzle types and overly ardent suitors. Be aware of any familiarity not explicitly granted, for example calling you "honey" or "kid" when you've just met, or stopping by and then settling in before being asked.

Survivors who know say that if they have the slightest hint that something is wrong, if they feel a little twinge of a strange feeling, or a little sinking feeling, or are even just a bit frustrated by someone's behavior, then they do not put themselves in a relationship with that person. If at all possible they have no more contact with that person. It is healthy to show yourself the same protective caring you would show your own child.

Once this controlling personality has "hooked" you, what abuse can he do to feel in control?

to dominate you?

to tell you what to do? or

what to wear? or
what you think? or
what you feel? or
what you said? or
how you are?

Here are some additional guidelines for evaluating relationships.

❏ Does he express an interest in your thoughts, ideas and achievements?

❏ Do you truthfully feel good and nourished after spending time with him?

❏ Do you find your conversations with him rich, interesting, and satisfying?

❏ Do you share some interests?

❏ Is he tense—or relaxed?

❏ Are your values similar?

❏ Is he rigid—or mellow?

❏ Is he happy—or depressed?

❏ Is he pleasantly outgoing—or withdrawn?

❏ Is he naturally conversational with others—or does he put on a show?

❏ Does he tell you what to do?

❏ Does he hear what you say and honor what he hears?

Take off Running
Get away from him immediately if he:

says hurtful things, even if—*especially if*—he says they're a joke.
betrays your confidences.
breaks agreements.
lies to you.
is addicted to (or abuses) drugs or alcohol.
has a secret or shady past.
has temper outbursts.
gets into fist fights.
has hit or threatened you.
has hit his former partner.
has verbally abused you.
tells you what to do.

Warning

He is not a best-choice relationship just because he:

> says he is.
> says he needs you more than anything.
> says he would die without you.
> says he can't live without you.
> says he can love you better than anyone else can.
> says he wants to show you off.
> says he will give you everything.
> says you belong together.
> says your destiny is with him.
> says you wouldn't understand (and won't give you a chance to).
> says he loves you so much that:
>> he doesn't want to see you talking to another man.
>> doesn't want you out of his sight.
>> doesn't want you to have to work.
>> doesn't want you to bother your pretty little head about it.

Proceed with Caution

He may be a better choice if you:

> have a wonderful time with him.
> have a meeting of the minds with him.
> share important values with him.
> have long and interesting conversations with him.
> laugh at the same things together.
> respect and admire him.
> value each others ideas.
> feel "yourself" with him.
> feel warmth and kindness from him.

Awareness and self-esteem are keys to healthy relationships. First, be aware of the person you are relating to. Are there any signs or indications that he is not a whole, healthy person? Second, recognize your own worth and decide what is good and healthy for you. The ability to say "no" to the unhealthy and "yes" to the healthy is closely tied up with self-esteem. A woman with low self-esteem, or an untaught woman, or an unmothered or poorly fathered woman may develop ties to a man *she would not have set out to find* but who happens to be available or who has set out to "get" her.

The following letters are like red flags, warning of what can occur if one is not aware and alert.

I could not understand his meanness and hate toward me. I did not do anything nor did I deserve the anger towards me.
— L.K., DULUTH, MN

I met him when I was twenty-one and married him a year later. We were married for five years. I am still wary of a relationship. I was confused, forlorn, lonely, frightened. His protestations of love were intense but it was love without any joy or even hope for happiness. Until I could name what happened as verbal abuse, my only explanation for my divorce was that I couldn't deal with it.

He was gentle and courteous during courtship and spent all his spare time with me. I was certain he preferred me and that I was the love of his life.

He would reject me coldly, disdainfully, then he would start winning me back. I seldom knew where I stood with him. He would discuss nothing about the relationship. There was a cycle of distance then closeness then distance again for no reason. I felt like I was being killed. I remember waking up crying.
— V.T., DETROIT, MI

Before I thought I was always "too sensitive." Now I know I have lived with verbal abuse for as long as I can remember. I am now seventy . . . Some therapists don't fully understand verbal abuse. Maybe because they have self-esteem so others don't put them down.

In some ways I haven't experienced some of the traumas that rob you of your self-respect. My mother never hit me but she was critical of me. I was sexually harassed during the time I worked but I was not raped.

Operating on the power of low self-esteem is a rough way to travel through life. If I hadn't been able to ignite some self-respect and self-confidence in successful work I would be having a harder time coping with the verbal abuse I now experience. However, many times I have cried and lived with a "death" wish.
— V.H., DURHAM, NC

We dated one and a half years steady and I never experienced any verbal abuse. Then he became a stranger and still is after all these years.
— T.A., SAN FRANCISCO, CA

Before we married he verbally abused me—but I thought I caused all the problems. He's getting worse, of course.
— G.R., LODI, CA

I don't know if I love my mate anymore. I wish I would have seen the signs before I got married. Only saw two incidents during our one-

year engagement and I ignored them thinking they were due to nerv-
ousness—When I am verbally abused I usually think I've done some-
thing wrong, feel sad and hurt and wonder what I'm missing or what
my abuser thought and then I withdraw into myself and feel terrible
the whole day. If I say anything to try to understand it makes matters
worse—feels like I'm walking on eggs.

— B.W., Minneapolis, MN

Generally when an abusive relationship ends, the abuser goes on to abuse someone else and the survivor goes into recovery. If the process is rushed and the partner seeks a new relationship too soon, she may make another poor choice. Why does this happen? Primarily because she doesn't have all the knowledge necessary to evaluate a new relationship. She may also overlook certain things, feeling she needs to be with "somebody" even though she hasn't yet worked through her feelings and come to understand herself and her needs. The fear of being without a mate may be part of her low self-esteem. In this situation, the one most important sign she may overlook is a little sinking feeling, a flash of anxiety, a touch of fear, a nervous twinge.

Before they awakened to the awareness that they were being verbally abused, many survivors believed that they must be doing something to hurt or anger their mates, but they had no idea of what that something was. They didn't think so much, "I am doing something wrong" as "I should have said or done this differently." Some believed that they must further prove their love by being:

kinder
less sensitive
more accepting
more understanding
more able to laugh at his "jokes"
more able to build his confidence
more able to make him feel important

Whatever they believed, their beliefs reflected what their mates told them and camouflaged the realization that they were being abused. Why? Because verbal abuse was never named or spoken of. It is as if the awareness that their mates were doing something abusive *was itself a taboo.*

With awareness, the unthinkable becomes thought: *He's actually saying this to me* not *because he misunderstood my motivations or because I did something awful or because I am stupid or missing something important. He is saying this to me because he wants to control me.*

Even after leaving a verbally abusive relationship, many women were surprised to find out that they were not the only ones who had experienced this kind of abuse. Some were stunned to learn that most abusers used the same methods. A survivor who had left her relationship was aware that her mate was verbally abusive, but when she found that his methods were also used by others, she was shocked. She wrote,

> *I knew my husband was verbally abusive. Very excessively controlling. That is why I left. The thing he did that most upset me was laugh when I shared something or got upset. That tore me up! I was shocked to find out that this is a common weapon for abusers and I feel much better knowing it wasn't me.*
> — V.M., ARLINGTON, TX

A man who realized that he had been abusive and had enacted all the categories of verbal abuse discussed in chapter 2 wrote,

> *My upbringing taught me many of these very successful tactics for putting down my wife.*
> — D.R., SAN FRANCISCO, CA

While the abuser hones his controlling skills and practices them on a daily basis, usually with no awareness of the pain he brings, his mate may live in the illusion that she just has to try harder. Awareness comes when distinctions can be made. The partner may not see the abuse for what it is until the abuser makes a shift in his tactics or does something out of the ordinary, so that a contrast is created and the dark incident emerges out of the gray fog. It becomes clear. In the case of the following survivor, all the disturbing incidents coalesced into a clear realization that "This is abuse" with one event.

> *I finally realized I was in an abusive relationship when I needed surgery and my husband was incredulous and scornful that I wanted him to take me to the hospital. He didn't take me to the hospital (I took a train) and later he said I wanted to take the train. I realized—no, that was not true. Suddenly I realized he was deliberately refusing me. I was hurt and it was a real shock.*
> — K.S., CHICAGO, IL

As we have seen, the confusion of the partner and her unawareness stem in part from the fact that there is such a great disparity between her experience and her mate's. A survivor wrote about how difficult it was for her to come to terms with this disparity.

When I was verbally abused I felt confused, unsure, sad, hurt, shocked and thought I was missing something or he didn't understand something and I wanted so badly for him to understand me.
— L.P., NASHVILLE, TN

Another survivor says,

I found out religion isn't much help. Too often, books, speakers, tapes parrot the line of "wifely submission," and prayer to save the marriage, open up the husband to talk. Be loving and submissive and all is well. (HA!)
— M.T., WORCESTER, MA

Most religions have not addressed the problem of male control in relationships. Some have still not even resolved these issues in their own institutions.

Survivors repeatedly express their need to know that they are not alone. Their hope is that the insights, realizations, and experiences they offer will be of benefit to others. They have often felt alone and that no one else in the world could understand their experience. Some felt that it was wrong to feel hurt by "the one who loves you."

I know now I've been a battered woman, just as if I'd been beaten. Thank goodness, now, verbal abuse is being researched, and admitted to by others. We who have been hurt by words have suffered alone long enough.
— B.H., MINNEAPOLIS, MN

I was never able to face my marriage. After years of nightmares and blocking out terrible pain of the marriage, I am now able to identify what the issue was: verbal abuse. I always thought I was alone—that no one could possibly understand how painful and sad my marriage was.
— E.S., URBANA, IL

Although verbal abuse doesn't leave the outward signs of physical abuse, a survivor reminds us that we can recognize many physical signs that *might* point to verbal abuse. She says,

There are many physical signs of verbal abuse that I, and I am sure others, experience: The physical signs are there but very subtle, shallow breath, tight muscles, eye strain, headaches, and poor posture. Possibly many stress-related illnesses develop from being beaten down for no reason.
— P.W., BRISTOL, RI

In the following letter excerpts, survivors share their growing awareness and describe their feelings and hopes. Some who had spent years trying to identify the cause of their pain and confusion tell how they felt as they learned the truth about their relationship—a truth that had been, for the most part, completely denied by their culture.

I suddenly realized that anger was not the issue, abuse was. I now feel emotionally strong just to know.

— M.O., LAFAYETTE, CA

I doubt if I could convey the work I've put into understanding our relationship during these thirty-six years. I settled for seeing my nearly total compliance as a gift of peace to my husband. I wanted to send the first ripple of joy I felt in knowing verbal abuse is identifiable and absolutely unacceptable.

— R.F., WASHINGTON, DC

Verbal abuse is what my life has been like for the past twelve years. My marriage has always been confusing to me. Until recently, I did not realize that I was being verbally abused.

— E.T., FORT WAYNE, IN

I never thought I did or said anything wrong—I just thought he didn't like or understand what I did or said.

— P.N., LAGUNA BEACH, CA

I was so glad he quit drinking I accepted being called foul names, ordering, undermining, control, criticizing, judging, extreme anger, on and on the list goes. I figured I had to put up with it, now I know I don't have to.

— R.S., BEAUMONT, TX

Now I understand the hell of the last twenty-five years. It was my miracle. It was like being in a dark room and the lights came on—already there are changes being made. He knows I'm different. I feel as if my life's just beginning and I'm forty-three years of age.

— J.K., RENO, NV

For the first time I believe that it's not me, that I'm not stupid, dumb and weak.

— E.M., CHICAGO, IL

I am trying to believe more in myself, but it is difficult when the person you live with puts you down. The first eight years I was not even aware that there was such a thing as verbal abuse. When I was verbally abused I thought that I could be better or do better.

— W.K., AUSTIN, TX

He says he is trying and says he's getting therapy. He did tell me that he is afraid I will leave him. I just might do that.

— R.S., SPOKANE, WA

If there is no relief, this partner may be compelled to leave her mate. The experience of thousands of survivors tells us that a verbally abusive relationship does not improve unless the abuser becomes aware of his behavior, admits to it, and wants to change *more* than he wants to control. The abuser faces a tremendous amount of fear when he isn't keeping this stranglehold on his mate. A man wrote,

When I first met her I wanted her to like me and I wanted to like her. Now, I wouldn't want to be treated even for one day the way I treat her. She doesn't know about verbal abuse and I don't want her to know. I might not be able to change fast enough.

— J.T., OMAHA, NE

A survivor wrote,

Use any parts of my story—anything that may help others. Why did I not see the red flag early on—I am angry with myself for not being aware years earlier that I was a victim of a verbally abusive relationship.

We both were young survivors of the Holocaust, both orphans of the war.

The early abuse started by making demands on me that I was not able to meet emotionally—this combined with the demands of raising a family. The incidents are etched into my brain.

A "lifetime" later and years after his death I talked to a doctor. When I told the doctor that mine is not a pretty story, he asked, "Did he beat you up?" I said, "No, only with words" and he said, "I have seen people shredded to pieces by verbal abuse; it is worse than by beating."

I took courses, they helped. In one, a question was: "What qualities do you most admire and treasure in your mate or significant other?" From the several suggested answers, I could not find one. I was shocked. Have I been living in a trance all these long years?

I did not think of it as abuse then. It escalated. I was yelled at, insulted, humiliated. I was made to believe I was stupid, I was constantly criticized, I was made to feel inadequate and inferior. I could never win.

I was resigned to it. I felt so belittled. If anything went wrong, it was my fault. I was made to feel guilty. I got blamed. I could never do enough.

— J.B., NEW YORK, NY

In the above letter the survivor was resigned to the abuse her husband dealt out on a daily basis. Why? Because, she tells us, she accepted the assumption that it was her fault. She experienced demands (Did she shirk her duty?), criticism (Was she really so incompetent?), his anger (Why did she somehow make him mad?), and disparaging comments (Did he really believe that of her? Then she would have to explain better), but she did not know it was *abuse*. The belief that one will "get it right one day," that one will discover what one's fault is and correct it and that then one's mate will be accepting, warm, and kind forestalls the horror, pain, and (though unjustified) shame of recognition. In the next chapter we will see how blame by spouse, family, culture, and history all conspire against the partner of a verbal abuser.

Many survivors write of similar experiences. Many have wondered how they could have had such difficulty, especially those who went to therapists, psychology classes, self-help groups, libraries, hospitals, and so on looking for understanding. I believe it is very important for them to know that their quest was duplicated by thousands, that it was not their fault they could not find the truth, and that by its nature verbal abuse in some respects "brainwashes" the sufferer.

As we have seen, this is accomplished through the shattering of integrity described earlier, as well as by cultural denial. No wonder the survivors are often tormented with doubt. "What should I do?" or "What should I have done?" This is especially true if the abuse has been covert, undermining, and subtle. The wives of ministers, laborers, legislators, judges, therapists, physicians, educators, school principals, and scientists have spoken out:

> *I didn't realize that he was a verbal abuser for so long. Actually, it took me ten years to recognize it.*
>
> — S.P., REDLANDS, CA

> *He's been verbally abusive for twenty-six years but I didn't recognize our problem so was terribly frustrated and felt mentally disturbed.*
>
> — K.J., TOPEKA, KS

> *I never could identify what he was so angry about, or why he thought what I did was so worthless, and twenty-eight years of this have passed.*
>
> — V.C., MORRISVILLE, PA

> *I had always thought verbal abuse was only name calling. Boy, was I wrong!*
>
> — M.K., GRAND RAPIDS, MI

I have never had a black eye or a broken bone but my heart has been broken time after time.

— L.H., DURHAM, NC

I can now see that this is real and that I am not alone.

— M.L., NEWARK, NJ

I now realize that there is a name for what I endured for twenty-five years. With this validation my resolve is to never again allow myself to be subjected to this behavior.

— G.F., SILVER SPRINGS, MD

Some survivors who suffered verbal abuse for years have said that they were at the point of wanting to die. Learning about verbal abuse can bring unexpected relief, along with some sadness. Women who had experienced very covert abuse and had begun to believe their abuser wrote of their new awareness, expressed faith in their own sanity, and were glad to be out of the confusion.

Once you've realized he has lied, you can then question the validity of everything he says and has said. And it is that realization that is the first key to gaining your freedom.

— T.M., PORTLAND, ME

This is real, it's not my imagination! I'm a lot stronger now. At this point in my life I think I'm able to recognize abuse and don't see myself getting into another abusive situation!

— R.C., NEWARK, NJ

When I became aware of what the abuse was I felt as though a fifty-pound weight had been lifted off my shoulders.

— A.J., READING, PA

With awakening awareness, women say they feel a release from feelings of incompetence and confusion and guilt. Those who have been in confusing relationships, who have sought answers, who could not pinpoint what gave rise to their feeling that "something is wrong," experience both the pain and liberation that awareness brings. One woman who wrote about her suffering made notations on every page of my first book on verbal abuse, then mailed the whole book to me so that someone would know her pain.

A woman who went through her life "never knowing quite what was wrong and always being blamed," tells us her story.

I was working long weeks in a demanding job. I was well-educated and had been treated with respect and kindness by my family and by the men I dated. We met and I fell in love with my handsome, "charming" husband. He was "different" but super nice the year we were engaged. Never had anyone treated me better than he had! He was a perfect gentleman. I was doing very well and had gained a national reputation in my field. His friends envied him. His family treated me like a princess. They were always nice to me.

When we had been married four months the verbal abuse began. I was in shock. I couldn't believe it. It was like a nightmare.

He said, "If you had known how I really am, you would not have married me." I replied, "I would not have dated you!" I was shell shocked. It was a nightmare. I wanted "out." I was told "no" the wedding was too expensive. Try for at least a year. I did. The children came along and that was it.

When I went to my mother she was very frightened of being burdened with the children. My mother said she didn't want to help. My family said they would disown me—not help in any way if I left. Again I was told, "stand up for your husband."

Never knowing quite what was wrong and always being blamed, I suffered the agony of being trapped in the relationship. Now I know what was wrong.

— V.R. Aurora, Ontario

In this chapter we examined the survivors' experiences of recognition and awareness. With the realization of their value and their rights came the painful awareness of how the human spirit suffers from disparagement and invalidation. Unfortunately, abuses are sanctioned in our culture. Is it any wonder we can be undermined and oppressed without even knowing it?

In the early 1990s on a TV sit-com, a father figure yanked a hair from a young teen's face because the boy was happy about his "first beard." While the boy acted stunned, laughter emanated from the set.

In an earlier time, "When Archie Bunker called Edith a dingbat and admonished her, 'Stifle yourself,' we laughed. But in real life verbal abuse is anything but funny." (*Newsweek,* Oct. 12, 1992, pg. 90.)

In the next two chapters we learn more about being blamed and feeling trapped as the survivors continue to tell us their stories.

Chapter 5

Blame

I just wanted to talk things out and go on, but he would be silent for days.

— M.L. CHICAGO

The destruction of integrity is a primary factor in the perpetuation of verbally abusive relationships; this destruction of integrity (the congruence of thought, action, and result) is achieved in part through blaming. One of the surest ways to destroy one's perception, to unravel the thread of connection between inner and outer, between action and result, between thought and its expression, is to abuse a person *while blaming that person* for the abuse that she or he experiences. Abusive blame is to place responsibility and fault on the person being abused.

As a consequence of blame, partners frequently stay in relationships that are dangerous to them. Their primary connection to nature, to their best instinct, to their consciousness of what is good for them, is shattered by the blame they receive. The partner's integrity is impaired, and the impairment, in turn, hinders her ability to act to remove herself from the suffering. Furthermore, her suffering leaves her vulnerable to being blamed for the fact that she is suffering. Being blamed for her own abuse is in itself abusive, and so it continues.

Thus, blaming is not only destructive of one's integrity but also impedes one from recognizing that one is being abused. Even so, with great awareness and courage, many of the survivors of verbal abuse have spoken. They say that they will not be blamed for the abuse they have suffered.

A survivor said, "Don't you understand, I could stand on my

head and spit nickels and he would still abuse me. The abuse has nothing to do with me. He abuses because he is an abuser."

It often takes time for the partners of verbal abusers to realize that the abuser is the one with the problem. Most women who are verbally abused spend time focused inward, soul-searching, taking inventory, trying to identify their "sins," trying to find out what they did wrong. Because they have been blamed for their pain, they look inside for solutions. With no place even to turn their anger, unless against themselves, they have nowhere to go and no one who would understand. So they believe the lie. "There must be something I can do."

Looking back on their lives, survivors have wondered why they spent any time at all in the situations they were in. Was it just low self-esteem? I don't think so. I believe that never knowing quite what was wrong because they were always being blamed did much more than erode their self-esteem. It so totally denied their experience and invalidated them that eventually there was nothing they felt they *could* know for certain, nothing on which to base action. Being blamed is one of the most common experiences of the partner of an abuser and may do more than any other abuse to disempower the partner.

Beyond the relationship, blaming is often a part of the survivor's culture. This culture, reinforced by the abuser and sometimes by family members, tell many survivors that if they are unhappy, it is their fault. They are to blame. They must try harder.

Blaming abuse occurs not only in couple relationships but also in parent-child relationships and relationships of adult children to parents, as well as those between employers and employees, students and teachers, and every other kind of relationship.

Almost every survivor, before she became aware that she was not to blame for her unhappy relationship, believed that no one else was such a failure as she in getting along with her mate—so unable to think right, to not upset and irritate him, and so forth. She believed this not because there was anything wrong with her but because her mate told her so, in many ways, often every day.

Blame perpetuates verbal abuse, so it is well that we understand the magnitude of the problem. Exploring this issue may well shed light on patterns of abuse that extend across our society. *Note:* Although there has been a great outpouring of letters from women who are struggling with the issue of verbal abuse, we do not know what percent of relationships are verbally abusive. Early research suggests it may be more prevalent than anyone could have imagined.

Cultural Blame

For many years women have been devalued simply for being female, and have had their work devalued as well. Women live in a world that sanctions discrimination against them, implying that they are to blame for the hurts they experience. Let us look at our culture. "A woman is beaten every fifteen seconds, every single day in this country. Two million to four million women are physically assaulted each year." (*Contra Costa Times*, Feb. 2, 1993.) What is it like for a woman who finds herself in a verbally abusive relationship in this culture? As a girl she has likely grown up with a habit of self-searching and introverted focus, wondering, "What is wrong with me? How come I don't think those comments are funny? Look how he's laughing. Why can't I be happy like I should be?"

Sadly, many women go through their lives in pain and confusion trying to find out what is wrong while their culture tells them that "nothing is wrong." Women who went to many sources looking for help were told to try harder, as if the abuse was their fault and their suffering the norm. For them the whole world was crazymaking.

Once a woman is aware of the ways she is blamed by her culture ("What did you do to provoke him?"), she finds it easier to look outside herself. In a verbally abusive relationship, this is essential. She must come to realize that the abuse has nothing to do with her. It is very difficult for anyone, including the partner of an abuser, to grasp that a person who seems to get along quite well in the world, as many verbal abusers do, could suddenly lash out unprovoked at his partner for *no apparent reason*. Yet this is exactly what happens.

Blaming the victim is a kind of denial. In some cases acts of cruelty are so frighteningly senseless that we try to make sense of them by blaming the victim. It must be something about her.

A survivor who wishes to remain anonymous sent me a list of the many ways she was blamed for being verbally abused by her husband. She was blamed by counselors, authors, and certain segments of society. She was fed up with it. Blaming is telling the victim that she is responsible for the attack on her or for the hostility expressed covertly or overtly against her.

> *I kept believing all the blame the victim statements and so I didn't heal. In fact, I seemed to hate myself even more. And my rage was stuffed even deeper. Finally I realized my problem wasn't all the things society was telling me, my problem was that I was with a man who was abusive.*

> — A.K., Chicago, IL

Here is her list.

Blaming the Victim

1. I was told that I was responsible for my husband switching in a Jekyll/Hyde fashion from normal behavior to a snide remark against me because I somehow "allowed it."

   When I heard this I not only felt responsible for his behavior but also believed that if I was responsible, I *should* be able to make him stop even when he refused.

2. I was told that I looked for an abuser—sought one out.

   When I heard this I thought that even though he didn't switch his behavior until several months after our marriage, I should have known how he would change and therefore I could not trust myself.

3. I was told that because I wasn't abusive my "St. Mary act" gave me tremendous Power Over the family—even more than the abuser whose unpredictability terrified both me and my children.

   When I heard this I wondered how I could diminish myself in his eyes even further so that my "tremendous power" wouldn't aggravate him.

4. I was told that I have been worse to deal with than an abuser because with an abuser a person at least knows what he is dealing with. However, this isn't true in dealing with a non-abusive person.

   When I heard this I felt like dying because something was really wrong with me like my abuser always said.

5. Even though I was brainwashed by constant accusation and blame to believe that I was doing something wrong, I was told that I "shouldn't" have stayed in the marriage while I tried to find out what I was doing wrong.

   When I heard this I felt more ashamed and guilty than my abuser who never did feel ashamed or guilty.

6. I was told that by spending time searching for answers, seeking counseling, and trying to understand I had hurt my children as well as my abuser because I was guilty of "collusion."

   When I heard this I wondered how I could collude without knowing it.

7. I was told that even though I told my abuser "I feel hurt"

when he said hurtful things, I enabled him to be abusive.

When I heard this I wondered why no one told me how I might *dis*able him.

8. I was told that I was a masochist who wanted to be mistreated.

When I heard this I wondered how this could be when I was so angry at his broken promises.

9. I was told that the problem in the relationship was that I was a woman who loved too much.

When I heard this I thought that since he verbally abused me on my answering machine after I divorced him, I was a failure in not getting him to understand I didn't love him anymore.

10. I was told that I was addicted to high drama and excitement.

When I heard this I thought "I cannot remember feeling excited about anything in quite a few years—maybe I am crazy."

11. I was told that I must forgive if I wish to recover.

When I heard this I thought how could I presume to play God? My abuser will live and die according to what he has sown. Will this prevent my recovery?

12. That I was responsible for all my pain because I had turned him into a monster by being trusting and innocently naive.

When I heard this I wondered why someone didn't tell me we are not supposed to trust our mates.

13. That I was a martyr—and nothing is worse.

When I heard this I thought "All the confusion and hurt must be my fault. I've done the worst spending time trying to understand him and the relationship—trying to get past the confusion. But, don't martyrs clearly know the cause for which they are martyred?"

14. That in splitting up it is both partners who are responsible for the ending of the relationship.

When I heard this I thought this must mean, if I'm responsible for breaking up the family I should stay and die a tortuous death.

15. That I mistreated him too. I abused him.

When I heard this I thought, I don't belong in this world. Nothing is what I think it is.

16. That I am only attracted to abusive men. That if I hadn't married this abuser, I'd have married another.

   When I heard this I thought there is no hope for me on this planet.

17. That I didn't believe I deserved to be loved.

   When I heard this I thought, "Why?" when love is all I wanted. I'd even wanted to find out what I did that upset my husband so as not to lose his love.

18. That I believed love is being in pain and I don't know how to love.

   When I heard that I wondered why I was so happy before when we were first married and he hadn't started putting me down.

19. That I could only love a needy person.

   When I heard that I thought, "Why had I thought him a pillar of strength?"

20. That to become clear, I must not focus on him nor "take his inventory."

   When I heard that I thought, "How can I tell what's real and what to watch out for, if I can't talk about what he does?"

21. That I am co-dependent.

   When I heard this I wondered, "Is not knowing he lied my fault too?"

22. That I was in love with a dream.

   When I heard this I realized that I was being told it wasn't just that I had hope for a better relationship, but that I'm some dope who was dumb enough to be in love with, not a man, but a fantasy—a dream.

23. That I must stop blaming my mate and take responsibility for my own behavior.

   When I heard this I felt so frustrated and helpless I wanted to die. If only I could discover what I was missing, what I was doing wrong, I would take responsibility for it, for anything, if only I knew what it was.

24. And finally, that I will not grow nor "recover," if I do not accept and work on the above truths.

   When I heard this I spent ten useless years working on the above "truths."

   Finally someone said your problem is you are married to an abuser.

The Blame Game

One couple I talked with developed a method of dealing with abusive incidents that backfired. It was based upon a misunderstanding of blame that simply sped up the usual cycle of violence (first described by Lenore Walker with regard to physical violence). In this case the partner was verbally battered instead of physically battered.

The abuser and his partner had both agreed upon the method. The abuser said he wanted to stop abusing, but so far he hadn't. Both believed that, although he didn't stop to feel his own feelings but instead kept acting them out, he would sometime be able to stop. As an example of his abusiveness, he used cutting sarcasm against his wife during the interview I was conducting *for no reason at all!*

Their method simulated a common cycle of physical domestic violence. A verbal hit. She "leaves." He apologizes. She forgives. A verbal hit. She "leaves." And so on. Although this was far from their intention, their method actually gave the abuser the opportunity of verbally battering without having to take responsibility for the wound he inflicted.

The abuser in this scenario had admitted to being abusive, but he told his mate that if she said "Stop it!" or "That hurts!" she would be *blaming* him. In other words, "I can throw the dart or stab you with the dagger, but if you tell me how you *really* feel I'll feel blamed and you'll pay for it!" Here, then, is how they interacted.

He would wound.

She couldn't say "Stop it" or "That hurts!" If she did, he would either feel blamed, or enticed by her vulnerability to really go after her "like dead meat on a hook." So instead they agreed that she would say something that suggested she was "gone" to him, defended, behind a wall, like, "*I'm protected.*"

He would then apologize to win her back.

She would accept.

The cycle could begin again at any moment.

What this couple had done is take the concept of blame and make her guilty of blaming if she dared let him know he was abusing her. The one thing the abuser wants most is for his partner to take responsibility for his feelings—just as the rapist wants his victim to be blamed for his violence.

Even more astonishing is that in order to reinforce her agreement to endure her pain without flinching or revealing it (other than by saying, "I'm protected") the woman seemed to believe that if she expressed her pain by crying out, "That hurts!" she would be "being a victim." This fit nicely with her abuser's desire to inflict pain *without having to hear a complaint.*

Thus, the person actually being *protected* was the abuser. He was being protected from suffering the consequences of being an abuser. He was protected from having to feel his own bad feelings without hiding behind an abusive act, especially anger. You see, his bad feelings make him feel small and powerless. When he feels small and powerless he wants to feel big and powerful. In order to feel big and powerful he has to have a "win," that is, a Power Over fix.

"How do you know when you have a win?" I asked.
He said, "You draw blood."
"How do you know you've drawn blood?"
"You hurt someone."

— INTERVIEW WITH A VERBAL ABUSER

This couple's method of dealing with verbal abuse shows how strangely out of balance and distorted a relationship can become. It is interesting that after he abused her, she pretended that she was inaccessible, just as his own unfelt wounded inner child was. Sadly, this method: (1) victimized and blamed the partner, (2) protected the abuser, (3) led the victim to hold the false hope that eventually her verbal batterer would stop, (4) protected him from feeling his bad feelings (avoiding those feelings was the reason he abused in the first place), and (5) confused the partner and set up the same old verbally abusive relationship with new code words and a virtual guarantee that it could go on forever.

This couple unwittingly reduced the cycle of abuse—build-up of tension in the abuser, release of tension in verbal "cut," "withdrawal of his mate, and him winning her back—to a ten-minute exercise!

Therapy
Many survivors expected to find out what was wrong in their relationship from therapists. Although many received much-needed support from therapists who had insight into the dynamics of verbal abuse, some did not get the information they needed. A good number of therapists were not knowledgeable about verbal abuse and were unable to help their clients. Some could not help them to define their relationship, and some were not able to spot the abuser's tactics. Some who realized that they were observing a verbally abusive relationship did not know how to increase their clients' awareness.

Survivors said that they often found it impossible to describe the pain and frustration they were experiencing in their relationships. The typical survivor said she was greatly confused by the abusive blaming statements she heard. She often believed that she was inadequate because she was blamed so often. If she weren't inadequate, she reasoned, he wouldn't object to her or her thoughts, ideas, or actions.

Some who suffered abuse encountered another difficulty in getting help. They found that many therapists had not really studied verbal abuse, especially as a covert means of controlling another in a relationship. This is understandable; after all, most verbal abusers are not crazy, and so their mode of control has not been a focus of study for mental health professionals. In fact, the mode of control used by the abuser is sanctioned in some parts of the world and by certain segments of society.

A man who was working on change spoke to a national audience about his own verbally abusive behavior. He said that he could place the blame for relationship problems on his wife and *could always convince any therapist that he was not abusive to his wife*, which was the opposite of the truth. He described himself as a "master of control." (Of course, he had not encountered therapists trained in these issues.)

Survivors did have many tragic, painful, and debilitating experiences. Many checked themselves into hospitals for evaluation. Several submitted to shock treatments. One had a series of particularly nightmarish experiences while looking for help. Her therapist told her to wear sexy nightgowns and clean the house more. When her husband took away the car keys and ripped out the phone, she walked miles to a new therapist, told him what had happened, and felt validated, only to find that the next day her abuser had convinced the new therapist she was lying. Prayer kept her going, and finally, several months later, through a call to a hospital, she was referred to a therapist who knew the dynamics of verbal abuse and understood everything. No human being should have to go through the pain and anguish and crazymaking behavior this woman suffered.

Some survivors were put on drugs to relieve their feelings of depression. Some attempted suicide because they were constantly told to do better and try harder, and were then abused even more—because most abusers move quickly to put their mate down when she is vulnerable.

Women in the public eye, married to men in high offices, did their best not to let on what was happening. "After all," they thought, "If I just knew what to do this wouldn't be happening." One said she was in pain and her stomach was in knots for three-quarters of her life with her spouse.

I believe that the issue here is not so much that some counselors didn't understand the dynamics of control in a relationship; it is that the culture has sanctioned the control of women to such an extent that a therapist might unwittingly advise a human being already suffering greatly to act like a slave.

Counseling is more readily available than ever before. So why hasn't the problem of verbal abuse and the controlling nature of abusive relationships been addressed long ago? Many survivors say that they had joint counseling with their husbands. Yet the issue was never addressed or even identified, despite the fact that the habitual methods of dominating and controlling through discounting, trivializing, diverting, and so forth actually took place *during the counseling sessions*. The counselor didn't necessarily indulge this abuse; instead, they often failed to notice it. In some cases, however, the counselor "bought into it," agreeing with the abuser that the partner was making *a big thing out of nothing*.

Survivors were told to try harder, to develop new interests, not to expect too much. One partner said that she was told "go shopping." Another was told to "be more submissive." Often, it seems, the problem of abuse is so pervasive that it is like gravity: it's there, but no one sees it and no one talks about it. This is perhaps the most horrifying aspect to the stories of verbal abuse—that while these women were being victimized with not a soul in the world to validate them, they had simultaneously to cope with an almost crazy feeling of helplessness and confusion that was "all their fault."

If you are seeking counseling and are not satisfied that your counselor is experienced in the control issues of verbal abuse and crazymaking behaviors, interview some more counselors until you are satisfied—until you feel, *This one really understands*. Don't settle for anyone who doesn't give you this feeling of support. Most of the women's service programs listed in the appendix of this book can refer you to a therapist who knows about these issues. Many therapists think they "know" about abuse and can deal with it, but unless it is specifically named and its dynamics uncovered and changed, the pattern will continue. Most women who are in, or suspect that they are in, verbally abusive relationships *can* get help from individual counseling. Too often, though, traditional marriage counseling blames the victim, telling her to try harder.

Repeated blame, overt and covert, leaves women feeling guilty and unsure. A survivor writes of feeling invalidated by her counselor when an issue of importance to her was questioned instead of accepted. This is the kind of problem you must watch out for when you are choosing a counselor.

My counselor asked why it was so important to me to have a name for what had happened to me. I answered that it made it real—I was validated. I hadn't "made it up" or been overly sensitive. It had happened to others too.

— M.F., WASHINGTON, DC

The following survivors did not receive help with regard to their verbally abusive relationships. They write,

My husband and I have been through many sessions of therapy and we were never made to realize that there was such a thing as verbal abuse.

— S.S., ALBUQUERQUE, NM

We began counseling and the counselor felt the problem was basically mine. It took three horrible years for me to get the courage to have [my husband] leave but when I did, I soared!

— M.H. RENO, NV

I've not been hit but have been threatened . . . I'm over fifty-five and have been verbally abused by my husband for more than twenty years . . . Now I do not know if I love him. He is a health care professional and advises women often.

— J.W., HOUSTON, TX

Women have been blamed by society for their unhappiness while being told by their abusers that they have nothing to complain about. Verbal abuse seems so inhuman, so bizarre to anyone seeking mutuality in a relationship that, no matter how deeply she understands that an abuser abuses because he abuses and not because of her, the survivor will almost always find it incredible that any human being would treat another that way. She will conclude, "He wouldn't do this for no reason at all." This is why the partner is confused by blame. It is as if she is just not *something* enough.

In order to avoid feeling responsible for someone else's behavior, no matter how blaming it is, the survivor must constantly remind herself, "Of course there is no *reason* for his behavior. I am not to blame, because abuse is irrational."

A survivor who had had no opportunity to learn about verbal abuse in her profession wrote,

I'm a health professional. I feel rather stupid that I haven't been more aware and knowledgeable of the problem.

— E.C., FLAGSTAFF, AZ

Understanding psychology does not make one immune to suffering verbal abuse.

I myself am a therapist, but I did not recognize the abuse in my own relationship for five years. I am embarrassed, but please tell people how subtle and undermining it can be.
— B.A., FOUNTAIN VALLEY, CA

This woman is not alone. The following letter excerpt is from another therapist.

I am a therapist, but it took me seven years to realize that what he did to me was immoral, destructive, and was not going to end.
— J.P., LOUISVILLE, KY

Many of the partners of verbal abusers have been told constantly that they are too sensitive. This may be one of the most common blaming statements. A verbal abuser tells about blaming his mate: "I always said, 'You're too sensitive.' That's how I got away with it."

"What," I asked him, "would have happened if she'd never recognized the lie?"

He answered, "I'd have gone on forever telling her she was too sensitive, if I could have gotten away with it."

Although some survivors gained support in twelve-step programs, others didn't. (See chapter 15 for more on twelve-step programs.) Some were blamed for bringing up the abusive incidents. In fact, they made a point of this fact. Some wrote,

The twelve-step programs I tried made it worse for me. Because in these groups, you're not supposed to talk about your mate. That's called taking his inventory. So, never would I do such a thing. I certainly wasn't going to blame him.

After learning this I felt it was wrong to tell anyone! Even when I went to a counselor, I felt I was "healthy" not talking about him.

In retrospect, I can say this doesn't work with abuse !!
— K.B., DULUTH, GA

I was in twelve-step programs for eleven years. They gave me certain kinds of support but when I said, "This is what he says to me . . . What could make him say such things? "They said don't blame him, talk about yourself."
— M.S., SEATTLE, WA

After about six years of marriage I began to seek psychotherapy. I even went into the hospital several times for "help" for my depression. My hus-

band was so good at looking good (church involvement and all that) that no one ever diagnosed the real problem—so it kept repeating.
— W.J., FAYETTEVILLE, AR

I have been repeatedly frustrated and discouraged when trying to explain to people what I'm suffering. No one seems to understand or believe that I am suffering abuse. Even professional therapists don't seem to see verbal abuse as serious, at least not the ones I've seen.
— E.M., BOULDER, CO

I knew something was wrong, just didn't know what. Three therapists didn't give me a clue. Now I know. I left for several days when he became verbally abusive. It made an impression. To leave permanently? I'm weighing things. My age: over fifty-five. My health: not great. My work: no retirement.
— S.P., ENCINO, CA

My relationship has been a major source of pain for the last thirty-five years. When I talked to a therapist about it she said to go shopping.
— L.D., ROCHESTER, NY

These appalling reports are *not* indicative of most therapists. They do, however, serve as warning signals. Some therapists are not trained in issues of control and communications. Your best source for references is your local women's service agency. You do not *ever* have to have been hit to get help. Many give referrals for both women's and men's programs. See the agency listings in the appendix of this book.

Men have also written about their experiences of therapy. Typically, they say something similar to what this man said:

I spent thousands of dollars on therapy. I never realized I was being abusive and I was indulging in every form of verbal abuse. It just never came up. I'd talk about my frustrations and that my wife and I were fighting. Her "Please don't yell at me" felt real antagonistic then.
— T.R., BUFFALO, NY

Blaming and Coming Back

Some women take the approach, "If it's something to do with me I'll try again." Survivors say that if they have accepted blame for being abused, they are inclined to come back after they have left the relationship. They believe that when they come back everything will work out because they won't "make him mad." Somehow they'll discover what it is they're "doing wrong." They may also feel that they are getting love and acceptance when he says he wants them back. Some may feel such total rejection from the pain of the abuse that the abuser's desire

to have them back makes it almost impossible for the victim not to return.

*"Why do you wound your wife with sarcasm and not, for instance, the
woman at the supermarket checking out groceries?"* I asked.

"It's simple," he said, *"The store could go after me. On the other
hand, my wife forgives me."*

Chapter 6

Killing the Spirit

Verbal abuse is bloodless murder. I feel like a walking dead person.

— J.M, Spokane, WA

Someday, You Have to Shout "Cut!"

Dear Ms. Evans,

I was going to begin, "It is a chapter that is closed," but I will re-open these pages for this letter. It was not a chapter I thought would have appeared in any book about my life, at least that is what I would have stated as a very young woman. I had vague images of partnership, concern, passion, and support that would surely materialize one day in my life with the appearance of a forthright and clear minded young man.

Together we would go into the world. You see, chapters follow each other naturally, to lead to a logical, cohesive work—an expression that, though meandering at times, winds up ultimately to have meaning, to have enriched some piece of the world, to have given something to the reader of the chapter of my life.

I was a passionate young person, idealistic and clear minded. It seemed natural to approach the world with my inborn optimism, and to expect the same commitment to life and to love and to intrinsic values from everyone.

I had not been coached in one powerful fact: Not everyone sees the world in the same way. And so what I endured, and what many suffer, does not seem logical and cannot be placed by logic into the certainty of our lives, or the vision we at one time believed would be: That at some time all the fragmented pieces, the inappropriate battles, the accu-

satory words, the unthinking disregard, the humiliation would become part of one proper, coherent and majestic whole. That somehow, eventually, both I and God could smile and say, "Yes, this is the right plan, the right story."

Instead, one year became five years, which became a significant five years given up and replaced by a fragile system of belief, faith, hope, wish and prayer. That could not be called a chapter in this life of mine. It looks more like a scene from an old black and white film where I see myself acting out the scenes like a macabre and exaggerated mannequin where pain and confusion are the order of the day.

I think that when we believe we have been cast in a leading role in a warm love story of unselfish support and rich laughter, painted in golden tones, we don't want to let go of that vision to the garish black and white that it is.

When your words are not heard, when conversation has become a series of bored one-syllable responses to your questions, when plans are made without regard for your schedule, when your partner talks more, and more lovingly, to your dog, when your accomplishments are received by patronization, when your laughter is met by silence, when you begin to feel like a different person than you were growing up . . . it is a terribly wrong picture.

Now, today, I look for my feelings. Back then, I buried almost all of them, except for hope. Now I respect my tears. Then, I dishonored them by hiding pain as though it were shameful, like a dog learns to hide its tail when it is kicked. Now, I believe in myself above all else. Then I believed all else before myself. Now, I can trust myself. For a long time, I could not.

I have asked myself how a person's own compass, the one that says, "This is right for me" or "This is not right at all" could be dismantled. I realize that the answer is: A little piece at a time. If you are involved with a con artist, a controller or any abuser, they eagerly take pieces of your self-esteem, your spirit, and your ability to make your own choices for yourself. How do they do this so easily? Because we who have been hopeful and faithful have left our souls unguarded. Who would have imagined that they had to hold on to their beliefs, feelings, and heart with two hands, tightly, in the company of their loved one?

We lay our forthrightness on the floor to be stepped on. And then we don't cry out in pain because we think it shouldn't hurt—it was only our beloved, not a mugger. We openly bare our thoughts, only to have them shot down right before our eyes out of the clear blue sky. We should have guarded the precious property of our minds—our dreams, plans, passions, and talents—to keep them undamaged and as filled

*with vigor and purpose as when we were children. But who would
have thought to protect their very identity from their life mate?*

*And so, bit by bit, what makes us feel good and sure of our identity
and direction, is given up freely to these erring mates. To err may be
human. To forgive over and over again goes against all that is human,
the spirit and the soul. Even a horse learns not to repeat the ungracious
dumping of the rider.*

*Look at the horse and take a hard look at where you are. Are you ly-
ing in the dirt again in an old black and white western, wondering how
you wound up in such an alien country? Is there, buried deep, a
screaming in your heart that you are afraid to hear—a screaming "It's
not the right story! It's a scrap of film left on the editing room floor,
decades ago, that wound up in the middle of my life!"*

Someday, you have to shout . . . "CUT!"

Sincerely,
C.H., NEWPORT, RI

Domination and control kill the spirit and may be so extremely
covert that the partner in the relationship is unable to define the problem. If, like the writer just quoted, you find that it isn't life that is getting you down but your relationship with its broken promise of
companionable partnership, you should ask yourself: Is there something screaming in your heart?

The mental pain of covert abuse is horrifying. Later in this chapter we will hear a survivor describe this covert cruelty in her own
story. She, unlike the writer above, suffered half a lifetime trying. And
her heart, I know, still screams, "Why, dear God, did he do it?" Our
screams are questions, are they not?

Now, in the perspective of time, she knows that what she experienced was one of the worst forms of abuse. Her spirit languished
while her "loving" husband played with her mind. She knows, as do
many survivors, that verbal abuse is killing to the spirit. "

Although verbal abuse is harmful to anyone it touches, it is particularly harmful to all those who experience it in family relationships.
Where but in the safety and comfort of home is one as trusting, as susceptible; where is one least wary and most easily destroyed, all under
the guise of love?

Although this book is based upon women's experiences as expressed by survivors of verbally abusive relationships, it is important
to remember that verbal abuse can be perpetrated by anyone. Most of
us can recall a time when we were "not ourselves," overly demanding,

thoughtlessly critical, disagreeable. Most people, seeing someone "out of sorts," wonder, "What's wrong with her today?" The verbally abusive *relationship* is something different. It is characterized by one person's continuing need to dominate and control the other.

If it is so subtle and so denied that the partner is confused as to what the problem is, she had best ask herself the question, "Am I feeling emotionally supported by what I'm hearing, or am I feeling emotionally hurt or beaten down or confused?" The spirit may die slowly, unnoticed by anyone, even the victim, if it happens very gradually and she adapts slowly.

As we have seen in previous chapters, although the abuser violates the basic human rights of his mate in many ways, the abuse often goes unrecognized for what it is, and its victims suffer a great loss of spirit. Any creature that loses its freedom to be itself and to live in a naturally healthy environment loses its spirit. We may say the spirit dies, although the spirit doesn't so much die as become "lost" to the sufferer. When a person has lost her spirit, she wonders why she is still around. Though she isn't necessarily suicidal, suicides *are* often fostered by verbal abuse.

We know from life experience that the spirit also "comes back," is felt again. One is revived, rejuvenated, inspired. The word *inspired* means "to be infused with spirit," as by divine action. Even while we contemplate the death of spirit, we may keep in mind that through recovery, the spirit is revived and the joy of life returns.

Secretly Abusing, Openly Denying
"His denial is so strong he says I lie about him."

Verbal abuse usually takes place in private. Usually the abuser is so good at "crazymaking," presenting a different side to others and convincing all who know him that he is a great guy, that the partner may begin to believe *she* is the abuser. She may also believe that no one would believe her even if she was sure she was being abused.

Many survivors say something along the lines of, "I am not one of the 'lucky' ones who gets hit." Why would they say such a thing? These survivors were often constantly (and very subtly) abused. With no witness, they were told it wasn't happening. They felt crazy. No one ever spoke of such a thing. They felt alone and uncertain. They could hardly understand what was happening to them. How could anyone else? These survivors wanted to get help. They wanted to understand their pain. Their friends and family said they were lucky. When they confronted their mates and said, "I don't like what you said," they were told they didn't know what they were talking about.

No one in their world seemed to. At least a victim of physical battering, they respond, can point to a bruise.

Diminishing

A man said, "I grew up with verbal abuse. I honed my skills in childhood." This man learned early to *diminish others* while his mate learned to *encourage others*. Consequently, she was unaware and vulnerable. No one had coached her, as the writer above told us, in "one powerful fact, not everyone sees the world in the same way." I might add that not everyone is in the same world.

Women who had lived through very difficult childhoods looked forward to the promise of adult freedom, never dreaming that the one who said he loved them would think so little of them. Women who did not have difficult childhoods and had not been verbally abused at home were often at a serious disadvantage. They did not know what to expect. The betrayal of love that often began in the first months of married life was an often subtle and insidious killing of spirit. A survivor wrote,

> *Being that I was marrying a "Christian" gentleman I thought it would make a world of difference. What a dream. Married less than a year and I have never felt so belittled or so degraded by one man in my life.*
>
> *I wanted to die but I was not suicidal. I kept thinking if I'm this unhappy he must be. Then I started realizing, he wasn't.*
>
> — E.P., SARASOTA, FL

> *I may leave with nothing. That or die. He seems to like to make fun of me. I said, "I don't like that!" as firmly and strongly as I could, then he started mimicking me. I felt so frustrated. I said, "Stop it!" and then he got madder—said I was a zero and he was sick of my complaining and that I was going to be sorry.*
>
> — K.W., OMAHA, NE

In the letter just quoted, the survivor was ridiculed, diminished, mimicked, called names, and then blamed for the verbal assault. The abuser sounds almost like a child, mimicking and name calling—almost more pathetic than dangerous. Except that a child's emotions in a 280-pound body are deadly serious.

Usually oblivious to the effects of his behavior, the verbal abuser pursues his course of disparagement. How else to feel "one up" with Power Over his partner? With skill and accuracy, the abuser takes aim at his partner and fires the shots that kill her spirit.

There are many ways to diminish another. The behaviors listed below are drawn from the List of Controlling Behaviors compiled by women of The Marin Abused Women's Services and by men in the Men Allied Nationally Against Living in Violent Environments (MANALIVE) Program. These behaviors rob the partner of her dignity and humanity and are employed to make the partner feel as disrespected, inconsequential, and worthless as possible. These cruel and hurtful behaviors are particularly killing to the spirit of the one who seeks a word of kindness, a word of support, a compassionate response. Most insidious, they are often immediately denied by the abuser.

Behaviors That Diminish Your Partner

- ❏ Belittling your partner
- ❏ Laughing, smirking or joking
- ❏ Mimicking your partner; for example, imitating her tone of voice when she is angry
- ❏ Infantilizing your partner; treating her as if she were an infant
- ❏ Repeating what you say to your partner as if she were too stupid to understand you
- ❏ Patronizing your partner; being scornful, disdainful, contemptuous
- ❏ Edifying your partner; for example, responding to her concerns by instructing her
- ❏ "Knowing it all"
- ❏ "Last wording"
- ❏ "So-ing" or So-what-ing"
- ❏ "Bafflegabbing"; talking in ways intended to mislead and baffle your partner
- ❏ "Eloquenting"; using high-flown words and phrases to appear superior
- ❏ Running on
- ❏ Insulting your partner
- ❏ Ignoring your partner
- ❏ Making inappropriate sounds
- ❏ Sentence hanging or dropping off

Making a Thing of the Other
Sometimes oppression is so pervasive it goes unnoticed. A classic example is the drama of two men fighting over a woman as they would

over an object—fighting as if she were not a human being with the human right to choose for herself. Any time someone is called a name, that person is being told she does not exist, that she is nothing but the *thing* she is being called. In fact, whenever one attempts to have Power Over another, to control another, one has already begun to view the other as a thing. Things are to be controlled, moved around, shown off, put aside, ignored, used, owned, and kept.

> *I was a thing, an object, he was totally indifferent to my needs . . . He was just as indifferent to his children unless they were waiting on him. I'm separated and I am also developing a zest for life that is great and new to me.*
>
> — E.W., St. Louis, MO

Threatening the Other

Body language that accompanies verbal communications can make the abuse more threatening. Body language is like speaking with your body. Following are some examples.

- ❑ Threatening with facial expressions, such as grimacing, glaring, and rolling the eyes
- ❑ Threatening your partner with your tone of voice; for example, speaking with a commanding or a scathing tone of voice
- ❑ Threatening your partner by your body stance while you are talking by wagging a finger, getting up in her face, or making a fist
- ❑ Invading her space by getting up close while you are talking
- ❑ Threatening her by making sudden movements to startle and scare her

There are numerous kinds of verbal threats. Some can be very subtle, and we don't consciously realize we're being threatened unless we think about what we are experiencing. In all matters of communication it is helpful to ask, "What am I hearing? What is he really communicating?" Following are some examples of verbal threats.

- ❑ Whispering or muttering to your partner.
- ❑ Swearing and cursing at your partner.
- ❑ Threatening to do or not to do something.
- ❑ Threatening the pets.
- ❑ Threatening the children.
- ❑ Threatening to throw something.

- ❏ Threatening to hit something.
- ❏ Threatening to destroy something.
- ❏ Threatening to have an affair.
- ❏ Threatening to leave the relationship or marriage.
- ❏ Threatening to take away the children.
- ❏ Threatening to restrain your partner.
- ❏ Threatening to restrict your partner's physical movements; for example, "I'll make you sit!"
- ❏ Threatening to prohibit your partner's social contacts; for example, "If I hear you talking to her again, the phone goes."
- ❏ Threatening to hit your partner.
- ❏ Threatening to maim your partner.
- ❏ Threatening your partner with a weapon (including cleaning it in front of her).
- ❏ Threatening to kill your partner.

A survivor wrote,

> *My therapist and I wonder whether verbal abusers carry out their threats because my husband, whom I am separated from, has threatened to kill me. Actually, he has threatened to slit my throat.*
> — D.W., OLYMPIA, WA

I answered this letter in short order! This therapist and survivor needed to know that many controlling personalities *do* carry out their threats. Of course, the partner suffers greatly from simply being threatened. Each time it happens, her spirit dies a little. But threats of violence must not be ignored. They are important reasons to make workable plans to leave a relationship and immediately seek shelter and support.

Threatening the loss of the relationship, threatening with abusive anger, threatening to hurt are just some of the ways threats can be used to control. One can become so used to hearing such threats, one can forget that at one time they would never have been tolerated for a moment.

Some readers may find it almost impossible to imagine that threatening could take place in many relationships in "this day and age." Yet threatening behavior is much more prevalent than is generally thought. We live in a culture that still fosters "not feeling" and "not crying." Verbal and physical abuse both originate with the abuser's attempts to control his own feelings. Although millions of verbally abusive relationships continue without physical abuse, it is hardly surprising that many do escalate to physical abuse. Survivors "walk on egg shells" to avoid abuse, although the abuse has nothing to do with them. And of course, there is no justification for abuse of any kind.

I have heard people in the media suggest, in planning an event to inform the public of the issue of verbal abuse, that couples should take part in the proceedings "so we can hear 'both sides.'" There are not two sides. Abuse is not a conflict. It is not a fight. Some survivors suffered an unnecessary ten years or more of torment because they were told that they were engaged in a power struggle that "needed to be resolved" or that they were just having normal fights "which you've got to expect . . ." They lost time and the chance of happiness trying to deal with a battery of nonexistent issues.

When a child is molested or abused, there are not two sides. Similarly, when an adult is verbally abused and threatened, there are not two sides. One person is not attacking and the other counterattacking. On the contrary, one is trying to understand and not upset the other, whose behavior is directed toward maintaining *control* and *dominance* with overt or covert attacks.

The following letter speaks for many in conveying the perplexed feeling many survivors have at trying to come to terms with these issues. The victim suffers from her mate's behavior, which she strives with all her being to understand. She also tries heroically to get her mate to understand that, even if he thinks nothing of what he is doing (as he so often says), she doesn't like it; it hurts her, and "silly" as her feelings may seem to the abuser, it is a cruel way to behave. To all of this she is usually told yet again not to get all worked up about "nothing."

Victims often do not know that the abuser enjoys the constant winning. And all the while their spirit slowly dies, as the following letter attests.

The Erosion of Spirit

I knew my marriage wasn't great—but I couldn't seem to figure out how to describe it to a counselor. I felt embarrassed to say things like, "He has to control the thermostat. He nags at me. Everything about me is wrong. He teases me in a way that I feel put down."

I couldn't seem to feel like anything but a fool if I described these things to a counselor.

I told myself that it was "affectionate teasing" and "no big deal."

*He'd tell me I'd just done such and such a foolish thing. He didn't seem
mad. Or he'd "tease" me that I couldn't get to the point in telling
something. Or "tease" me about the way I walked. Or the way I drove.
Or how I'd go around with one eye open, when first waking up.*

*Yes, it all seemed harmless. He didn't seem to be mad at me. In fact
he seemed to smile at me, as if my stupid little ways were cute. But I
was beginning to feel stupid.*

*He'd laugh to others about the way I answered the phone. Or, he'd
tell them how I spent so much time combing my hair. Or how he was
always ready first.*

I'd laugh. Try to be a good sport.

Isn't this just the way people like to tease one another?

*But I never teased him. It would seem too cruel. Isn't that a contra-
diction? I couldn't figure it out.*

*It was always something else wrong with me. The way I talked, the
way I gestured, the way I laughed, or how I dropped something, or forgot where I placed something.*

I kept telling myself, as he did, it was "affectionate teasing."

*It went on and on. I told myself it was harmless, but it hurt. Was
I really annoying him?*

*One day when he teased me about how I packed my suitcase, I re-
member beginning to feel really embarrassed. There were so many
things I did "wrong."*

*I learned much later that what was actually happening to me was
that I was continually being kept "off-balance" and made to feel "wrong."*

How cruel.

Chip. Chip. Chip.

My self-esteem was being chipped away.

*Without realizing it I was monitoring his expressions. A look of ir-
ritation—I was wrong again! But how? I had no idea. But, something
I was doing was embarrassing or irritating him.*

*As unlovable as I was now feeling, wasn't I lucky this wonderful
man chose me?*

How subtly he stole my soul.

— W.A., FORT WAYNE, IN

This survivor's spirit was gradually eroded by constant ridicule.
The correspondence between what she did (action), and how it turned
out (result) was destroyed. It was as if, while she was making the bed,
for example, she was being convinced by her abuser that in some way,
of which he was certain, she was messing it up. And it was in her best
interests that he let her know.

The destruction of integrity—the correspondence between inner and outer, cause and effect—is doubly debilitating to the spirit when it is secretive and when it is denied, as if any pain on the part of the victim indicates yet another of the "defects" already so "humorously" pointed out.

She was completely convinced of her mate's good intentions, so much so that teasing him in return would "seem too cruel." His pretense of kindly good humor made it seem utterly wrong to accuse *him* of cruelty. In fact, to accuse him would seem to break a taboo. To dare to say he didn't love her when all he did was for her. Didn't he always say? If there were only a way to say, "Your joking and your teasing are intolerable to me. They hurt too much." But, she went on to say, if she complained, he would erupt in a terrifying rage, declaring the mere implication of unkindness to be outrageous.

> *I probably would have . . . just tried to buffalo her into backing down if I got angry enough.*
> — INTERVIEW WITH A VERBAL ABUSER

His rage would be so real she would believe him. And her spirit would die a little more. It would seem that any man who could disparage another as this one does has lost the capacity for compassion in the process of losing touch with his feelings.

I mentioned the torment of teasing to a young woman in her early twenties. She told me how awful it seemed and how it was amazing to her that anyone would put up with that sort of thing. A few minutes later, however, she said that on several occasions recently her boyfriend had said things that made her feel bad, things she didn't think were funny—and that when she told her mother about this, her mother explained that she was being too sensitive, and that it was just her boyfriend's sense of humor. In a way she was glad to hear that *he really did love her after all*. Her mother had probably been glad too, when she first heard that she was just "too sensitive." Hearing this, it was a little easier to squelch the initial pain and go on believing, *It's not happening.*

The letter below is from a young woman married just six years. Her disintegration and loss of spirit are like a "hold" on her mind. Seven years ago, she too believed, "It's not happening."

> *My self-esteem is so low I don't think I can face life on my own. I have been trying to get away from my husband since the day I met him when I was 17, but he has such a hold on my mind I can't do it yet. He threatens to have me hurt if I try to leave.*
> — H.B., MOUNTAIN, WI

This young woman, who might be enjoying life with her family and other young people, is instead experiencing the existence of a prisoner, her spirit so shattered she can barely face life. It sounds as if her soul, too, has been stolen. However, she may yet save it. Recognition is the hardest step; after that, nearly anything is possible. Without recognition, nearly nothing is.

This sense of impossibility is the grief of verbal abuse. It is killing to the spirit, enervating, withering—all with the horrifying twist, "You're making it all up."

The following letter excerpts are from more survivors.

When I look back on it all now, the lack of love he has given me—even hugs or kisses—they were nil. I feel I've wasted so much of my life on a man, perhaps incapable of love—I feel he's cheated me.
— D. F., Caldwell, NJ

My spirit has died once again but I know it will come back to life.
— T.N., Tucson, AZ

Knowing about verbal abuse can help a lot of women like myself who were not aware of the cause of their broken spirit.
— E.B., White Plains, NY

Shortly after the birth of our second child I was pretty sure we were in major trouble, but it was still nothing I could put my finger on. It was all so subtle and always done in private. My spirit almost died. My joy, my trust in everything dried up.
— L.M., Portland, OR

Verbal abuse . . . It killed my spirit—I'm wondering if I'll ever feel alive in a relationship again.
— J.S., Lynchburg, VA

I was prepared to leave my husband thirty years ago. The family, relatives and friends said "stay" don't disrupt the home. This was in the sixties. We were upper middle-class. There was no physical abuse.

I was most stunned and shocked as a bride. The verbal abuse increased over time. In the late forties I was told marriage is forever. I was verbally abused until the children came along, then they were verbally abused. I didn't think of "abuse" then, just "unhappy."

He started again very much on me when the children left home. The abuse then exploded with his retirement. Both sides of the family knew of the verbal abuse to the children and me. They said "stay!"
— V.N., Los Angeles, CA

I need to regain my self-esteem. I have no spirit left. I am very badly damaged and I know it will take time and professional help to overcome the consequences of so many years of verbal and emotional abuse. It is especially bad because I loved him so much and wanted a wonderful, happy, and healthy family.

— P.C., CHICAGO, IL

Below, a survivor of age and wisdom spoke out. She wrote and wrote, using up stationery, then loose sheets of paper. This excerpt from her letter says it all.

No one's dealt with this terrible diseased painful stripping of human beings. It is in effect like cancer. A major underground epidemic. A systemic disease sometimes in remission, not contagious—but predisposed. It can—often does—kill. It affects one's health. I testify to this. It robs you of energy, drive, certainty, talent, spirit and love.

— C.M., TOPEKA, KS

Verbal abuse *is* insidious. So few see it. Each victim is alone. No one speaks of it. It destroys its victim's spirit as cancer destroys healthy cells. And for too long it has grown in the dark, in hiding.

I cannot tell you how emotionally tired I am. I cannot listen to it anymore, anywhere, without contempt. Verbal abuse is a metaphor of AIDS. Why are they verbally abusive on all economic levels and educational levels? One would think education and fluency would eliminate these problems somewhat.

— G.L., MOORESTOWN, NJ

Even when I realized that I was being verbally abused I thought that I could tell my husband how I felt and he would stop being abusive. Actually, talking to him was like talking to a fish underwater in a big bowl. He'd look at me occasionally, then not. He'd move, sometimes my way, sometimes away. He would comprehend no more of what I had to say than a fish which keeps moving, seeming to know what it is doing, seeming to have a purpose, seeming to take me in with its eyes, seeming to realize that I was there.

If I shared my heart, my self, trying to tell him how things were with me, I found that I was sinking into the water, myself drowning. I could not go through the motions. I could not act as though everything were always the same, as if the atmosphere were fixed and nothing could ripple the waters, as if life were just a series of repetitious movements and the world were no bigger than a pond. Year followed year on time and no one mentioned the circuitous route which always brought me back to the beginning, only one level lower, in my downward spiral as I went down with him trying to reach him.

Eventually I came back up alone.

— M.H., Mountain View, CA

The following letter is from a woman who left a verbally abusive relationship after eleven years. She spent years walking on egg shells. Her abuser never stopped verbally abusing her; finally she gave herself the gift of peace of mind. She saved her soul and the spirit of life at her center.

My husband verbally abused me and the children. The three of us walked around on egg shells and tried to stay out of his way when he was in a bad mood.

Finally I had to get out of there. It was very, very hard. I left with almost nothing and when my lawyer asked why, I told him "I can't ever win with this man. But it doesn't really matter because he can't have my soul."

It has been hard, but I can't tell you how much better I feel about myself since I left and how much peace of mind I have now.

— B.H., Washington, DC

The Dying Spirit

The symptoms of depression are strikingly similar to the symptoms of a spirit dying from abuse. Of course, this does not mean that all depressed persons are verbally abused. However, if you are depressed and also unhappy with your relationship, you may need to reevaluate your situation based on current information about verbal abuse.

Please keep in mind that depression may have other causes. Following are a list of symptoms commonly associated with depression. Persons who are depressed may experience two or three of these symptoms, or many of them.

- ❏ Feeling in a depressed mood part of the day or most of the time
- ❏ Feelings of hopelessness
- ❏ Low self-esteem
- ❏ Low energy; fatigue
- ❏ Poor concentration or difficulty making decisions
- ❏ Difficulty sleeping
- ❏ Wanting to sleep all the time
- ❏ Marked lack of interest or pleasure in all (or almost all) daily activity

- Significant weight loss or gain
- Noticeable nervous habits
- Feelings of worthlessness
- Recurrent thoughts of death
- A suicide attempt
- A plan for suicide

Chapter 7

Trapped in the Dragon's Realm

I feel trapped. I'm terrified—I don't know what he'd do. I feel like running away continuously but have no place to go. I need to learn how to get healthy so I can get out of here.

— T.M., JACKSONVILLE, FL

When verbally abused women realize, "This is abuse," they say, "Stop it." They set limits and ask for change. Yet when change isn't forthcoming, they may still stay. Why?

There are many reasons. Often they are without economic security or job skills. They may have young children; they may be in poor health; they may be at an age that rules out most possibilities of gainful employment. Many are too frightened to leave, have lost all confidence and self-esteem, or feel it is sinful to leave. And in their deepest heart, many may still hope that a partner will change.

We do not know how many women and men in this country feel trapped in frightening, painful, and debilitating relationships. There seem to be a great many, far more than therapists and social workers had imagined only a year or two ago. I have selected excerpts from just a small percentage of the letters I have received describing this shocking situation, which I truly believe to be a wide-ranging societal problem—indeed, a tragedy, and one ignored for too long.

It seems almost impossible to comprehend the extent of this tragedy. Almost every writer believed that she was alone—that no one had a relationship like hers. Can we begin to imagine the destructive impact of verbal abuse on the lives of people who, if they were not isolated, undermined, trapped, and disempowered, might be enjoying the benefits of a full and satisfying life?

We need to let the public know what really goes on behind closed doors and when we are not around other people in public who could help defend us in this time of need. I know I am a victim of verbal abuse. We need more laws to support and help us. I feel stronger to know there is some help to go against this crime.

— A.O., GILROY, CA

Women are screaming for help and don't know where to turn—no one ever sees or hears it. No adult would ever believe the things that go on.

— H.B., LUBBOCK, TX

For years I thought I had done something wrong, and would sit there in shock and numbness, thinking "What was that all about?" It was like a bomb had dropped on you from no where and makes you devoid of all rational thinking, leaving only mass confusion.

After years of this, the abuse was so obviously irrational, I realized it definitely was not me. But this did not help me to fend it off, and the resulting feelings of helplessness it created—or the pain and sadness that nothing I did/do will counter it—Never a compliment, never a thank-you, never a sorry, never I was wrong, never forgive me.

— M.H., INDIANAPOLIS, IN

I have worked so hard to try to figure out and determine what more I can give or do to make him happy and not cruel. In contrast, I believe it's finally beginning to sink in deep within my soul that it is abuse, and I don't deserve it any longer. I am so tired of the struggle and fear.

— A.C., WICHITA, KS

I believe he is the cruelest man I have ever met. He is a master at verbal abuse. The Golden Years they say! When he yells at me for no apparent reason, I just quiver inside. I can't believe he is doing this to me.

I always thought marriage was to enrich each other's lives. He didn't learn that chapter. I would like to know more about what makes a man be so cruel to a woman who has been so good to him. I am afraid of him more now than ever. Over thirty-five years and it's gotten worse and worse.

— S.L., CONCORD, NH

We cannot enter a mind and know the source of irrational behavior. We can, however, catch a glimpse of his world. In attempting to answer the question, "What makes a man be so cruel?" we might conjecture that the abuser cannot experience a ground of being, or feeling center within himself, that would lead him to honor life with true compassion and empathy. His abusive behavior is evidence of this lost connection. If this is true, we can then assume that this loss of feeling bars him from deeper experience, and that his pursuit of Power Over is a misguided quest for his lost feeling-self. This lost self has been buried alive, so deep and so long ago he does not even want to smell it. No wonder he wonders why he does what he does. No wonder he seems so cold.

Power Over, dominance and control, seem to be the primary motivations for the verbal abuser's behavior. Severed from his connection to the Creative Force that brings us forth and is brought forth by us, he does not know his Personal Power. Bereft of his feeling self, he would sooner disempower another than know his own grief. In this way he lives upon the life of others—stealing power, stealing spirit.

The Dragon

While the partner feels trapped in the relationship, the abuser, in turn, is trapped in a never-ending cycle of avoidance and control, control of his own feelings of powerlessness—forever fighting their increasing Power Over *him*.

The abuser's need for Power Over looms so great it is like a wall—the wall of an impenetrable fortress. To attempt to understand his partner he would have to leave his fort and, unprotected, confront his fears and feelings of helplessness. At the same time, behind his impenetrable wall he lives with a hidden dragon—the dragon that breathes the breath of *fear*, the fire of *rage*, and the smoke of *powerlessness*.

If you were with him when last he felt the breath, the fire, and the smoke, he *knew* it was coming from you. Seldom was anyone else around when it happened. Where else could it come from? It was obvious to him. Didn't he feel its breath, its fire, and its smoke? He felt and saw the dragon—heard its roar, a rush within his head. He did not have to think or even reason. There was no place else where this dragon could be—at least, not where he knew to look.

Didn't the dragon always await your appearance before its dreaded breath touched him, cornering him, threatening him? Didn't it? *You* must know. "You know what you did," he lashes out, forcing back the breath of fear, the fire of rage, and the smoke of powerlessness; feeling at that moment a strength so great that the dragon disappears, taking dread with it, for a time.

Back in its lair the dragon skulks, waiting to be awakened by a quiet voice that hopes not to disturb. Dragons sense their prey from far away—a tiny quiver, a small movement they do not control, brings them roaring into action.

More and more often the dragon stirs, more and more often he comes to do battle. The abuser must make a hit, see a wound. Nothing else will banish the dragon. "Master" abusers say they can draw blood with one cutting remark.

If you were with him when last he felt the breath, the fire and smoke, it is no wonder you found him unpredictable. You would never know when he would lash out, nor could you see the dragon he does battle with. Not knowing about the dragon you would understandably try to *say things so he won't get mad* and walk on egg shells very carefully to avoid a misstep.

In the verbally abusive relationship, the abuser is fighting the dragon of threatening feelings. The dragon rumbles and roars whenever it wants. The abuser fights the dragon by "becoming it"—acting out its rage and beating it down . . . killing if he can the spirit of his mate mistaken for the dragon he fears. Just the presence of the partner or the thought of her can bring the dragon out. But the creature holds a secret. If the abuser accepts and feels his dragon—every feeling, every memory, every tiny speck of the dreaded dragon, it becomes his own source of Personal Power. It carries him across a threshold into a new reality.

The Dragon's Roar

How many feel trapped in the Land of the Free? Following are letter excerpts that tell what it is like for women who feel trapped in relationships in which the dragon often roars.

He seems to get angry out of the blue, and living with him is often like walking through a mine field—you never know what will trigger an outburst. Sometimes I feel trapped.
— M.K., NORTH PALM BEACH, FL

With his snapping and snarling I feel like I am with a mad dog. I am seventy-seven years old and have been married for forty-nine years. Where can I go?
— H.D., RENO, NV

It has occurred to me to leave but money, lack of education and skill and the physical and financial needs of my children all keep me trapped.
— M.J., PASADENA, TX

I've been abused fifty years in my fifty-year marriage and have been advised by two lawyers that I am financially unable to leave. The house is divided and we live in separate sections. Nonetheless, I am harassed.
— G.A., BROOKLINE, MA

I feel I am never free of the emotional abuse even when I am away from him. It has me paralyzed and imprisoned. My abuser has a long history of past abusive relationships, all of which he either denies or blames on his partner at the time.
— C.K., ARLINGTON, TX

I do feel "trapped," because I am finding it difficult to find worthwhile work that will support me and my children.
— C.L., MOAH, UT

Survivors often express a feeling of incredulousness about their mate's behavior because it is so foreign to them. They try "very hard to make things right." This is another reason many women stay so long in unhappy relationships. Others, whose abusers will not change, have stayed so long they have nearly lost the strength to leave. They just can't seem to get a picture of what is wrong—especially when they are told nothing is wrong.

The following letter speaks of the fear of never knowing when the next attack will come.

I have lived in an abusive relationship for twenty years, knowing for the last twelve years that something was wrong and trying very hard to make things right. I finally realized that no matter what I did to appease my husband, his anger and criticism of me remained. Fortunately, I had contact with the outside world and knew I was a competent person. In the last years, I could see how irrational his behavior was.

The verbal abuse escalated and he began pointing out news stories in which men had killed their wives and said how justified they were in doing so. I walked on egg shells, trying not to "provoke" him, but of course it was always some unexpected thing that would trigger an explosive outburst. I lived with that confusion of wanting to leave for my safety and sanity, and staying with the hope I would find the solution to our problem. The worst part of my experience was that he was a counselor, so underlying all my doubts was the constant notion that maybe there really was something wrong with me.

We're divorced but the court allowed him the freedom to come on my property as long as he gives me notice. I try very hard to avoid personal contact with him.

It seems as if he will never be out of my life, but at least I have a clearer perspective of what has happened in the past and am beginning to reclaim my life.

I have freed myself from daily contact with him, and I have the peace of mind that I am not alone: there are people in the world who understand what I have experienced.

But he is still full of anger. It seems more contained, but I know it is there and I live with the fear that as long as he knows where to find me, I am in danger.

— B.D., MARIETTA, GA

This survivor writes of two very important needs, *the need to be safe* from her abuser and *the need to be validated.* These primary needs are not met in a verbally abusive relationship. All verbal abuse invalidates the partner, and no one who experiences verbal abuse is really safe from its harm.

The writer knows her former abuser is still full of anger. We know he is still living with his dragon. Moreover, although she severed all relationship to him, the court allowed him the right of access to her residence and gave him storage rights as well. This is surprisingly common. She lives in fear, knowing that "He knows where to find me."

"I want to raise the consciousness of this country that women's civil rights—their right to be left alone—is in jeopardy." (Senator Joseph Biden of Delaware, chairman of the Senate Judiciary Committee on Domestic Violence, October 1992.)

The fear of irrational and abusive anger keeps many women feeling trapped. The next writer seems to speak for thousands of survivors when she says,

I read about verbal abuse in hiding. I knew my husband would be explosive at seeing the title. He belittles all my self-help books and tries to undermine any beliefs I have.

Recently I recognized that his ways were like a thug although he has a high standing in this state. I told him so. After eight years of extreme verbal abuse, I was gaining an insight into his real world.

He is very changeable, good or bad, rewarding or depriving me. It "starts" with a comment or two about things in general, then towards me, the glare, the tenseness, the clenched jaw.

All the while I think, "He really loves me because he doesn't hit me." So I console myself wanting to believe in his "I love you's."

He knows ways to cut me deeply—"I'd like the fern planted here in the shade," ever so gently I made my request, softly, not to anger him. Only to face a tirade, "You're never content. Why can't you just accept my direction? Why do you always try to run everything?"

My childhood was so happy I had no doubt I could trust the one

who loved me. I totally trusted my husband and his judgment. My father had always had my best interests at heart, so why shouldn't my husband, who said he loved me also? The loss in self-esteem occurred with me simply because I believed that he was saying it, what was wrong with me, with truthfulness; otherwise why would he say it?

I have tried so very hard to make this marriage work. I am even willing to "back down" to keep the peace but nothing has worked. At counseling I told my feelings from my deepest inner self; my husband exploded, how dare I feel these things!

When I was laid off from a job I loved he said, "Admit it, you really are glad you don't have to work. I know you are." It was then that I started to realize that my own feelings, thoughts and emotions were never realized by him. As far as he was concerned, I was simply his extension.

When I wanted training in another field he said he wouldn't support me in getting it (he's in a high income bracket), because I was where I was by making bad choices, like having our children when my peers were in college or starting careers. As if my life had been easy.

My will to live has been drained so often that I've considered suicide. Your very soul is taken away. They play God with you. No one sees the torture you endure inside.

I am presently seeking a way out, but it is slow and painful. With every positive step he sees me take he delights in pulling the rug out of my efforts and dreams. My job skills and earning powers are limited, but I know I must take responsibility for my own life.

No one can love another human being and still devalue them at the same time. It hurts to realize my love, almost worship at first, was never returned.

What a waste.
What sadness.
What now?

— M.W., LONG ISLAND, NY

Alone with the Dragon

Very often the survivors of verbal abuse have found themselves isolated not just from the comfort of family and friends but also by their mate's emotional distance.

One cannot help but feel trapped if one is constantly feeling sad, confused, unsure, hurt, stunned, and shocked. Survivors are often so debilitated, so filled with pain, that leaving is very difficult. Because of their isolation they are not sure of their strengths and have no emotional support. Many must build an entire life anew, as if immigrating to a new land—despite the years invested in the life they thought they had. The following letter excerpts attest to the fact that isolation and abuse go hand in hand.

> *I feel lonely with him, I've been verbally abused almost all my life. My career was raising my big family. Now he wants to retire to a mountain cabin. I'm filled with dread when I think of it. At sixty I am leaving. No matter what, I will survive.*
>
> — V.N., Selah, WA

> *I must leave because all I do is cry. I do not work because he wants me at home. My friends and family are far away. He accuses, blames, judges, and criticizes me numerous times a day. He is always ordering me and when I stand up, say "Stop it," or just leave the room he tends to be angrier. Why have I stayed in this awful relationship—obviously my husband is just a mean man.*
>
> — S.T., Dallas, TX

> *It is so hard to accept that I am the kind of person who has allowed this to continue. What is it about me? I will take a stand. Stand up to it. Then if he doesn't change, I'll walk away from it.*
>
> — Student, Houston, TX

> *I have wanted to run away many times.*
>
> — L.N., Denver, CO

> *I can't stand this life. He once told me he would "break me." I've been verbally abused in every way constantly. I am afraid to leave. He won't help me in any way when it comes to going to college. He doesn't want me to succeed or I'd leave and he wouldn't have anyone to bully.*
>
> — S.T., Boston, MA

> *I am married to a man I've grown to hate and I am afraid to leave.*
>
> — L.W., Naugatuck, CT

> *I feel trapped financially. I feel and have felt for a long time that my husband is a really awful and evil human being. He has no worth; nothing I could respect, let alone love. I adore life, and live it as fully as I can as an individual. It would be nice to have someone to relate to, though.*
>
> — R.H., Venice, CA

Traps

Many methods used by survivors for dealing with problems in an abusive relationship actually turn into traps to keep them there. Some of these methods would have been entirely effective with a nonabuser.

For example, a woman might *explain* to an nonabusive person why she did something (the person would have asked about it, not yelled about it), and understanding would be reached. In a verbally abusive relationship, explaining often is a trap.

As we examine this and other traps, you may begin to suspect that you are often in a trap. Ask yourself these questions: "What beliefs do I hold about my relationship?" and "What is he really communicating?"

Your beliefs are disempowering if they revolve around ideas like, "If I do this differently, talk differently, or act differently, he'll change or be nice."

They are also defeating if they revolve around ideas like, "I can take it," or "I can ignore it," or "It really doesn't matter."

Analyze your mate's communications with a few questions. Is he communicating in a nonthreatening and kindly accepting way? Is he abusive or respectful? Most importantly, ask yourself how you *feel* about the communication in your relationship.

Following are ten common traps.

1. The Explaining Trap

I've tried for a long time to get my abuser to understand my good intentions. I'm in extreme isolation and am working toward finding friends. I have given up everything to try to stop the anger and to please him. I am now trying to get some of my life back and I intend to end the relationship no matter what.

I need to find the courage to leave and a plan to protect myself mentally and emotionally.

— K.F., Eugene, OR

This survivor, who has found herself extremely isolated and who did everything she could to try to stop her mate's abuse, writes, "*I've tried for a long time to get my abuser to understand my good intentions.*" I think this is a key to the partner's struggle, the reason she spent years trying to make the relationship work. It is the same reason many women stay in physically battering relationships. She believes that she must explain and convince him of her good intentions; that once he knows her good intentions, he will be happy with her and nice to her. To her it is incomprehensible, unbelievable, incredible, and inconceivable that he would say those hurtful things if he knew her good intentions. It is equally incomprehensible that the abuse has nothing to do with her.

The partner of the verbal abuser believes there is some way that she can explain herself, her intentions, her motivations, her meaning, her plans, her hopes, her views, her actions, her experiences, her needs, her feelings, her thoughts, or her interests so that her mate will be respectful, considerate, and understanding of them. Survivors report having been caught in this trap for years and even decades. It is the nature of this trap not to know you're in it unless it has been defined for you. Many survivors thought that at some point, with enough study, insight, and observation, they would find out how to express themselves so that their mate would understand them.

2. The "If You Feel Your Pain, You Are a Victim" Trap

No matter how good you are at hiding or suppressing your pain, he knows when he's "scored." When you try to hide your pain and act as though nothing has happened "so he won't get the satisfaction," he is free to do it again without ever being accountable for the abuse he inflicts. You *both* pretend it's okay. This is not healthy behavior.

If you become really numb to your pain, you will find you are numb to everything. Your spirit is "playing dead." On the other hand, when you feel your pain, you become motivated to act on your own behalf.

3. The "He Doesn't Really Mean It so It Shouldn't Hurt" Trap

This is similar to the trap just described. In this trap, however, the partner believes she isn't supposed to "take it personally." Actually, all abuse originates with the abuser's malfunction. In some way he would like not to be, say, a batterer (verbal or physical), but he is. Self-knowledge hurts!

If he denies the "dig," saying, "It was only a joke," tell him it was no joke to you and that you don't ever want to hear that kind of talk again.

4. The "I Should Be Able to Take It" Trap

When he totally denies having said something hurtful by telling you that "You're too sensitive," tell him, "Cut it out. No more accusations." Don't fall into the trap of trying to take it. There truly are relationships in which no one has to take it from anyone else—in which both parties feel emotionally supported and both give emotional support.

5. The "Saying 'I'm Hurting' Is Blaming" Trap

Remember the woman in chapter 6 who became convinced that if she told her mate her real feelings she would be "blaming him"? This is insidious. *Not* to cry out from a wounding goes against nature and instinct.

I knew of a couple in which the abuser would frequently stand on his mate's foot "accidentally." He would put on his surprised did-it-by-accident look, and she became convinced that if she got angry enough to say "Stop it!" she would be blaming him, "because it was only by accident." Of course he was to blame! *He* was responsible for his bizarre behavior. No one else!

6. The "Setting a Good Example" Trap

In the "Setting a Good Example" trap, the partner of the abuser believes that if she is especially respectful and considerate of her mate, he will learn from her. She believes that by not losing her temper, by asking instead of ordering, by giving him the "benefit of the doubt" rather than judging, and so on, she will model appropriate behavior and he will learn from her example. Actually, he will see her consideration as *affirmation* of his dominance.

I do not recommend that she instead be angrily abusive, demanding, and judging. It is, however, important to know that expecting change from example is unrealistic in a verbally abusive relationship.

7. The "I Am Responsible" Trap

This trap is the result of being blamed, as discussed in the previous chapter.

> *Over twenty years, and even after I insisted on counseling, he hasn't changed. But now he is always so sorry after a verbal attack. It seems that since the counseling he knows exactly what to say to make me feel that he will come around in time. He says I don't have enough faith in him and that's why he keeps failing [to stop the verbal abuse]. When he seems to be so sorry I think, "It wasn't that bad."*
> — E.K., Patterson, NJ

In this letter, the survivor describes being blamed. She is in the "I am responsible" trap. If we ask what is he communicating, we find that her abuser has said in effect, "I am a verbal batterer because you don't have enough faith in me. You are responsible for my cruel and unfeeling behavior toward you. If you had more faith in me, I would be able to stop acting out abusively and I would give you warmth, empathy, and understanding." This is crazymaking behavior. A person could be persecuted for a lifetime while trying to prove her faith in her persecutor by not acting persecuted.

She is also in two additional traps: the "He Loves Me, He Loves Me Not" trap described below and the "I Should Be Able To Take It" trap described earlier.

Some survivors went to extraordinary lengths to deal with their abusers. Feeling responsible, wanting more than anything not to be abused, they stayed too long where they *were* abused.

> *No one has ever explained this tragedy. Mainly I was led to believe if I would just try harder to understand him and "be patient" with him I would find peace.*
>
> *The responsibility for his behavior was always placed upon my shoulders. I was young when married and from out of town. I was told that I expected too much. No one had ever treated me before as he did our first year of marriage.*
>
> — M.T., NEW WILMINGTON, PA

> *I was walking on egg shells and sweeping hurts under the rug. I was only relaxed when he was out of the house. That's when the tension lifted like a fog.*
>
> — J.S., NEW ORLEANS, LA

> *I was on guard, because he'd run down angrily my opinions and belittle them. "You don't know what you're talking about." I seldom expressed my feelings and said only what I felt he wanted to hear.*
>
> — MEMPHIS, TN

Feeling responsible for their abuse, they thought, "I should be doing something differently." Feeling confused about the abuse, they thought, "It must not have happened the way it felt because he acts like nothing happened." Believing they could explain, they thought, "Now he understands."

8. The "He Loves Me, He Loves Me Not" Trap

> *Why do I want to go back when I know how abusive he is?*
>
> — E.H., INDUSTRY, CA

The greater the survivor's deprivation, the more the promise of tomorrow holds. When a survivor has suffered much, she may, paradoxically enough, stay in the relationship that is not nurturing to her because every now and then her mate holds out the possibility that *tomorrow* she will receive respect, warmth, and validation. She may believe an abuser can change by an act of will and not in a long slow process. The longer she has been deprived, the greater her need, and the more likely she will be to live on hope, as the following writer describes.

> *One day it is as if all things are hopeless, and the next day there is some hope. The idea of starting over scares me to death. I know it can be done, but I don't seem to have the energy or the guts needed to make that decision. I even feel when I am trying to tell someone that I am be-*

ing verbally abused that I don't know where to start, it seems so trivial when you talk about it. There are no visible scars. So how can someone know what is being done to me?

I'd think of leaving and then would get "hooked" again by his seem-ing to understand a problem between us. I'd hope again and get stuck again.

— R.F, GREAT FALLS, MT

The way out of this trap is to give up the hope about him and to look to what is hopeful in yourself. Many survivors describe how they too thought "Now he loves me. Now he doesn't."

Over the past ten years I have wanted to leave. He would seem to un-derstand and then the sarcasm, the withholding and the angry snaps would start again.

— N.S., FRESNO, CA

I leave and then I come back thinking he may be different. He only is for a little while then in a day or a week it starts again.

— L.B., TORONTO, ONTARIO

A partner who leaves and comes back wrote, "I want advice on how to leave gracefully."

The leaving-and-coming-back cycle could (and often does) go on for years. Why? Because the partner doesn't really leave when she re-mains in contact with her abuser and is available to be convinced by him that he has changed. Thus, it is of the utmost importance that con-tact be severed completely. As one survivor wrote,

Three years later I saw him at a wedding. There had been no contact—no relationship whatsoever. I wasn't talking to him—but he told me to "shut up." I thought, "How odd he is to speak to me this way. He doesn't even know me. But I know him; he hasn't changed a bit."

— M.H., BOSTON, MA

Typically, the survivor experienced a repeating cycle of abuse. There were a series of "ups and downs" in the relationship, or she may have noticed that, periodically, "things" got worse. Then they got better. If she left her relationship because she was abused and then came back because her mate seemed to change by being nice, she did not know that his "niceness" was a ploy to get her back and was just another aspect of control.

The abuser's cycle is typically to be nice to get his partner back after she leaves, then to verbally abuse her when he gets her back to keep her under his control. Some abusers who do this are so subtle that their criticism sounds like concerned advice; nevertheless it brings their partners down and keeps them trapped until their confidence is shattered and their self-trust disintegrates.

To be sure, some people go through entire lifetime relationships without experiencing any of the abuses described in this book. But verbal abuse victims often do not know this, and become convinced that "He didn't mean it," or "It was by accident," or "Now he's changed."

When the abuser gets his mate to believe she is "too sensitive," or that he "did it by accident," or that "now he's changed," he has scored another win. He has managed to get her to believe him instead of her own perceptions, feelings, and intuition. He has widened the gap between inner and outer, cause and effect, perception and reality. She is feeling just a little more disintegrated—a little more likely to fall into a trap.

9. Emotional and Financial Traps

The next survivors we hear from feel trapped emotionally and financially. Like many, they are looking for a way out of the dragon's realm that is their relationship.

> *I have been in an extremely abusive relationship for a very long time—I am sixty years old and I would give anything to get out of this—I have nowhere to go, nobody I can talk to and no support group.*
>
> *In order to deal with verbal abuse now I need to develop interests in order to meet people; this seems to be an impossible hurdle. I've been depressed and isolated for thirty years and can't get out of an abusive relationship for financial reasons.*
>
> — J.M., WATERFORD, CT

> *For the longest time I felt if I just did this or that "things" would be better. Not! He'd just change his method of abuse. Every time I told him he was hurting me he'd do something worse. I want out but I haven't figured out how to yet.*
>
> — L.D., LOVELAND, CO

All survivors, whether they realize it or not, need the support of their community. There is often a choice, a beginning to make, a support group to find, a friend to call, a way to walk out, be one's own advocate, tell all the neighbors, call all the relatives, find some support.

Some survivors spend two years, five years, or more studying—becoming trained or certified in work that will support them. Some manage by finding a room to rent or an exchange for housekeeping or child care. Over time, as the abuse continues or increases, the options may decrease.

I know I don't have to accept his verbal abuse, but I do if I have no money of my own and am too old to get a job and have spent all these years losing my self-esteem and self-confidence.

He was a good provider. It wasn't too bad while raising our children, who are grown beautiful adults. He was gone a whole lot.

Over the years he grew more verbally abusive. I've been shocked to see how this man has turned out to be so extremely abusive. I have never anywhere else heard such gutter language. He even accuses me of vile things. I am embarrassed to even write the words. Each day he says many bad words to me. I keep a journal of how he is to me, and if he is nice to me for a few days, I think it's all over and he's going to be nice to me from now on. So I rip up the journal.

No more I don't. Sometimes after a bad siege I feel so dizzy or mixed up, I hardly know what I am doing. I am not perfect but I can honestly say I strive for peace and harmony. In all fairness to myself I must say I have been more than fair.

— P.R., Eureka, CA

Sometimes abuse can become so intense that the abuser's mental health can be called into question. Sometimes he can become a danger not only to others but also to himself. In the case of such abuse as the writer described above, help should be sought through a women's center, a medical doctor, or a social service agency.

The following letter is from a survivor who has come to the realization that her mate will not go through the long hard work of change. Her letter reveals her determination to heal. Even though she is alone in her "effort," it is important for her to know that there are others making a similar effort and that in that respect she is not alone.

I am still so much in the midst of this effort. I am working through the feelings of entrapment and hope to achieve my freedom from this web of misery this summer. My self-esteem was decreased and my self-doubt grew over so many years. I still have a lot of difficulty in trusting my own perceptions. I have survived weekends with my husband as my only adult contact and by Sunday afternoon I would be convinced that I was losing my sanity.

— M.K., Berlin, NJ

10. Trapped by Beliefs

A survivor in despair, betrayed by her mate and her culture, stands as a reminder to all that protecting our spirit is our first priority.

I have most often been verbally abused in the following ways: withholding, discounting, accusing, blaming, judging, criticizing, threat-

ening, denial and abusive anger. I am a Christian and have been taught to turn the other cheek. It has resulted in my "shutting down." It has occurred to me to end my life.

— D.P., Sioux Falls, ID

Perhaps we *are* meant to turn our cheek—as we leave the dragon's realm. Then, with the abuse behind us, we can begin to work to save our souls, hungering for the spirit's return.

Fear

Reality-based fear tells us something is wrong. It is a warning signal. Fear is a communication from one part of ourselves to another. The feeling of fear says, "This person, place or thing is dangerous or may be dangerous to my well-being. I must get away from it as quickly as possible."

Another kind of fear is fear of the unknown. This fear has to do with our own ability to manage the course of our life. This kind of fear is about the future: change, loss, competency, loneliness, abandonment. This is the kind of fear we must confront and deal with.

Fear can be a very valid, real sign that there is danger to body or soul. A survivor tells of her relationship in the letter below. Years later her pain is still vivid. Her fear was real. The "temper outbursts" brought flashbacks of the terrors of Hitler's Germany. No wonder she felt imprisoned. Her fear shouted, "Run away as fast as you can. This is not a good place to be." She says,

I felt like a prisoner whose life is disciplined, controlled, dictated, and told what and when to do—who gets punished if she disobeys the rules. My punishment was temper outbursts which I could not take, I just cowered and hoped it would blow over fast. His demonstrations of rage were overwhelming. I was terrified. I felt like a prisoner.

The memory of the pain he caused me is still very vivid after nine years. I had no strength to stand up for my rights, to assert myself. [Author's note: I don't believe standing up to him or being assertive would have done anything to lessen his rage.] *I always looked for a way out. I weighed my words before saying them in order to avoid outbursts. He'd beat his head or fists on the wall when something went wrong in business or personal life. And to walk out on him while the display of his temper was going on would bring an even bigger temper tantrum.*

I was never hit but my life was unhappy, miserable, and extremely stressful on a daily basis. There were no pleasant days. I was so brow-

beaten for so long that I had no self-esteem. Every time I heard his
voice, my stomach literally was turning, and my mouth got dry.
— E.H., SCARSDALE, NY

The survivor who wrote the above letter was in too much fear to
"stand up" to her mate. Without support, without equal strength,
without a role model, without knowledge (without a bodyguard?),
how could she? She believed, like so many, that there was some way
to affect his behavior, to stop the pain, by weighing her words.

Fear of Escalation

Many survivors wrote that as they tried to stop the abuse, it escalated.
Any abuser who is unwilling to change and believes he has the right
to treat a human being abusively will increase the abuse when his
partner stands up to it, even if she tells him, "It's your behavior, not
you, that I don't like." Why? Because when she says, "Stop!" he feels
he's losing control. If the abuse then increases, one is with a *confirmed*
abuser.

I was confused because I thought if I could detach from him, I could
still be with him. Also, I tried to separate the behavior from the person
and both of these seemed to intensify his abuse.
— E.C., MAYNARD, MA

The abuse increases as I set boundaries.
— G.S., TULSA, OK

My husband was an extreme verbal abuser. As I started gaining inde-
pendence he became much more abusive. He followed me while con-
stantly verbally abusing. I could not retreat to my room, outside, etc.
He'd take my keys to keep me from going.
— R.W., LONG ISLAND, NY

I am hesitating to leave because he is vindictive and I fear for how the
children will cope and how they will be used.
— N.G., MADISON, WI

Leaving has been on my mind, for what feels like twenty-four hours per
day for the past several months—I know I am unable to keep a job due
to ill health. There is some put-down every day. I am afraid of him. His
abuse is so caustic that I do fear that it may escalate—One thing I do
find myself saying to him on even the smallest thing: "Now, before you
get mad and blow up, let me tell you what I think."
— P.A., LINCOLN, NE

It is a fact that I am so exhausted from the stress and strain of the relationship I can hardly think. I don't have the energy to leave and fight the fight I know would be ahead.

— J.W., CHARLOTTE, NC

The experience of a man's rage is frightening to a woman. Many *men* are also afraid of a raging man. This is reality-based fear that needs to be respected. Violence may follow rage. In a June 1992 report from Surgeon General Antonio Novella, violence was listed as the leading cause of injury to women ages fifteen to forty-four.

Fighting Fear

I feel this is a fight for my life and my children's lives. I cannot seem to convince others I have been abused. He's so good at hiding abuse—I am shaking as I write to you because if I tell others of my abuse he will "punish me." He still verbally attacks me when no one hears or in front of my children to prove to them he is stronger. It's very hard to fight something he says doesn't exist.

— O.T., LEXINGTON, KY

Many women experience "being punished" when they bring up their abuse, especially after joint counseling. Usually they suffer a rage attack directed at them by the very spouse who was supposedly going to counseling to improve the relationship. Some women who were abused by physical violence have said that they felt verbal abuse was worse than physical abuse. A survivor shared this information and many pages of her notes, her thinking, and her insights with me. She said her purpose was to share what she has learned about verbal abuse and to understand what happened to her. After ten years, she says that she is still gaining clarity and coming to grips with her abuse. She contributed the following.

To learn more about verbal abuse and control issues, I attended a support group for abused women for over two years. Week after week, women would walk in with broken bones, bruises, cuts. They'd tell about being taken to the hospital emergency room, some more than once.

With woman after woman, I'd ask: "Which was worse in your relationship, the physical abuse or the verbal abuse?"

And without exception the answer was the verbal abuse, "Truly!"

— H.S., AKRON, OH

Survivors' fears include the loss of love, being abandoned, being ostracized by society for not having a man, struggling alone. In the letters below they share their concerns and their recognition that they must confront their fears.

> *When I was abused I thought it was my fault and I felt very anxious and afraid of losing my husband and his love.*
>
> — V.E., SCRANTON, PA

> *Although I have a major concern about being able to financially survive on my own, my biggest fear is that I have not acted soon enough to help my daughter. I wonder, if because of my modeling, will she seek a man who will follow the pattern of this sick relationship? I do intend to make her aware of the necessity of financial independence.*
>
> *I hope to impart to her, her inherent value as an individual; that she may be guilty of wrong actions, but there is [not] and never will be anything wrong with her as a person. If it seems that I am overly conscious of monetary interests, it is because I am not sure of being able to find a job that provides sufficient income. It is a fear that kept me in the relationship when I used it as an excuse to stay, and now a similar, but reality-based fear, now affects my prospects for autonomy.*
>
> — R.B., DOVER, NH

> *I felt broken, I feared change, financial insecurity, and leaving the familiar.*
>
> — E.H., SACRAMENTO, CA

In the next chapter we will hear from survivors who, after trying everything they could to make their relationship work, found that it does take two. They could not make it better while their mate made it worse. They are escaping or planning escapes.

Chapter 8

Escape

I don't think anyone other than another victim of verbal abuse could totally understand the tremendous damage that is done to a verbally abused person.

— M.B., DALLAS, TX

Although many couples in verbally abusive relationships have recognized the issues of control and Power Over within the relationship and are making progress toward change and mutuality, others are not. In these relationships the survivors of the abuse, realizing that their mates are not changing, either feel trapped, as we saw in the previous chapter, or have resources and are in circumstances that allow them to leave or to make plans to escape the terrible pain of the abuse.

In some relationships the survivors are diminished and verbally beaten down even when they try every conceivable way to stop the abuse. Very often they have spent many years trying to be somehow better so their mates would not find so much wrong with them. Once they realized that they were being abused and that the abuse had nothing to do with them, many chose to leave or began planning their escapes.

Survivors who had lived in pain and confusion, trying to "make a go of it" and "hoping for the best" for many years, saw their children raised and found their relationship worse, not better. As they began to identify the abusive nature of their relationship and realized they were not to blame, they felt free to leave. Then, even with sadness, many expressed a newly found sense of freedom, clarity, strength, determination, and awareness.

A survivor who had hoped her mate would grow better as he

grew more affluent and more established and was freed of the responsibilities of a young family, wrote the story of her giving, living, striv-
ing, and finally yearning for freedom and the return of her spirit.

I Married a Man So in Fear He Could Not Be in Love

*For over thirty years, I have been married to a man solely motivated by
fear. I am his verbal beating board, his leaning post, his anxiety reliever,
and his place to hide when he has nowhere else to turn. What do I get
in return? Nothing—no sharing of souls, no friendship, no caring of
heart—only sporadic material rewards and a day or two sick in bed,
when he fears that I am breaking down under the strain of his demands.*

*I resisted and I was able to withstand his violent fits of verbal
abuse, withholding (emotionally and financially), his denial, discounting, countering and trivializing for over twenty years because he trav-
eled a great deal. Even with three children to care for, it was heaven
when he was gone.*

*Too soon he would return to tell us what was wrong with us, to
criticize and blame what we had done and even our environment. If not
that, he would collapse into glaring silence—not speaking for days. I
tried to make things better, I would be cheerful, and considerate and
thoughtful of his needs, making sure he knew I loved him—wondering
why he didn't seem to think so from the way he acted. I also was on
guard for our children. I didn't want them to realize that their father
was such a jerk, so I would try to make light of his attacks on me and
his withdrawals, as if it was a one-time thing, or there were some reason or a way to make light of it. When I did approach him in private
about his "unhappiness" or his "depressions," he would spit out some
nasty comment, trivialize my concerns, or continue his silence.*

*In his mind the REAL world is out to get him so he will get them
first, and how naive I am to think that good things happen. And, in the
meantime, I am like the rest he has to deal with. He'd best get me down
or I might get him first—devious and hard-hearted soul that I am, to
have tried for so long to prove my love.*

*He has our money in his accounts. When I confront him with my
knowledge of these accounts he passes it off that he is straightening
"things" out. If I pursue further, I am in for an explosive, very threatening fit of anger. Yet I have never hidden our money from him. If I
persist he leaves—returning later as if nothing had happened. If I confront him again, he explodes, or leaves again until I tire of the cycle.*

Since the children are grown and he is traveling less the verbal abuse has escalated. He tried to "look good" in front of our children, family and friends so they didn't see it. Now that I am alone with him he thinks he has free reign. When he isn't being out rightly abusive, he ignores me like a hired housekeeper. He allows me to cook, clean, and accompany him to business affairs.

I kept thinking that he would realize that he doesn't have the "pressures" that he thought he used to have—raising a family, establishing his career, lacking leisure time. But no, he has replaced those fears with new ones.

I realized a long time ago that there was no room for me in his life of fear, although he would tell me when he was "down" that he needed me more than anything in the world. I always knew, after his begging and apologies that I was no more in his life than our lamp post. He confessed of affairs while the children were still young. I wanted to leave him, but he promised me it would never happen again, which I came to know just meant he would never tell me again.

I tried to help him understand a better world not run by fear, by confiding in him my thoughts, dreams, and hopes for our future. But he would listen, take it in, and use it against me at a later date—attacking me as a "flake," a future "bag lady," or a confused, naive person.

While telling me we could not afford car repairs he made major purchases without my knowledge, even boats, cars, and real estate.

My only vacations have been his business meetings and conventions, which often are at inconvenient times for me. He is furious if I don't go. I know that I "stand in" as the personable side of him because it is such an effort for him to pretend to be without fear of something all the time.

Knowing many years ago that nothing ever changed, I began to make plans. By choice, I decided that I would forego luxuries to be home while my children were growing up. I decided that finishing my college education would be a step towards my independence. Through the years of child raising I took a college course or two whenever possible. Later I enrolled full time. Then his verbal onslaughts increased dramatically. He wanted every minute of my time, and especially disparaged me when I was trying to study. He was making a six figure salary then and wanted me to quit school for a minimum wage job. I had to get therapy to get through college because I was so torn between my time and his time—my confusion.

After graduation, I wanted so much to go to graduate school. I approached him on the subject, thinking that it was a major decision that he should be in on. He smiled sweetly, but said that we had several big conventions coming up, and also that business was kind of shaky, and

I should consider getting a job. So, I jumped into his fear. I thought my presence at the conventions would ease his fear of possible failure. The trips, as usual, were miserable. He verbally attacked me at every turn. I would return more confused than ever. I could not understand why he was so angry with me when I'd gone with him and had done what he wanted. I thought his anger and irritation at me had something to do with me.

I ended up with a little job I hated with little pay, pushing papers, punching a clock, doing what I had once hired people to do. But he felt better, I think, knowing I was trapped while he was freewheeling out of his own office, enjoying a huge income, a fat expense account, luxury accommodations, first class flights and many mid-week sailing outings with clients on his boat.

He was still hiding the income. And, just before I would get my little paycheck he would say such and such a bill needs to be paid right now or they'll "whatever."

I could no longer stand up to him. I became depressed, frustrated and confused. I lost all hope—moreover, I lost what I valued most—my spirit.

I succumbed. I quit my job and sat on the couch in the living room most of the day for months. I didn't want to talk to anyone—not even my family. I was frozen. I could not face the thought that in fact my marriage was a failure. I guarded the image of our "happy family." I didn't want my family to know how bad things were. I lied and made excuses for his behavior and my reclusiveness. I became numb, passive, and even more susceptible to his influence.

Soon he began telling me that we needed to get away—live somewhere else, because everybody was too close—everybody wanted something from us. He said that he was tired and he knew that if we had a change that our relationship would flourish. Hope!!! I could not but grasp at any hope.

I said "Yes." Off we went into total seclusion to a very small town with no family or friends around. I decided to get into artistic endeavors. This was good. I wasn't frozen any more. But fear followed my husband as sure as the sun comes up in the morning and now I was completely alone with him and his fear. Alone together, he began to see me as his prime enemy. He rejected my efforts to help him with his business. He became upset if I wasn't around for lunch. He questioned my every phone call. He kept our income hidden in his account only. He brushed off my confrontations with the promise that he was putting my name on the account and that it had been just an oversight. It never happened.

Here I am a year later. I have come to the end of the line. My heart is bleeding with sadness and grief, but my soul is yet yearning for the return of my spirit. I feel the death of a life-long dream. I feel that I have tried everything to adjust, to fit in, to change, to ignore, and to rise above the ways of this man—my husband. Strangely now I only see him as a huge stone wall that I keep running into.

Lately though, I see there is no real wall. I can step forward on my own behalf. I can gather up my own resources, make my own plans, take in what is best for me and let the rest fall away. I must take responsibility for my own life and value it to the utmost, so that I can be free to be who I really am.

— D.M., HAMPTON, VA

This life-story letter covers everything discussed in the first eight chapters of this book. We see a survivor who, living with her abuser, felt the *oppression and control* of abuse gradually bringing her to a state of *disintegration*. Over time, however, with new *awareness*, she realized her abuser was not going to change. She took steps. While raising her children she completed her degree, and was about to move forward on her path when she was *blamed* for possible imminent financial difficulties. The blame was *killing her spirit*. She felt responsible and gave up her path. "I succumbed," she wrote. No financial difficulties occurred, but by then it seemed too late to turn back. She became passive, *trapped in the dragon's realm*. Finally, her grief brought forth a new young yearning from her soul to *escape* into the freedom to be "who I really am."

In the following letters, other survivors share their hearts and souls that they may pass along their strength and resolve.

It's been a struggle to sort and clarify and deal with my abusive husband. To leave takes faith in yourself and the ability not to listen and not allow yourself to be confused or deflected. I am filing for divorce, knowing it is the best thing for me, but I am still frightened. "What if he is right and I really am an awful person." But for the most part I no longer accept his definition of me and can sort interactions much more quickly. Still—he says the relationship problems are my fault and if we divorce it is because I am not capable of having a good relationship. My response? "So you say!"

I will proceed to save my soul, and in the perspective of time I know I will bless myself for having had the courage to act for myself.

— D.W., CHICAGO, IL

He was the King. I was the serf. I saved myself one month ago. I am free now and have my first real peace of mind in years. I wrote this right after I left.

— S.B., INDIANAPOLIS, IN

I have been "confused" for twenty years and only came to realize in the last few years that I've been verbally abused almost daily since my marriage over twenty years ago. It is now clear that Power Over me and control of my life was my husband's goal. Although we presented an image to the public of a "happy family" our home was a prison of constant tension and fear. I usually felt emotionally drained.

Please try to get the message across to others that living with a "verbal abuser" is just as damaging as living with an alcoholic or physically abusive person. It is not something to be taken lightly—I have moved away but am not divorced.

Incidentally, for some reason, I often thought of "Hitler" when attempting conversations with my husband and felt he would have made the perfect soldier in Hitler's army.

— B. L., WASHINGTON, DC

For ten years I have had all forms of verbal abuse constantly. Counselors and ministers and doctors have all told me to do what I have to, to keep peace because he's such a good provider—the last five years he has made me support myself totally all the while discounting my talents, yelling anger addict that he is, so I feel I have to tip toe in my own house. I don't need it. I'm planning my escape.

— A.W., ATLANTA, GA

In letter after letter, the survivors of verbal abuse told how they had found that, despite the assurances of their culture, their family, and their churches, the womanly thing, the thoughtful thing, the caring thing, the loving thing, the thinking-of-the-other person thing, the doing-the-best-one-can thing, the putting-yourself-in-his-shoes thing, the thinking-of-what-you're-saying thing, the respectful thing, the giving-him-the-benefit-of-the-doubt thing, the trying-to-understand thing, the taking-it-lightly thing, the seeing-his-side-of-it thing, the not-letting-it-bother-you thing, the brushing-it-off thing, the taking-it-with-a-grain-of-salt thing, the not-being- sensitive thing, the letting-it-roll-off-you thing, wasn't *the* thing that would guarantee freedom from abuse. These approaches, paradoxically, were *the* thing that guaranteed that they would stay in an abusive relationship.

How did this lie come into our culture? Very likely, I believe, it was a way for women who had no rights, who could not leave their abusers, to stay alive.

Survivors today constantly speak out against the lie, which ensured their vulnerability to manipulation and control. Many have offered their experiences, their dreams, their journals, and their poems. The following poem powerfully presents a survivor's pain and frustration over being born into a world in which she felt betrayed by abuse.

The Top Dogs

Wagging tales of platitudes
Baring their teeth in grins,
Feeding on scraps of indifference
The indigestible
Symbols of power.
While life, the human tree
Is devoured
By their overriding power.

Self proscribed, inscribed
Seeking more to devour
Of hope, of freedom, of life
Determined within the Self.
Shadows of themselves,
Afraid.
Flushing out
With fear and rage
All who do not swallow
The prescriptions of their
Sage dictates.
Demanding, decreeing,
In awe of themselves
Shouting louder
Smashing harder
Atoms,
All.

— A.R, Green Bay, WI

Other women also felt betrayed. We will hear from one survivor who says, "I see that what I have been led to believe all of life about myself was at some level abuse." How true this is for the betrayed— and how motivating of escape.

He is a leader in the church. Had I known about this side of him I would never have married him. We dated for five years and I did not see the anger. It began after marriage. I was shocked at his language. For some reason, marriage has put him in the mode of controlling and managing me. I'm sick of it and want to be free.

— D.S., MOORESTOWN, NJ

He was only capable of negative hostile emotion and nothing else. He used to say "a negative emotion is better than no emotion at all."

— K.W., WILMINGTON, NC

There was no physical violence but lots of cruelty. He was severely physically abused as a child.

— F.L., MOBILE, AL

I've been verbally abused for thirty-five years. I have no intentions of waiting for my husband to change. I see him now for exactly what he is: An abuser. I see that what I have been led to believe all my life about myself was at some level abuse but I could never put my finger on what it was.

— A.N., COLUMBIA, SC

Many survivors, once they realize that what they are hearing is abuse—that it is not only not true but has nothing to do with them—do not stay in their relationships unless the relationship changes dramatically. These partners choose not to live in abusive atmospheres. Once awareness begins, determination follows—survivors everywhere express their great determination to see changes or to leave.

Some may bide their time while raising their children or developing their resources, then leave if their mates have remained abusive. When they understand the dynamics of verbal abuse, they are released from the confusion of unnamed and unacknowledged disparagement.

Leaving the Dragon's Lair

Many survivors tell why they consider leaving their relationship, some for the sake of their children, some because they cannot endure the abuse getting worse, some because they realize their abuser won't change.

I'm leaving next week—threatening was maybe not the most often experienced abuse, but the scariest and most damaging—He hasn't hit me but has threatened not only to hit me but to kill me explicitly. In order to deal with verbal abuse now I need to be more alert to it and stay away from abusers! Maybe stay away from men altogether after this. It has been bad.

— C.S., ERIE, PA

I plan on leaving—I just haven't done it. I no longer believe he'll change.

— H.K., AUGUSTA, GA

I need to move on with my life so that my three young children do not consider this behavior normal.

— V.T., SAN JOSE, CA

I have been in a verbally abusive relationship for six years and the pain I felt was extremely intense. However, I could never understand why he did it. Recently my spouse yelled at me for seven days straight. Of course it was behind closed doors. I cried for an entire month every day. I must truthfully say, he never did strike me even once. He is extremely intelligent and he is in complete denial and not ready to accept help. Now, however, I have decided to make a change in my life and do not intend to put up with any more abuse.

— W. C., DALLAS, TX

I will go and keep going. I cannot say I love my mate. I feel too injured. He has said too much and gone too far.

— M.C., AKRON, OH

I would like to know how to get help. I am getting out of this relationship.

— O.L., NEW ORLEANS, LA

I have suffered through thirty plus years of terrible abuse from childhood to adulthood. What my outcome in my marriage will be remains to be seen. But I'm sure of one thing. The abuse will stop here. At least in my life it will.

— M.T., EUREKA, IL

I felt a good deal of anger against my husband for using abusive words and for slapping me. He denies any wrongdoing and says he didn't hurt me. I told him if he does it again I will be gone. I mean it too.

— D.K., ROYAL OAK, MI

I will not accept abusive anger. I'll say "STOP" and leave the room and if the above doesn't bring improvement I will leave.

— G.J., BLOOMINGTON, MN

I have known for a long time that my relationship with my husband isn't nourishing. I have tried for so long to be a better wife, better homemaker, better cook, better lover, better looking, thinner, etc. and the list goes on and on. Despite all my attempts at being better our relationship has just gotten worse. I think the open hostility is one of the worst things I have to deal with. It is so true that the partner in the re-

lationship ends up feeling like the abuser's enemy. I remember thinking early in our marriage that I would not talk to a dog like my husband talked to me.

Well, I am through living with the enemy. I give up.

— I.W., Oakland, CA

I do not need my husband financially and emotionally. He does nothing but hurt me. The abuse really got bad once I was pregnant, before that there were indirect outbursts that I attributed to his fear of losing me (before we were married)—silly me! I do not know if I love him, I do know I do NOT respect him, since he cannot respect me, our child or himself for what he does.

He is his own worst enemy. He has severely damaged our marriage and my feelings towards him for absolutely no valid reason. His tantrums, outbursts, threats have nothing whatsoever to do with me. I refuse to live like this. I never know what will happen next. I am escaping.

— M.B., Tucson, AZ

Understanding that my husband can't even comprehend my feelings allows me the option of leaving him without so much guilt. I now understand there is absolutely nothing I can do to change him. I hope to get strong enough to walk away from this toxic marriage.

— L.D., Columbus, OH

It was nine years before I began to realize mine was a verbal abuse situation. I've been with him now twenty-one years. Leaving him is a last option: few job skills, a rural area, kids, make staying the best I can do, for now. I know now he has an attitude problem. Our relationship is full of hostility, one-up-manship, manipulations, judging, blaming— eventually a messy breakup—when it goes public. The end isn't far off.

— A.P., Carson City, NV

If you decide to end your relationship, it is often wise to end direct contact with your abuser. After all, if you do not want to hear yelling, ordering, or any other verbal abuse, you will need to eliminate contact with your former mate as much as possible. One way to view this is to think of the effects of his behavior toward you as being toxic. The toxicity of being around him may be like exposure to a poisonous gas. One doesn't take periodic whiffs of poison.

If you have left a relationship and you decide that you do not care to see your former mate, you may be able to make arrangements so that you will not have to endure any situation in which he verbally abuses you. You can:

1. Leave messages for him with a neutral party.

2. Use a voice mail number for messages.

3. Decline to keep anything of his stored at your residence.

4. Keep your phone number unlisted.

5. If you have children with him: Find a sitter where you can drop off and pick up your children before or after he is there.

6. If necessary, move to a secret location.

7. Keep family communication on your terms. Don't ever discuss your abuser with your children except where their welfare is concerned (for example, if they seem disturbed after being with him).

8. Let your children's relationship to their father be separate from yours.

9. Use a P.O. box for communications.

10. Get further help and referrals from a women's agency (listed in the appendix).

Out of the Dragon's Lair

The following survivors left their verbally abusive relationships. They now seem committed to living their lives free from abuse. Many express the recurring theme of secrecy—"when we were alone," or "always when we were alone"—and the unreality or strangeness of the interactions—"how crazy it was"—experienced by so many survivors. The secrecy of the abuse makes it doubly difficult for many partners to realize what is occurring. Usually their mate tells them that they are crazy and their unknowing friends may actually tell them that they are *lucky* to be in the relationship!

> *When someone asks why I am divorcing I tell them I didn't want to be in an abusive relationship anymore. To deny to others the type of relationship I was in is to deny it to myself. My husband has the problem, not me.*
>
> — W.J., LAUREL, MD

> *I moved out this year, secretly because I was afraid of him. I'm looking for a job now—It is sort of scary to be fifty and be on your own. I'm learning that I have rights. I can do as I please. It is so much better. My friends and family have rallied around me. He does not know where I live.*
>
> *When I tell about some of the things he said and did when we were alone, my friends cannot believe I lived with it. Now that I am out of it I can see how crazy it was. I know the divorce is really going to be aw-*

ful, but even if it takes forever and is really hard, it is still better than what I lived with.

— A.S., MARIETTA, GA

I never witnessed anyone behave or use the language that my husband displayed, and always when we were alone. Always afraid of him. I left. Now I need to put my life back together. At age forty—homeless and jobless, that's a tall order—I have hopes of leading a productive life again.

— G.K., NEWBERRY, SC

I felt confused, unsure, sad, hurt, stunned, like I was in a land mine-field daily. Then a nervous breakdown entitled me to disability and a way out.

— K.N., WESTFIELD, MA

I feel lucky to have gone to a psychiatrist about ten years into the marriage. Really thought I was going crazy. He gave me confidence to get a job and start putting money away for myself. I don't know where I would be now if I hadn't seen him. He gave me self-esteem and helped me to realize I was right and my husband wrong. I stayed because the children were young. Now they are raised. I have been divorced a year and though I wish he would have changed, I am free and have grown so much.

— G.C., CHAMPLAIN, NY

I tried everything (marriage counseling and individual counseling) to make this work, all to no avail. Through the years I have grown spiritually to a point where I finally realized that I could no longer tolerate his sarcasm and ever-present opposition, and that it was tearing me apart and shattering my spirit. I am thirty-two and on my own. I chose to leave.

— M.W., SAN DIEGO, CA

Usually, no one wants to save her marriage more than the partner of the abuser. Almost all separation and divorce is undertaken with great reluctance and as a last resort. The evidence seems to indicate that in most cases, if the partner of the abuser chose to leave, it was because she felt there was no choice. Many verbal abusers so adamantly deny the abuse that they make up reasons for the breakup of their marriages and relationships that have nothing to do with abuse. Sometimes when an abuser knows his partner knows he is abusive and will not "take it," *he* will end the relationship rather than face his problems.

It seems that the verbal abuser does not usually pursue all the avenues that the partner does to improve the relationship. He does not ask her to get into a group to make the relationship better. He does not ask her what is bothering her. Most abusers refuse to discuss the relationship at all, a reliable sign that one is dealing with a verbal abuser. One verbal abuser quoted earlier in the book said that he would have told his partner she was too sensitive forever if he could have gotten away with it. In fact, covert abusers usually pick their times and modes of abuse so that the abuse is hidden both from his partner's awareness and from others. The abuser will usually not admit that there is anything wrong in the relationship at all. *His attitude is often reflected in society. This is the attitude of complete denial.*

This writer was in her verbally abusive relationship for four years when she wrote,

> *I give up. I'm tired and I want some peace and freedom to be me. Whatever my standard of living becomes, it'll be a small price to pay for my peace of mind.*
>
> — J.W., LIVERMORE, CA

Survivors Seek Assistance

> *I don't know anymore if I love my mate—I would like to know more about how I can get stronger while I'm still being abused, so I can leave.*
>
> *I would like to know more about how I can leave this situation. I need help. I'm in my late sixties. Still working. He's a great guy to other people. No one would believe this. His two children know from his first marriage. I was led to believe his first wife was promiscuous. Not so. She left because of physical and verbal abuse. I now have found out. The abuse is starting to affect my work.*
>
> — R.S., BOSTON, MA

> *I've seen a counselor intermittently for four years and have attended support groups. Throughout all these years, all help has been oriented toward understanding him and trying different ways to work and talk things out—tell him it hurts, laugh more at his jokes, praise him, set up times to talk about the relationship, etc., etc.) None of which has had a lasting effect. The verbal abuse continued each week. The counselor I see always talks about his childhood and how difficult it must have been.*
>
> *Then she discusses ways to express my feelings to him and to talk about these hurtful situations. I am always left frustrated because these methods never worked. He has always refused to get counseling. We*

went to a support group a few times. I finally gave up because of his criticism of the group and because he hated going. I have thought in the past of leaving him, but that has always brought mixed emotions and I think a small hope that our marriage will get better with time.

I've kept thinking the verbal abuse is still there, but if I wait long enough, we will eventually have a happy marriage. Now I realize more than ever he will probably never change. I will not live the rest of my life this way. I will not allow him to inflict his abuse on our children. He will never get the opportunity to erode their self-esteem. How sad that he may never understand this. He definitely refuses to look at himself.

I am sure I will be making a life transition away from him in the future and will definitely need help along the way. It won't be easy and will cause even more anger and rage from him. He hates not having full control of everything, but it is better than listening to his verbal abuse month after month, and year after year.

— R.T., SEATTLE, WA

Well, the straw that broke the camel's back—well, it's there. And now it's time to get out—after twenty-one years while I still have a little bit of get up and go left.

— T.W., LONG ISLAND, NY

In order to deal with verbal abuse now I need to separate from my husband. Legally. Finally.

— E.M., RICHMOND, VA

Relationships break up all the time. Some women can leave more readily than others. If you are planning to leave the dragon's realm, your first step is to gather information. Find out your legal rights. Find a group for support as well as information and referrals. (See chapter 15, "The Support Group.") Women's services and other women's organizations may be of help. You do *not* have to be a battered wife to find support, legal services, and support groups.

Many victims who have been raising children and/or working at minimally paid jobs have financial concerns. Some want to raise their children before leaving. Some want to spend some time standing up to the abuse to see if their mate will change. Some need time to build emotional and financial strength. Persons who suffer in verbally abusive relationships must make their own choices, weighing everything in order to choose their best course of action. We each have our *own* path.

Saying, "Stop It! Enough! No More!" doesn't always work.

Strong and courageous women leaving long-term relationships brave the uncertainty of life, which is much more difficult to face when all that has been is gone, and all that might be may be faced alone.

> *I've been married more than thirty years. (How could I have been so blind?) I am leaving in the next month. After asking my spouse to stop it, please, I came to the horrid realization that he's hostile. I felt his rage and my grief, oh so much grief, and also a growing sense of my own power.*
>
> — E.L., SAN RAFAEL, CA

This survivor's husband would not respect her limits and would not respect her. If the feminine—all that represents the feminine and all that is attributed to the feminine—is not respected, then all of humanity suffers. Men, as well as women, suffer because all aspects are within each and require development. For example, if a man is not nurturing and protective of the less able, all suffer. If a woman does not take a stand and act for what she believes in, all suffer. Has there been a time in the history of our world when more people have suffered from a lack of mutuality in our human relations?

Tragically, there are still parts of the world in which a woman has so few rights she must face complete poverty to escape abuse. If we are to bring about a balanced, healthy society, we must draw upon the potentials, gifts, genius, and creativity of all. It is essential to the well-being of our planet that we bring awareness and support to all who are subject to abuse. Anyone who is abused is most able to heal from that abuse when she or he is no longer being abused. Can we solve the complex problems of our age if the voices of so many facing *this* problem are silenced?

Part 2

IN PART 1 OF THIS BOOK we heard from many survivors of verbally abusive relationships who told how, with little or no knowledge of what was happening to them, they had been controlled and their integrity assaulted. They had endured this abuse while unable to name or describe it. We saw how their anguish, intensified by blame, afflicted their spirits. Finally, we heard them speak out about their fears, their sense of entrapment, and their need to escape.

In Part 2 we will look at the pervasiveness of verbal abuse and explore the results of a survey on the feelings and thinking of women who have suffered in abusive relationships. We will look at the top five verbal abuses and find out why abusers use them most. Finally we will explore how, despite the suppression of their spirits, survivors find ways of coping within their relationships while they build their strengths and their resources.

Chapter 9

The Survey—and the Wildcat Story

What a shock! What a relief to know I'm right about him. How sad that it may not work out.

— T.N., BERKELEY, CA

I have received more than a thousand responses to a survey questionnaire on verbal abuse that I included at the end of my first book on the subject, *The Verbally Abusive Relationship*. This survey requests information from anyone who has recognized that he or she is, or has been, in a verbally abusive relationship. It is designed to provide information about these relationships and about the experience of being subject to verbal abuse.

The results of the first two hundred and fifty surveys received were tallied by an independent agency for inclusion here. This work was done about a year before publication of this book in order to meet publication deadlines. Surveys received later—and new responses continue to arrive daily—are immensely valuable for further research and are deeply appreciated. Most of the surveys have been accompanied by notes and letters. *I read them all.*

As I mentioned earlier, one writer found so much to identify with that she actually wrote on *every page* of her book—in the margins and between the lines—including dates, incidents, times, places. Then, wanting very much that someone else should know her truth, she turned the book, with its record of suffering, over to me.

Besides sharing their experiences, many survivors have questions. One asked,

Do these verbal abusers poison their own souls, when they hurt others?
Do they as well suffer, as we who are verbally battered by them, suffer?
— H.C., HOUSTON, TX

To answer H.C., I believe they suffer in a different way from the partner who experiences the abuse. The abuser's life is built around avoiding his feelings, especially his pain.

Some men wrote telling of their realization that they were verbally abusive. They expressed a tremendous desire to change. It seems that they had not realized the effects of their behavior. This was so even when they were close to becoming physically abusive. One man who responded to the survey from the perspective of being verbally abusive himself spoke for many. He wrote,

I am a married male thirty-five years of age and have been married for nine years. In my relationship I am abusive. I did, however, experience being verbally abused growing up from my parents, teachers and from kids at school.

Now, I realize that I am in a verbally abusive relationship and that I am the abuser. I definitely want to change, not leave. Rather than feeling trapped in the relationship I feel guilty and ashamed. I love my mate very much and it has never occurred to me to leave her. I can say that the frequency and intensity of the abusive incidents did increase over time. Furthermore, I fear that I was on the verge of escalating to physically abusing my wife.

Although I believe that I may only occasionally be verbally abusive toward others, I know that I have been constantly verbally abusive toward my wife. And, although I have never been hit, pushed, or shoved by my mate and I have never hit, pushed, or shoved my mate, nor has she threatened me, nor I her, I know that at times my mate is afraid of me.

I believe that the verbal abuse I encountered in childhood has very much affected my self-esteem, confidence and happiness in a negative way. What I experienced in childhood, discounting, judging, criticizing, trivializing, name calling and abusive anger is the verbal abuse I am most guilty of inflicting on my mate in my marriage. When I was verbally abused in childhood I thought I had said or done something wrong, felt confused and unsure, sad, hurt, stunned and shocked.

Now that I better understand what verbal abuse is, I need to be more alert to it, more confident. To change my verbally abusive ways I need to be more aware to recognize when I am slipping into old patterns.
— R.S., OMAHA, NE

When this writer says "I need to be more aware" he names the key to change, *awareness*. Change will be discussed in detail in chapter 12. For now it is important to know that if the abuser does not become aware of his behavior *and* its effects, and allow his partner to call him on lapses so that he can stop and feel his feelings without acting them out, *the abuse will in almost every case escalate over time.*

The issue of control through abuse has been an enormously difficult issue for women to deal with. Although thousands of women are beginning to recognize how verbal abuse has affected them, we have no sure knowledge in the following areas:

1. We do not know what percent of relationships are verbally abusive, defined as one person primarily dominating and controlling the other through verbal abuse. For example, we do not know in what percentage of heterosexual relationships the man is controlling his mate through verbal abuse, nor in what percentage of heterosexual relationships the woman is controlling her mate through verbal abuse.

2. We do not know what the differences are in the experiences of women and men with regard to verbal abuse.

One of the great difficulties in making any assessment at this time is that those who experience verbal abuse generally do not recognize it until they learn the name for their experience. Even a large poll on a national scale would not necessarily give us an accurate answer, because thousands or millions who suffer and know "something is wrong" do not recognize the problem for what it is. Until they realize that the way they are being treated isn't justified, that they are not doing something wrong and that they aren't inadequate, their self doubt will grow and they will not know why they are suffering.

Of the 250 respondents tallied, 94 percent were women who had been or were currently in verbally abusive heterosexual relationships. Less than 3 percent were males in heterosexual relationships. Of these, two volunteered the information that their abusive spouses were diagnosed as manic depressive.

Although no conclusions can be drawn on the basis of this extremely small number, the coincidence suggests that the possibility of a chemical imbalance could be explored. This is in no way to suggest that a person diagnosed as manic depressive would necessarily be verbally abusive, nor that a verbally abusive woman is necessarily manic depressive. However, further research may be called for.

I have insufficient information to write about verbally abused men's experiences. Less than 1 percent of the letters received were from men who had been abused. Several men and women have written wondering why the book *The Verbally Abusive Relationship* did not portray women and men equally as "the abuser" in the examples. Since no men came forward for that book, and since less than 1 percent of those writing to me with their stories are men abused by women, to write of anything but the feminine experience of control through verbal abuse would be conjecture on my part. Perhaps men abused as these survivors have been suffer similarly, in which case the material provided here will be of value to them as well. These are important questions to which we simply do not yet have answers. We await further information.

All 250 respondents in the survey analysis stated that they had experienced a verbally abusive relationship at some time. Of the total female respondents, two were in homosexual relationships and eight were in verbally abusive relationships with a boss, a sibling, a parent, or an adult child. Of the remaining 229 heterosexual female respondents, about 75 percent said that they are *currently* in a heterosexual verbally abusive relationship. The remaining 25 percent said that they are not now, but had been, in a heterosexual verbally abusive relationship in the past. Many had very recently left an abusive relationship. Most were desirous of learning more about why their relationship had not worked for them and of understanding the dynamics in order to avoid future verbally abusive relationships.

The respondents who are not females presently or formerly in a verbally abusive heterosexual relationship do not compose a *substantial* representation of their category. Therefore, to avoid drawing false conclusions, I have not included their data in the following analysis. This is not to say that their suffering is not real and worthy of response.

Do women feel trapped in their relationships?
Yes. 71 percent do feel trapped. Of these, about 40 percent believe that it would at some time be possible to leave.

Some primary concerns of a large number of the survivors who felt trapped in their relationships were fear, lost confidence, economic survival, and health. Thus, it is important that they receive as much support and validation as possible from their families and their community in order to cope with the abuse they suffer.

Are women in verbally abusive relationships afraid of their mates at times?
Yes. The vast majority of survivors (83 percent) were at times afraid of their mates.

Once we are afraid of someone, it is possible that we may feel some potential threat from them for a very long time to come. Displays of anger are made to demonstrate the potential for destruction. Most women who are not hit but see displays of rage are afraid of their mates. Many are afraid of the emotional pain of verbal abuse. These fears are natural responses to toxic experiences.

Do many verbally abused women experience physical abuse?
More than half. Fifty-six percent have been hit, pushed, or shoved by their mates. Many survivors say that they never totally relax or trust their mate again after being hit. Many also say that the mental anguish of verbal abuse is much worse than being hit. This may account for the fact that *more than three-fourths of the survivors fear their mates at least some of time.*

Do women who are verbally abused love their mates?
Only 43 percent said that they feel they love their mates. One percent is undecided.

Do the women who suffer verbal abuse from their mates believe their mates will change and give up their controlling ways?
A whopping 84 percent do *not* believe their mates will change. In their letters, however, many women expressed great fear regarding what their mate would do if they tried to leave. These women may need special support and assistance to help them leave situations they regard as hopeless.

Do women who are verbally abused think about leaving?
Yes. Eighty-three percent said that it had occurred to them to leave.

What about early childhood? How much abuse did the survivors experience?
More than half (55 percent) said that they had experienced verbal abuse in childhood; of these, 41 percent had experienced verbal abuse from their fathers and 41 percent from their mothers. Some had experienced verbal abuse from both parents, others from only one. These differences were not distinguished in the tallies.

It is interesting to note that 22 percent of female respondents said that they experienced verbal abuse from relatives, 22 percent said that they experienced verbal abuse from bosses, and 22 percent said that they had experienced verbal abuse from peers when they were in school.

Being verbally abused in childhood does not at this time appear to be a crucial criteria for ending up in a verbally abusive relationship, but feelings of abandonment from childhood do seem to play some part in maintaining, that is, staying in, abusive relationships. Some survivors said that they felt very loved and secure in childhood and never dreamt they would be in a verbally abusive relationship. Neither, however, did those with less secure and loving childhoods.

Does verbal abuse really get worse over time?
Yes, just about always. Ninety-two percent of survivors were able to identify an increase over time in the frequency and intensity of abusive incidents in their relationship.

Even though the partners of verbal abusers did everything they could think of to stop the abuse, although they were as kind as they could be, walked on egg shells, tried to bolster their mate's confidence, went on diets, took classes, got degrees, read books, tried new recipes, went to therapists, went into hospitals for evaluations, tried to explain, earned extra money, pleaded, cried, left, tried to say something abusive back, and told him what he was doing, the abuse escalated.

What does this signify? That the abuse was the abuser's problem and had nothing to do with the partner. The increase in abuse in these cases is like a tree that becomes unbalanced and starts to tilt because it was not planted in solid ground. Year by year, as it tilts a little more, it becomes a little more unbalanced, causing it to tilt even more—twice as much this year as the year before—until finally it crashes to the ground.

How did the survivors feel when they were verbally abused?
The survivors of verbal abuse said that when they were abused they felt, first, sad and hurt. This is the experience of rejection. Next they felt stunned and shocked. The abuse was completely unexpected. Finally they felt confused. This is because there was no correspondence between what they thought, felt and did just prior to the abuse and the sudden abuse they experienced.

If we are being rejected—and all verbal abuse is rejecting—we are liable to feel that there is something unworthy about us. If one never knows when or why a hurtful experience may occur, one does feel confused. If one imagines that the abuser has a sickness or malady that he caught in childhood from family and culture that grows progressively worse, clarity may replace confusion.

What did the survivors think when they were verbally abused?
The survivors said that when they were abused, their first thought was that they had said or done something wrong. Generally they had absolutely no idea that the abuse had nothing to do with them, that

they were not responsible or to blame. Next they thought that their mate didn't understand something. This led them to want to explain themselves so that friendship and communication could be restored. Finally they thought that there was something they were missing, perhaps the right kinds of words or the right kind of logic; or maybe growing up they had missed some important piece of information that would make everything understandable.

Did verbal abuse affect the survivor's self-esteem, confidence, and happiness in a negative way?
Ninety-nine percent said yes. Eighty-nine percent said they were *very much* affected.

Although we cannot yet begin to estimate the numbers of women in verbally abusive relationships, we may assume that millions of women worldwide are limited in their pursuits by low self-esteem and a lack of confidence as a direct result of having been undermined by verbal abuse.

The following story has been contributed by a survivor in the hope that it will help someone else who may be suffering from verbal abuse.

The Story of the Wildcat

There was once a young woman named Judy who had an unusual house companion. It was a wildcat. Judy had never for a moment thought that she would have a wildcat for a house companion, and so she was alarmed when she discovered that in truth that is just what she had. This is how it all came about.

When Judy first met her companion, it looked like a friend. It was young and seemed a lot like the companion she had always dreamed of. It was a warm and friendly creature. It wanted her to like it and she wanted it to like her. It seemed lovable, and cute and cuddly. And she enjoyed it.

But, with time, it grew into a wildcat. First it was a nice companion. Then it was suddenly in wildcat time—scary and mean and wildcat-like. For Judy, it was a whole lot bigger than a basket full of trouble—more trouble than she had ever dreamt of.

Judy spent a lot of her time trying to keep her wildcat happy so it wouldn't hurt her. But it was unpredictable. So she was very, very careful not to disturb it. She was so careful in fact that she felt like she was walking on egg shells.

Sadly, Judy didn't seem to have time for friends because her wildcat took most of her time and all of her energy. Sometimes it was lovable—

just like when she first met it. But when it snapped into wildcat time it tore into her and it hurt her.

Swiftly seeking a solution Judy went to a therapist sadly saying, "What should I do about my wildcat? I love him, but honestly, he's habitually horrible to me. I want to tell you what he says and does—I hope you can tell me if what he says and does makes sense to you or if I'm taking it all wrong, and making a big thing out of nothing, and provoking him as he says. I want to know if there is a treatment for our relationship."

The therapist said, "Oh, Judy, that's your main mistake: wanting to talk about the wildcat. I want you to talk about you. You need help! You need to look at why you are a person who seeks to have such a cruel, scary companion."

"But I didn't want a cruel, scary companion." Judy exclaimed. "When we were first together, he was cute and sweet and lovable. Then he started to change."

"No," said the therapist. "You really feel more comfortable being mistreated. You have problems. I'm sure you've had an unhappy childhood. You have low self-esteem. You are a martyr. At some level, you enjoy being mistreated. It's what you're accustomed to. If you didn't have your wildcat, you would merely look for another one—just so you could mess up your life again. You are addicted to wildcats and to emotional pain."

And Judy said, "Really?!?! Gosh, I just thought I had a mean companion."

"No," said the therapist. "You must work on yourself. The creature is not the problem. You've become obsessed with him to avoid your emptiness, your fear of relationships and your anger. You're using your relationship with your wildcat as a drug. You're addicted to it. You don't like yourself very much. And you seem to be a very angry person. You are drawn to situations that are chaotic. You crave excitement. You aren't attracted to nice, kind creatures. You find such creatures boring. You really have problems."

"Why?" Judy asked.

"Because you are a woman who loves too much," the therapist answered.

"Gosh," said Judy. "I must be really sick."

And the therapist slowly nodded, "Yes."

Sooooo, Judy kept talking with the therapist about all of Judy's personality problems. And Judy went to meetings too, and she got an advanced degree to make sure she wasn't depending on her wildcat for intellectual stimulation, and she made four new friends to make sure she wasn't depending on her wildcat for conversation, and she worked for extra money to make sure she wasn't depending financially on her wildcat too much and she kept trying to gain self-esteem and to grow by taking responsibility for all of her personal defects. But, the wildcat, in the meantime, just kept on enjoying himself and scaring Judy.

Finally, Judy heard about a different therapist, and she went to her. This therapist said to Judy, "We don't need to focus on you, Judy, as the problem. We need to focus on the wildcat. It's the problem. Get rid of it!"

"The wildcat or the problem?" Judy asked.

"Whatever will give you peace," said the therapist.

"But," Judy said, "Shouldn't we talk about why I have such a cruel creature? I have deep-seated problems."

"No. I don't believe so. Didn't you think you were getting a cute, lovable, cuddly creature?"

"Oh, yes," Judy said, glad at last to feel understood. "But he turned into a wildcat, except he isn't one when certain people are around."

"Yes," the therapist replied with wonderful understanding. "It's not really possible to live with a wildcat."

"But," Judy said, "my other therapist said if I don't work on me, I'll just pick another wildcat."

"I don't agree," replied the therapist. "I don't believe you enjoy living with a wildcat. I think the more we talk about the wildcat the more you will see him as he really is—and you won't ever live with a wildcat again."

But Judy, still remembering what the first therapist had told her, replied, "I still think it's partly my problem. Maybe the wildcat and I should go together for counseling."

"No," said the therapist. "That doesn't usually work. But your wildcat might change back to his original self in 'Wildcat Group Therapy.' You may want to wait to see if they can help him. However, I must warn you wildcats are hard to change back into kind creatures unless they really want to change."

Some time went by, and Judy saw that she must let the wildcat go. By then she knew all about wildcats and knew how to spot them very quickly. She missed the wildcat at first, because she loved him. But eventually she felt very happy because she didn't have to "walk on egg shells" any more.

Her self-esteem bounced back and she realized that the first therapist had not been quite right. She wasn't a woman who loved too much. She was a woman who had had a wildcat.

— J.L., MINNEAPOLIS, MN

Chapter 10

The Top Five Abuses and the Closed Relationship

It is hard to realize that I am a worthwhile and capable person when I am not treated as such.

— W.L., OKLAHOMA CITY, OK

The survey of 250 survivors discussed in the previous chapter asked respondents to identify the five forms of verbal abuse they experienced most frequently. Although nearly all respondents said that they had frequently suffered from *all* categories of verbal abuse, they agreed to rank the five most frequent. Here are the abuses most frequently cited, beginning with the most common.

Category of Abuse	Frequency
Abusive Anger	192
Accusing and Blaming	161
Judging & Criticizing	159
Withholding	124
Denial	106

Let us look at what this frequency chart above may indicate. We can see, for example, that the partner of an abuser is more often blamed than made the object of direct threats. Threats did not make the top five. It would seem that the abuser accomplishes his goals more through the intimidation of accusatory anger than by overt behavior. Of course, abusive anger is itself threatening and may intimidate the partner for long periods of time as she stays "braced for it."

These top five abuses together serve to alienate the partner from her mate. They completely close off the possibility of connection between them. They end the "relationship," exactly as if the partner of the abuser did not exist at all. All that is left is the abuser acting out.

Let's take another look at number 1, *Abusive Anger*. This is one of the most disturbing forms of verbal abuse. This anger is often combined with number 2, *Accusing and Blaming*. This is a primary reason that partners of verbal abusers are confused and unsure, often wondering what is wrong in their relationship. They are blamed for their mate's anger. If he is furious "with them" they can hardly help but believe that they *are* in some way to blame. Consequently they are immobilized. According to the abuser, they are the "culprit." They are the cause of their own pain. *Nothing is more immobilizing than a constant search within to find this culprit, who is really not one's self but one's mate.* If they also experience frequent *Criticism* (number 3), they are even more unsure of themselves and more likely to believe that "something" is wrong with them, intensifying the search for the culprit in the wrong place.

Finally, if her spouse *Withholds* (number 4) and is unwilling to discuss the relationship or to share himself, *Denying* his behavior (number 5), the partner is stuck in an unchanging and rigid relationship. The verbally abusive relationship is a closed system.

The top five abuses operate to "imprison" the partner in the verbally abusive relationship. The partner of the abuser has been made the enemy by the abuser's *anger*. Because of *accusation and blame* she comes to believe she is the cause, so the problem becomes unsolvable. She feels defenseless from *criticism* that seems to confirm that something is wrong about her. She is imprisoned by her mate's *withholding*. The door to change is closed—the discussion is ended. Finally, even future possibilities for freedom in the relationship are lost when *denial* is used—"It never happened at all."

Survivors have described feeling disempowered and trapped in abusive relationships. Most (71 percent) say they do feel trapped in their relationships. One reason this is so is that there is no exchange of thoughts and feelings in the closed relationship.

When an abuser will not actively discuss his behavior and listen with care and attention to his mate, or when he will not change, the relationship itself is inflexible. After all, a relationship is only as strong as its weakest aspect. Rigid relationships are prone to disintegrate and finally end because healthy and necessary change cannot take place.

Science tells us that when systems are closed, they collapse. A simple example is a plant, which must take in carbon dioxide and put out oxygen in order to survive. If its leaves are sealed—like a closed mind—the system will not survive. The plant collapses or disintegrates into compost, because the system which supported it became closed.

Imbalance may also cause a system to collapse in chaos. So it is with relationships. An example of imbalance can be observed in the escalation of abuse over time. Ninety-two percent of the women who experienced verbal abuse said that the abuse escalated over time. In other words, one can almost count on abuse becoming worse in the closed system of the abusive relationship.

When systems reach states of chaos, they must reorganize if they are to survive. Often a catalyst to change is needed. Some abusers reading about their own behavior are open enough to take in the information and use it. In this case, the information becomes the catalyst for change. In some cases when the partner says, for instance, "Cut that out! I don't ever want to hear you tell me what I think again," the abuser hears his partner speaking with a force he had never heard before, and is so startled that he actually hears what is said. He begins to realize he has developed some abusive patterns of behavior that will have to stop if the relationship is to survive. This kind of significant emotional event is often effective in bringing about change.

In abusive relationships, communication is not open and free. Any two living entities that live in relationship to each other must be able to relate to each other in an open and mutual way, meaning that each one must be willing to communicate. You can't have a relationship with a noncommunicator. Each, moreover, must respect the other as a separate person.

In an abusive relationship, this separateness is denied by the abuser. For example, if the partner of an abuser hears "You were" or "You are" or "You're just" or "You should" or "You don't" she is *usually* hearing this from a person who does not know that she exists as a separate person. Her own existence as a separate person is denied. In actual experience, only she can know if she "was" "is," "just," "should" or "doesn't" something. Only she can define her reality and her experience. Anyone else who presumes to do so violates her boundaries.

I heard a man who realized he had been extremely verbally abusive say, "I love my wife, she's everything to me. I love her more than anything, we're so close she is like an extension of my very self."

What is he communicating? He is communicating, "You do not exist as a separate person."

This means, "You must think as I think. Do as I say. And my behavior has no affect on you because I don't feel its effects. You are my extension; you can only feel what I feel."

I heard a woman say, with her adult daughter sitting nearby, "I don't know why my daughter says I verbally abuse her. Why, I love my daughter." She was very intent on convincing me that her daughter did not know what she was talking about when it came to her claim of being verbally abused.

A few minutes later the daughter, who was leaving for a very important appointment, expressed a need for some reassurance about her appearance—did she look okay? I saw that she was very well dressed.

I complimented the daughter on her nice-looking jacket. Before she could even respond, her mother said, "Well, it's okay, but it wrinkles." Immediately the daughter lost confidence. She was being criticized about her choice of clothes. She was being undermined when she needed confidence. Why? Because her mother forgot, and possibly never knew, her daughter was a separate person.

What was the mother communicating? She was communicating, "I am concerned about my/our jacket wrinkling." After all, if you are an extension of me, what you wear is a statement about what I wear.

When people do not see other people as separate from themselves, they are prone to be abusive. To invade another's mind doesn't feel wrong if you do not recognize it as separate from your own. To criticize another's apparel does not feel wrong if you think it is your own apparel.

If they are told to "stop it," such people may apologize—OR they may (and here we are back to the top five) (1) become abusively angry; (2) accuse and blame *you* for *their* anger ("You're picking a fight."); (3) criticize you more ("Well, it does wrinkle."); (4) withhold in stony silence, and if you say, "I deserve an apology," (5) deny their behavior ("You've got to be crazy; if anyone deserves an apology, it's *me*.")

Some survivors say that, more than anything else in the world (as far as their relationship is concerned), they want to be treated as a separate person, to be treated with dignity and respect, to have their individuality, their personhood, and their feelings acknowledged and validated. This is just what doesn't happen in a verbally abusive relationship. Validation is withheld.

Since withholding is one of the most disastrous categories of verbal abuse as far as a relationship is concerned, I will expand on it a little more here. Did you notice in the interaction above that approval of the daughter was withheld the entire time? Willingness to hear the daughter's experience was also withheld.

Withholding is in the top five because withholding is what keeps the toxic relationship going. There is nothing tangible to respond to if someone refuses to talk with you, or refuses to answer you, or refuses to inform you of actions that may affect you. The withholding of response and acknowledgment is one of the most painful of all abuses and is a potent form of rejection.

Withholding isn't about having time and space alone. Having time and space to oneself is healthy in a relationship. Telling your mate, "I'll be in my room reading," or "I'll be chatting with Smith next door," for example, is a courteous and thoughtful revelation of your activities and leaves the door open for anyone to mention anything urgent or to dispense any messages.

Withholding isn't being quiet. It is a choice not to reveal oneself and not to give approval, acceptance or validation to one's mate. The withholding abuser simply will not respond to his partner. This is a major control issue.

Withholding may be used to keep a partner off-balance and to ensure that there is no change in the relationship and no equality of communication. This strategy of keeping his partner off balance is demonstrated in the following story, called the "Car Scenario." It is not about verbal or physical abuse, but it is relevant here because it is abusive behavior designed to control the victim's time and energy. It is *withholding dramatized*.

A woman I know told me this story. She watched it as it was played out.

Car Scenario

A young man backed his friend's car out of the driveway. A moment later the friend came out and approached the car. As she got within about six feet of it, the young man backed the car up five to ten feet more. The young woman started off in that direction. Just as she got close, he moved off again. Then, as she approached, he did it again. At this point the young woman walked to the garage, leaned against it and stood there waiting. Finally the young man drove forward, got out of the car, and gave her the keys, and she drove off.

This young man was on a power trip. He needed to control. His method: withholding. He withheld the car because he could, like an older child holding a toy out to a baby and pulling it away just as the baby's hand is about to grasp it. The older child feels powerful; the baby, frustrated and powerless.

The young woman gave up after a few tries. Completely powerless to gain access to her car, she withdrew. The young man then came forward and "won her back." He can then start the process over again in some other way. This is another version of the cycle of violence described in the chapter on blame.

The young woman has since been seen with the same young man. Power trips are abusive, and it would be easy to imagine this young man becoming verbally abusive toward this young woman, if he isn't already.

Just as the abuser will pull away emotionally, the young man pulled away physically. Survivors have described a movement first toward them, then away from them. It is like this drama except in reverse. First he is warm or friendly, then cold and unfriendly.

In a healthy, nonabusive relationship, both parties generally experience warmth, respect, and consideration from the other. In a non-controlling relationship one has a comfortable feeling of well-being when with the loved one. No one in this relationship is experiencing unexpected outbursts, or criticism, or the "silent treatment." Though one or the other partners may sometimes seem irritable, any unkindness is usually apologized for with an explanation of what was really going on, such as, "Oh, I'm sorry, honey, I'm feeling irritable because . . ." On the other hand, a verbally abusive relationship is *characterized* by dominance and control primarily through diminishing and anger.

All of the issues I have been describing have to do with communication. What is being communicated? What is really being said? The young woman in the car scenario tried several times to move toward her boyfriend, hoping that "this time" he would not withhold recognition of her. Abuse is salt to the soul's thirst. In the mother/daughter story told earlier, the young woman thirsted for one word of approval from her mother—and the withholding of that word, like all abuse, was killing to her spirit.

Chapter 11

Coping

---

*There are quite a few of us out here. Aware or un-
aware, we are surviving, not living emotionally
happy lives, but existing because we feel we have
no other place to be and we love our children and
want to provide the best we can for them. We are
trapped emotionally and economically, living the
life of a servant to an abusive tyrannical king who
tries to control our existence.*

— R.T., PROVIDENCE, RI

According to the poll discussed earlier, 75 percent of those who are
currently in verbally abusive relationships feel that they are going to
be in those relationships for some time to come. Those with much at
stake, who, for instance, have young families, economic concerns, or
limited education and training, are looking for ways of coping with
the abuse while they develop themselves and their resources. They are
working to end the abuse by setting limits and stating their needs—or
at least to manage in the relationship for a time. They ask questions
and share their experiences about coping with verbal abuse.

*There is much to be done. I must take some time. I have given up my hope
that he would change. I want to know how to cope on a daily basis.*
— W.G., COLUMBUS, OH

*We need to know more about how to handle it—the times when you
can't walk away.*
— A.J., WEST PALM BEACH, FL

I would like to know more about effective ways of dealing with it.
— E.N., CHICAGO, IL

I would like to know more about how you can cope with being verbally abused until you can get on track again.
— M.H., NORTH BEND, OR

I would like to know how to enforce limits.
— S.H., MILWAUKEE, WI

I would like to know more about good responses.
— N.G., CLEVELAND, OH

After thirty-five years in this relationship I want to learn how to cope.
— M.J., LITTLE ROCK, AR

If you are coping with an abusive relationship, I recommend that you get all the support you can from trusted friends, family, counselors, therapists, and *especially* from a support group. Groups offer increased resources, friends, a feeling of community, and plenty of reality feedback. For more information, see chapter 15, "The Support Group."

Living with an abuser will never be easy. Every situation is different. Some abusers spend most of their time arguing and being sarcastic. Others spend a lot of time taking over, giving orders, and raging, and some stick to silence, countering, and sarcasm. Some do a little (or a lot) of all of the above. Most claim to be supportive of their partners and most are well thought of outside the home.

Because each situation is so different I have outlined only the most general suggestions for coping with abuse. These strategies have been gleaned from many survivors' experiences. For more specific information, check the recommended reading in the back of this book.

Be Aware

Following are some suggestions and thoughts that may support you in maintaining some sense of balance, with reduced fear, anxiety, and sadness.

1. Be Aware. Ask Yourself What He Is Communicating.

If you ask yourself what is being communicated to you, as did the woman in chapter 1, who analyzed her day in her journal, you may be more able to respond appropriately and be less likely to be manipulated by your mate when he is in an abusive Reality I Mode.

2. Be Aware of the Abuser's Purpose.

Know the abuser's motives and strategy. His motive is to control you, not to be with you in a mutual way, and his strategy is to diminish you so you will doubt yourself and be more controllable.

Generally, abusers say that they are completely unaware of the effects of their behavior. They like to feel in control, dominant, and at liberty to vent their anger by disparaging their mates; they certainly don't feel empathy for them. It seems that they almost automatically behave as they do in order to maintain a feeling of Power Over you. They want most to blame you, make you responsible, make you the scapegoat for any unpleasant thought or feeling they may have. Sometimes the abuser may just want to "score a win" when he doesn't feel quite up to snuff. One man described his "automatic behavior" as a knee-jerk reaction. If you are experiencing this, it is important to know that he isn't reacting to anything *you* have said or done, even when he says he is. He is reacting to his *own* feelings (the wounded inner child). By beating you down, tormenting you with teasing, topping you, countering you, or ordering you, he is feeling strong and powerful without noticing his own wounded and vulnerable feelings buried deep inside.

3. Be Aware that Abusers Make Their Partners Responsible for Their Happiness.

The abuser makes his partner responsible for his happiness by saying, for example,

"What's that doing there?" in an angry voice, as if you are responsible for where it is and his happiness depends on your doing what he wants done with it.

"You make me happy," as if you are responsible for his happiness.

"Where's my (whatever)?" as if you are supposed to find it.

"You make me mad," as if you are the cause of his anger.

"You made me do it," as if you could make anyone do anything (especially him).

4. Be Aware that the Abuser May Not See You as a Separate Person.

It follows from this that the abuser may not be willing to allow you to have a different opinion and may, indeed, be unaware on some level that you are a separate person. If he can't tell you are a separate person metaphorically speaking, he will swallow you in his shadow as you become "responsible" for everything he feels and become the object of his hostility.

Know about His Quickly Changing Behavior

1. When the wounded inner child (his dragon) is napping, your abuser may seem nice.

2. After the wounded inner child (his dragon) has been pushed

back down by great feelings of Power Over (you), your abuser may seem nice.

3. When the wounded inner child (his dragon) starts to come out and you aren't there to be the scapegoat, your abuser may try to get you back and so "be nice."

4. After he has you "back" he can at any moment switch to "Being A Dragon" behavior.

What to Avoid

1. Avoid Trying to Change Yourself.

> *When verbally abused I usually try to change me so it doesn't happen again so I end up verbally abusing myself silently.*
> — SANTA CLARA, CA

If you find yourself doing this, make every effort not to try to change yourself. Being abused is not your fault. You are not to blame. *You cannot cure his illness.*

2. Avoid Focusing on the Abusive Incident.

> *When abused I withdraw into myself and feel terrible the whole day. If I say anything to try to understand it, it makes matters worse. I feel like I'm walking on eggshells.*
> — W.S., ROCKY HILL, NJ

Focus on something you like and do it no matter how you feel. Don't try to understand or to get your abuser to understand because abusive behavior is irrational. It is "acting out" unfelt feelings. It can still be a killer. However, finding something to do for yourself, and someone to talk to, helps.

3. Avoid Isolation.

> *When abused I feel frustrated, helpless, defenseless, angry, frightened, crazy and indecisive.*

> *I'm afraid to tell anyone about all the verbal abuse.*

Find some support groups, check the newspapers, call a women's center. Get some feedback, reality checks, and validation; tell *everybody* who may be sympathetic. If you are ashamed that *he* is a verbal abuser, remind yourself that you are not the abuser and that *you* are a *separate person from him*. With that objectivity, you might imagine calling everyone you know well and saying something along the lines of, "Guess what, I unwittingly married a verbal abuser. I would like some support."

4. Avoid Trying to Make Everything "Better."

When I was verbally abused I usually did everything in my power to make everything okay—get up earlier, work harder, get the kids to behave better, apologize.

— M.L., LEHIGH VALLEY, PA

Verbal abuse is about control. Sometimes the abuser is testing his power. When the partner doesn't realize that her mate is testing his power and has no idea of "what is wrong," she becomes confused. If, however, she realizes that her mate is contradicting her, say, out of a desire for power and control, she will not be likely to try to explain or "make things right."

Trying to make everything okay is a common reaction to controlling behavior. Abuse carries so much rejection the partner wants to be "more acceptable." If this is your usual method of coping, try putting all that time and energy into a project for yourself—something you enjoy.

5. Avoid Trying to Change Him.

I want to know more about how to change him. I just want to help him get better.

The following survivor neatly summarizes the entire verbally abusive relationship in the following note:

If they never say I'm sorry or if they say I'm sorry and do it again, you know they have an abuse disease and you can't cure it. So protect yourself from it and be sure not to catch it, and see if you can stop it from spreading by saying, "Stop it."

— M.L., OXNARD, CA

No one can change another person. You can sometimes bring awareness, but only if he doesn't completely close you off. You can do this by consistently telling him "Stop it" or "I don't like that." In time some abusers do accept the truth about their behavior.

Some Additional Ideas

❏ Say "Stop it" to the abuse.

❏ Don't drink or take drugs to relieve the pain.

❏ Don't try to engage the abuser in conversation or discussion about the abuse.

❏ Meet your needs as best you can.

❏ Work to become as financially independent as possible.

❏ Leave the area the moment you feel at all threatened.

❑ Constantly affirm your reality and experience.

❑ Join organizations according to your interests.

❑ Make friends who are supportive to you.

❑ Avoid isolation.

❑ Join a support group as soon as possible.

❑ Protect your resources, your time, and your space.

❑ Protect your children.

❑ Get exercise daily.

❑ Maintain good health habits.

Survivors say: In order to deal with verbal abuse I need to
". . . have faith in myself and my feelings."
". . . put into practice what I have learned."
". . . leave as soon as I spot it."
". . . be consistent about not letting verbal abuse pass without showing that I am aware of it and don't accept it."
". . . take assertiveness training classes."
". . . be around women who stand up to verbal abuse and use them as role models."
". . . take a course in communication dynamics."
". . . learn about power issues between men and women."
". . . look more closely at the patterns of communication in my relationship and ways [I was] verbally abused . . . as a little girl so I stop recreating patterns."
". . . be more aware of subtle forms of verbal abuse in the workplace."

Strategies
Survivors share their own experiences of coping with abusive mates.

I need to be aware of what he is and his reality, and not accept any of it as truth.

— B.W., FAYETTEVILLE, NC

As I get stronger he respects me more.

— P.K., ROCKY HILL, NJ

If the abuse usually happens when you are alone, then when you have something to say to him, say it when other people are around. Otherwise don't say anything and try not to be alone with him.

— O.B., VACAVILLE, CA

I see a counselor. I learned to nurture, love and care for my own inner self; trust my feelings and intuition.
— G.L., SANTA BARBARA, CA

I have been deeply troubled by the verbal abuse in my relationship but because I am a career woman I've kept very busy and have put aside the problem to deal with later. Later is now.
— V.B., SAN FRANCISCO, CA

Protecting Your Material Resources
The first step to protecting your resources is knowing all your rights and responsibilities in the state in which you live. For example, you have certain liabilities and obligations regarding taxes. Separate property and community property, joint income and debts, and inheritances are treated differently in different states.

Your own car and your own money are resources that allow you greater independence.

Protecting Your Time
The following responses may help you to protect your time.
"I have to think that over."
"I'll get back to you on that."
"I'll sleep on that and let you know tomorrow."
"I'll be free to do that . . . (name the day/time)"
"I'm not willing to take that on/undertake that project/do that."
Don't wait for long periods for your mate if he is late for an appointment with you. Go on with what you want to do after a reasonable time.

Protecting Your Space
Everyone needs a space of her own where she can be by herself. It may simply be a desk, chair and shelves or it may be a room or office. If you don't have one, see whether you can create one. Keep your favorite books, papers, pictures, art objects, flowers, or keepsakes in your place.

Tell your mate when you want to be alone.

Be firm and clear when saying "no" to what you do not want.

Protecting Your Health
Do the best you can to take very good care of yourself. Prolonged stress or traumatic abuse can lower your immune system and cause anxiety or depression. Don't ever stay where you feel threatened or where another's behavior is disturbing to you. A survivor writes,

Please know I take full responsibility for the fact that I'm addicted to pre-scription pain killers. I'm in recovery now. It seems that was only one more way of coping with the pain that didn't work. Please tell others.
— W.A., FARMINTON HILLS, MI

Abusive "Complainers"

Are there other abusers who feel constantly sorry for themselves like my husband?
— M.W., POTOMAC, MD

Are there other constant complainers out there?
— S.T., SIOUX FALLS, SD

Do other abusers take every opportunity to show how misunderstood and under-appreciated they are by absolutely everyone?
— M.P., BRISTOL, CT

Constant complaining and "feeling sorry for themselves" are ways abusers want to make you responsible—to get you to handle *life* for them. These abusers often leave the partner feeling guilty and more to blame for the abuse she suffers. As if she were supposed to fix everything, and as if he would not be angry and complain if she did!.

If you are with a complainer, don't take responsibility or try to fix things for him. An appropriate response to this kind of complaint is, "Oh," said sympathetically. With no additional suggestions. Period.

Managing

1. Respond clearly and firmly to all verbal abuse with any of the following or similar statements:

   > Stop it.
   > Cut it out.
   > I don't want to hear it.
   > Enough.
   > Don't raise your voice to me.
   > I will discuss this with you later when you are calmer.
   > Is that a request? (when you hear an order)
   > I'll be available to talk with you at _____.
   > I will not accept that.
   > Hold it. I'm not through talking.

2. Take care of your own needs.

   > Education and intellectual stimulation
   > Employment and financial security

Entertainment and friendship
Enrichment and arts
Exercise and health

3. A survivor wrote that she "felt constrained" when her mate verbally abused her in front of others. The constrained feeling may be fear or shame. You can deal with the false shame by simply saying in front of everyone, "I will not accept . . ." repeating it until he acknowledges you and apologizes.

4. Know that there is nothing you can do and no way you can be to have him be kind and supportive. He will change only if he wants to change. Therefore put every bit of energy you have into taking care of yourself in every way: physically, spiritually, intellectually, emotionally, socially.

5. If you find he isn't changing and you realize you have an opponent, not a partner, allow yourself to grieve your loss.

Keeping a Journal

Many women find comfort and clarity in journal writing. It is a way to track events, evaluate, and clarify your experiences. A survivor says,

> Writing is for me sanity saving. Writing down your experiences and feelings helps to keep reality clearer for you. It is a confirmation of yourself and your experiences that is eroded by your mate, your family, friends and the general world you live in! They wipe out, negate and invalidate your pain and anguish, not meaning to, perhaps, but as they're programmed to do.

> — E.H., PORTLAND, OR

Another survivor offered her very personal perspective on journal writing, which she says enables her to converse with herself. She writes,

> My journal is a conversation with myself as though the different parts of myself speak to each other. What is said would be left unsaid were it not for my journal. Where would I be if this conversation did not take place? When and where and how would I hear myself?
>
> Would "knowings," thoughts, feelings hidden in my soul bubble up to the surface of my consciousness in the midst of my daily life, or would they stir and rumble, ferment, if you will, and rise to the surface only slowly, if at all? I think I might not hear and might not answer, if that were so. Would I recognize myself? How much of me would I know if I knew only my surface self?

The pen becomes the instrument of my knowing. What there is of me, at this moment, that needs to be heard is heard. I hear myself. I am my own audience. I am my own speaker. And, if I am a seeker of truth, then I shall find it in myself. Here I collect the pieces, the unspoken words, the feeling fragments, I speak them all within my heart and form a new mosaic of self-awareness each day. I ask, "Is this who I am now? How much more of me is there?"

— J.W., MENDOCINO, CA

Taking Time to See Whether the Relationship Improves

I have been the partner of a verbally abusive man for six years. I tried to think of every excuse and explanation for his behavior, as well as trying to be patient and understanding, and now I can recognize the abuse for what it is. Fortunately, my mate is now taking steps not to be so abusive, although our relationship is very up and down at times—if things go the way they've been going, my situation will have a happy outcome. Maybe I'll be one of the lucky ones.

— M.N., LUBBOCK, TX

Coping with Extreme Hostility

I would like to know how to set limits when you are terrified in the first place of explosive anger, and also, when every single comment indicates hostility. If not against myself, against the world at large. Then what?

— R.M., INDIANAPOLIS, IN

I never know what kind of mood he will be in, so am wary of open talk unless I'm sure he's in a good mood. I like to broach some subjects in front of other people, then he won't yell or snap at me, but will seemingly be a real partner.

— T.C., WOODBRIDGE, VA

On abusive anger how can I protect myself without getting him angrier?

I would like practical ways, day to day things, that can be done to diffuse the abusive anger.

If you are coping with this kind of hostility and can't get out of the dragon's realm as fast as you would like, make every effort to *build your feelings of independence and strength.* Hostility tears down these feelings; consequently, one needs to learn how to counteract its effects.

Generally, it is important that you keep means at hand to leave immediately if the abuse escalates or you feel upset or in danger.

It is doubtful that a man who is as closed to his feelings as a pressure cooker would be open enough to hear his partner's requests for change or her statements of her limits. Men who are this closed are always building up explosive rage. They are extremely dangerous, and most dangerous if they catch on to the fact that their partner is not only *not* enjoying being around them but is also terrified enough of their behavior to want to leave. Here are some further suggestions.

1. Join a support group for women, preferably through a women's shelter agency (see the appendix of this book).

2. Stay away from your mate as much as possible—by, for instance, working up to one and a half jobs, trading baby-sitting, taking a class, going to school or graduate school part- or full-time, putting in volunteer hours for a women's service group or shelter, joining a hiking, walking, or biking club, or visiting relatives.

3. Keep a getaway bag hidden, and, if possible, make arrangements with a friend or relative in advance so you can leave the premises if he starts raging.

4. Tell family, close friends, neighbors, classmates, and relatives that you are terrified of your mate's explosive anger and verbal battering. The less it is a secret the safer you are. Just don't tell people in front of him, or he may think you are putting *him* down.

5. Do some things alone so that you become used to relying solely on yourself. If you don't already, you may come to enjoy doing things for yourself by yourself. But be sure to avoid isolation. It is not the same as solitude.

6. Take some classes in self-defense for women. Call the colleges and schools for information.

7. Keep any journal or other personal information hidden.

8. Call the police if your mate hits you, breaks things around you, or threatens your life or safety.

Trying to Make Sense of the Past

The following excerpts express survivors' courage, their hopes, and their questions. They are representative of too many who have suffered too long from the unseen epidemic that is verbal abuse.

> *I want to know how to keep Personal Power while remaining in a verbally abusive relationship. I've been in it for more than twenty years not knowing what was wrong.*
>
> — C.N., WINCHESTER, MA

*Realizing that what I was hearing was verbal abuse opened my per-
sonal "prison cell" door. I've yet to get past the "guards" and over the
"wall" to total freedom, but that too will come in time.*
— A.T., CEDAR RAPIDS, IA

*I wonder if it is possible to get enough self-esteem and "tools" to live
within the marriage boundaries. I am fifty-nine now—it's late for
starting over.*
— B.R., JACKSONVILLE, FL

*I need to be validated by someone. I still feel terribly ashamed and an-
gry that he controlled and humiliated and fooled me and never had to
apologize and was never seen as a "bad guy"—he was brilliant at hiding the side of himself that he showed me.*
— B.F., ALBUQUERQUE, NM

*This process of healing and freeing myself from him on emotional and
psychological levels hurts like hell. The grief? I gave myself permission
to feel it all along. Now it's time I owned my anger, loved myself
through it and then released it to God.*
— L.P., JOPLIN, MO

*The fundamental quality of my dealing with this changed from one of
doing it alone, with self-doubt even when I knew I was right, to one of
certainty. I'm not wrong, I'm not making it up and I am no longer
alone. When just one other person knows the truth, it sets you free. I
feel as though my spirit has broken out, but my life is still in prison.*
— W.E., SUNNYVALE, CA

*I only hope that I can be strong enough to carry out my requests for
what I would like in a relationship. However, if this relationship fails, I
hope I can recognize it in a man next time.*
— G.H., WICHITA, KS

*I now know what was wrong. I have laid down ground rules to my
husband about what I will not accept as behavior from him. He knows
I won't tolerate it anymore. I have a bag packed in case I have to go. I
have alternatives and my sanity is my top priority now.*
— P.L., OLYMPIA, WA

*I am an independent woman, professionally employed and financially
independent. Emotionally, however, I am dependent on his love and approval. I think I have a better perspective and overview of the situation
now. I am going to try to change my way of dealing for a while longer.*
— B.S., TULSA, OK

I consider myself a living miracle—It is with His [Jesus'] love that I love my husband, because I could not do it by myself on the natural level.
— H.M., La Jolla, CA

I have not given up on the relationship. I am learning to set clear firm boundaries with my spouse, to seek support in other relationships, to communicate my needs.
— N.L., Toronto, Ontario

I am trying to make sense of the past thirty-six years. Explanations and defense have become such an automatic, fixed response pattern after all of these years that I know it will be a great effort on my part.
— S.W., Frankfort, KY

Coping with His Reality

If you are coping with a mate's controlling and abusive personality, you may discover that he has a distinct difference in perception and understanding from your own. Take gifts and giving. Partners of abusers give because they care and because they want to show their love. To give a gift may take real effort, getting up early for it, saving up for it, setting aside their own interests for it, or spending a lot of time on it. The partner may also see her preparation of meals or doing household tasks as a gift of time and energy to the relationship.

In seeking mutuality and harmony, the partner may put forth an effort to express her good will and to assure her mate that she is not "the enemy." She may bake his favorite cake, bring home his favorite take-out, or in some other way gift her mate. A partner who didn't know her mate's anger had nothing to do with her but was simply being blamed on her told me about a special meal she was fixing for her spouse.

He'll know I really care. Sometimes he thinks I don't. He got mad when he thought I didn't do something "on purpose" just to "be obstinate" which wasn't true at all.

The problem is, the abuser, because he sees his partner as "the enemy," does not experience her gift in the way she intends but as a retreat or as a manipulation to get something, or as a statement of subservience—i.e., *a pleasurable reinforcement of his abuse.*

While the partner is trying to show her mate her good will, demonstrating that she cares, her mate perceives it as retreating from an offensive position she never took in the first place. In his reality, Reality I, everything has to do with "I win, you lose."

Since the abuser's goal is control of his partner, if he gives her a gift, it is often given to "get" her back after he's been abusive, or to put himself in charge. A survivor told me that her spouse, who hid her money from her, also bought her clothes *he* liked that were *not* her style. Abusers view compliments and acknowledgments in much the same way. The abuser uses these to manipulate his mate.

When he seems normal and even pleasant the next day or an hour after being abusive, it is very difficult to know what to do. However, this is the pattern. Abusers verbally abuse for exactly the same reason they physically abuse, to maintain power and control, and they also try to get their mate back in the same way physical abusers do— by being nice. Some apologize; some are in complete denial.

The survivors of verbally abusive relationships have expressed their understanding in the following statements.

I thought that if I gave him a gift of my time and energy, he would recognize it as an expression of my love. Now I realize that he took my gift to mean he was superior.

If it's his anger and his problem, I thought, I can rise above it or disassociate from it. Now I know I've had enough.

I thought it was one of his "moods." Now I've put the pieces together and understand his "moods" were verbal abuse.

I thought that I was a terrible wife for saying the wrong things or voicing my opinions, now I realize I don't deserve to be pushed out of the way just so he can walk through.

I thought I needed bruises or broken bones so people would believe me, now I can describe it because verbal abuse has a name.

I thought I ought to be able to rationally figure out the problem and fix it. I see now that the problem is that it isn't rational.

I thought that if I was careful I would find a way not to set him off. Now I know I've got to tell him, "Stop it," every time he's abusive.

I tried to make him feel more loved and more secure so he'd be reassured. Now I see how silly that was.

I thought that if he really knew I loved him he would love me enough to hear me. Now I know he will never change.

I thought I was the only one to have experienced this horrible abuse. Now I know how widespread it is.

When I was living in the abuse I was either confused or sad—never indignant, resolved or self-protective. Now I am.

I was unwilling to lose the relationship rather than demean myself. Now I am willing to lose it, but earlier in my life I was too terrified.

The Children

I have been trying to change my husband's ways. The name calling has quit but there is always something new to replace it. When he finally stops one thing with me, then he will begin it on our oldest daughter— But his son can do no wrong . . . He can be so mean and cruel and then come and apologize and sound sincere. I don't know when I will ever fully wake up to it all. It is so hard.

Please write and try and help me out some. I guess I really do know what I have to do—just have to bring myself to do it. But how when things always seem better the next day!!!!! Now my young son is starting to act like his father.

— S.H., Detroit, MI

Dear S.H.: Verbal abuse has nothing to do with you or your daughters in particular. If you or an older daughter were magically replaced by somebody different, he would still have *his* problem of being verbally abusive to a wife and oldest daughter. Being abusive to the oldest daughter is a common pattern. Another is that the son is "king" and all the daughters are nothing. A variation is that the son can never do anything right and is "picked on" constantly while the daughters are ignored or favored. Whatever the configuration, however, the problem begins with the abuser.

It sounds as if your son is afraid of the abuse, and that by being like his dad, he hopes "nothing bad" will happen to him. Adults in recovery from abuse in the home often say that it was so horrifying for them as a child to see a mother or sibling abused that they just "decided" that it really was okay behavior and wasn't that bad. *"What are you making a big deal out of nothing for?"* Sound familiar? Unfortunately, some of the worst abusers come from this kind of family dynamic.

Many survivors have fears regarding their children. They fear for their children's emotional well-being if they are subject to abuse. They also worry about losing their children if they choose to leave the relationship. Following are some of their concerns.

My greatest fear was, "He'll take my child." The more afraid you are of him the more afraid you are to leave him. What if our daughter were alone with him? I absolutely don't leave her alone with him. I always tell her what is real and what is not. I tried to protect her. I couldn't always keep her from taking the brunt of his temper. I couldn't leave un-

til she was old enough to voice her own feelings about his behavior. He never hit either of us.

— C.F., BOISE, ID

The children are part like me and part like their father. They all have difficulty with relationships. Sometimes they are abusive and sometimes very sweet.

— M.S., LOS ANGELES, CA

All categories of abuse are used on me and he pushes and shoves me but doesn't hit . . . I desperately want to get away. I have three children and one on the way. I want to protect them when I do leave but don't know how. He threatens to take them away from me all the time.

— G.B., SPRINGFIELD, IL

My husband was very subtle—besides verbally abusing our children— he was able to leave us with the impression that we could do the job— do much better—have a better attitude—if we really wanted to, and if we tried hard enough. But it was never enough.

— M.R., HARRISBURG, PA

Now my mother and all my family understand it wasn't and isn't our fault about my father's verbal abuse.

— C.D., AKRON, OH

The abuse got worse after dad retired.

— V.I., TYLER, TX

I had fifteen years of a nightmare marriage. I raised two strong wonderful sons who are not abusive.

— K.L., MADISON, WI

My teenage daughter is now talking to me exactly like her father did.

— M.T., RALEIGH, NC

I want to know more about how children are affected and survival techniques.

— M.K., JACKSONVILLE, FL

I just saw my six-year-old daughter verbally abusing my three-year-old daughter. I know now I have to find a way out of this relationship.

— S.P., CAMBRIDGE, MA

I would like to know more about the effect this relationship has on male children in the home.

— D.B., BOULDER, CO

I would like to know more about how to make my children feel better about themselves and to help them understand about abuse, verbal and physical.

— T.O., VAN NUYS, CA

Children need

1. protection
2. a sympathetic witness
3. a healthy role model
4. no secrets
5. open communication

The evidence indicates that if the child is not directly verbally abused and has good nurturing by at least one parent, the damage of growing up in a home where a parent suffers from verbal abuse is not nearly as severe as if the child is also verbally abused by a parent.

If verbal abuse is directed toward a child, it is very hurtful. I have had more than one letter arrive to tell of a teen suicide who, too late, was recognized to be the victim of verbal abuse.

If your child has periodically been verbally abused, has witnessed a sibling being verbally abused, or has witnessed a parent being overtly abused in rage attacks, name calling, and so forth, the child might do well to receive some therapy from a specialist in child psychology.

In the book *The Verbally Abusive Relationship, How to Recognize It and How to Respond*, I wrote about the sympathetic witness, the person Alice Miller's work reveals as crucial to healthy development in children. This is the parent or caretaker who *validates* the child's experience. Survivors wanted to know more. One wrote,

If the partner was able to emerge from Reality I into Reality II as a consequence of having a sympathetic witness in childhood and the abuser wasn't able to cross the threshold into Reality II because he didn't have a sympathetic witness, who is this witness that she had and he didn't?

— C.E., HAMPTON, VA

The sympathetic witness is the empathetic care giver—the person who is emotionally available to the child, who can hold the child—even one who is too young to say why he is crying. This person who gives validation and understanding to the child can say:

When the child is blamed, "It is not your fault. Yes, it is cruel. Yes it hurts. I will stand by you."

When the child is diminished, "It is not true. You are special. I am so glad you are my child."

When the child is afraid, "Yes, you are frightened. I will protect you. I will stay with you."

When the child is tired, "Yes, you seem tired. Come and rest."

When the child hurts, "Yes, that hurts. It is sad. I will give you my strength when you feel your pain."

If a child is raised with respect, responsibility, and loving nurturing from both parents, the child is not so disempowered that he must diminish and control someone in order to have a sense of power. A child needs to learn to identify his feelings or he grows up not knowing what he is feeling. Some appropriate responses to a child are,

You seem very happy.

It sounds like you are bored.

Do you feel frustrated when . . .

It looks like you are determined to . . .

That took courage.

The sympathetic witness mirrors to the child the child's feelings, so that he does not grow to adulthood ignorant of himself and the validity of his own nature. In some ways, a sibling may fulfill this mirroring role. One of the worst things that could possibly happen to a child would be to have his feelings be, not just ignored and undefined, but also denied as if they were not real, and suppressed so that they could not be felt.

If the child grows up ignorant of himself and his nature, he is still a child walking around as an adult. This child is likely to be angry, manipulative, and controlling. This child within runs the adult.

In the next chapter we will look at how the survivors of verbally abusive relationships have seen change and hoped for change in their relationships.

Part 3

WE HAVE EXPLORED THE RESULTS of the survey on verbally abusive relationships and learned that many women fear their mates, no longer love them, and/or feel trapped. We also discovered which categories of verbal abuse are most frequently used by verbal abusers and how the partners of verbal abusers cope with their mates.

In the next chapter, "Changes," we will explore the effort some couples are making to bring about healthy changes in their relationships as well as such questions as, "What motivates change?" and "In what context will change be effected?"

Chapter 13, "Healing and Recovery," offers the survivors of verbally abusive relationships methods and tools to aid them in their recovery. These include ways of increasing self-awareness to bring about greater autonomy and satisfaction, as well as ways to reweave the thread of connection to the Creative Force that nourishes the spirit at one's center. In chapter 14, "The Sixty-Minute Me," I offer a simple way to remember to take care of yourself in a holistic way. This chapter concludes with an in-depth discussion of how verbal abuse destroys self-esteem. Chapter 15, "The Support Group," answers survivors' questions on how to find one, start one, and benefit from one.

Some affirmations are offered in the final chapter, along with ways you can work with them to give your life meaning and purpose, set limits, and establish boundaries to protect your personal integrity.

Chapter 12

Changes

---

*I want to change—My wife recognized the abuser
in me that I could not see, and had the fortitude to
bring it out into the open.*

— S.R., WHITE PLAINS, NY

---

*When he's angry I look him in the eye and softly say, "What are you
really angry at?" and I do not even enter into his arena of discussion,
but keep repeating "What is angering you—what is it really that is angering you?" (Not what did I do.) He usually breaks down and cries
and pours out his anger. We look at it, discuss it (me, usually very nurturing) and we come to an understanding of his "dragon in the dark"
as we call it.*

*We are coming to a wonderful communion of souls and desire to
grow old and happy together. It is back-breaking, heart-breaking work,
but everything else we have is worth this effort. One thing: He has always been remorseful. One day I said, I will no longer accept your
apologies. I now want change. I will accept nothing less. Your apologies
only buy time. It is time to change because I will not live the rest of my
life like this.*

— M.W., AUBURN, CA

The survivor was living in Reality II, where mutuality prevailed.
The abuser was still in Reality I, where the dragon lurked. He had
never opened the door and looked into the world of mutuality and
personal power where his mate lived, but despite the horror and pain
she felt, she *could* look into his reality. To see into that world was to realize that what he said and what he did had nothing to do with her. She
also realized that a strategy would be required, for when you are abused,

when the dragon breathes on you with its toxic sarcasm or poisonous put-down, you cannot allow it to get too close. You must set limits, saying "Stop it," or leave to avoid the abuse.

A great many survivors wrote expressing the hope that everyone who knows of verbal abuse will teach others. How can we bring about change without awareness? If every child knew that his or her feelings were real, and if every child knew that what was hurtful was abusive and that abuse was not a manly or strong thing to do, we might effect change.

> *I would have given anything to know about verbal abuse years ago. We need to teach our children and their parents about it. It should be taught in schools, in parenting classes, in relationship seminars, in psychology class, in women's and men's study programs and in the work place. How else will we see change. If abusers don't know that bullies are wimps, it's time they found out.*
>
> — T.D., NEWARK, NJ

A man who wanted change but who was also very frightened that his wife would realize what he had been doing wrote the following.

> *After learning even just a little about verbal abuse I realize it is a study of my life. Recently, my wife has begun to fight back, which has helped me to begin to see that I have basically forced her to either resign to a non-existence or stand up for herself.*
>
> *I am terrified as I realize my abuse of her is a daily occurrence in our relationship. I feel as though I have not really understood who I am. I am confused and scared as to what to do to maintain my relationship and begin to allow my wife to become a person and be happy for her.*
>
> *I have always seen myself as a good 'Christian' and caring individual. I really do care for my wife and family. As my wife begins to find out who she is and feel good about herself, I feel I will lose her unless I can change, really change. Knowing about verbal abuse has brought me to the realization of some gut wrenching anguishing, troubling, mistakes I have made and am making. I'm unsure how to even approach my wife and begin to ask for forgiveness and patience and understanding (all of which I refused her) while I try to resolve my confusion.*
>
> — E.B., PITTSBURGH, PA

At some moment the abuser wakes up and says, "My God! what am I doing? Why am I doing this?" He *knows* what it is, this roar of the dragon. Through a mist he knows—*and through her eyes he sees himself mirrored for a moment.* Then again, turning away from his awareness, he strikes out harder, that once and for all he might slay the dragon. (After all, it's not easy to be the bad guy.)

Yes, the abuser glimpses his own reality. He looks. For so long he has seen her looking at him. For so long he has heard her asking, "Why?" For so long he has known he doesn't know, and now his secret is out. She knows, and he knows that she knows.

"Stop it!"

At some moment the abuser hears the warm sounds of caring, concern, life and aliveness—just beyond, elusive, another reality, barely glimpsed. All of a sudden, it's hard not to be in Reality II with her.

Only by glimpsing her reality can he acknowledge his own. It's his first admission. He knows now that he seeks Power Over. He wants to get better; *she* wants him to get better. He wants to be in Reality II. However, he doesn't yet know the extraordinary pain a sudden wounding brings. When she express her warmth in a caring gesture and he knows she is vulnerable, he is likely to strike even now. Why? Because when the enemy is weak, you strike.

Many survivors of verbal abuse want to see changes in their relationship. Some of the letters I receive are from survivors who are with mates who continue to deny they are abusive at all. Some are with mates who admit to verbal abuse some of the time but are still doing it most of the time. Some are with mates who do it only occasionally and admit it virtually every time. Some have left abusive relationships and are now with mates who are not only *not* verbally abusive but are kind, warm, and real—and do not live in the reality of Power Over.

> *What do you do about a verbal abuser who admits to the abuse, apologizes, and then continues the abuse?*
>
> — W.S., DAYTON, OH

A survivor gave us the answer to this question at the beginning of this chapter: "I will no longer accept your apologies."

From Reality I to Reality II

If you are a male verbal abuser and want to change, to feel the true love of a woman who sticks around because she wants to, not because she's become too immobilized or too confused to move, here are a few things you can do. Read everything you can about verbal abuse, and read it several times over. Listen to your partner with an open, accepting mind and feel your pain without shutting it down with anger. Re-

read the list of controlling behaviors: diminishing your partner, threat-ening your partner with body language, and threatening your partner with words. Make your own list of everything you've ever done that was abusive. Ask your partner to review the list and ask whether she would be willing to remind you if she hears these or other kinds of verbal abuse.

Including all the reading, this won't take more than a few days. A few days invested in changing the rest of your life. Can you imagine what it would be to have a *real* relationship with your partner?

A man committed to change wrote,

> *I am a verbal abuser. My wife has left me to rebuild herself. I am strongly committed to changing myself. I am truly hurt by my actions inside. I've never cried until now and have done so several times after realizing my behavior. It is indeed extremely difficult to see one's self as others do. It is indeed a very traumatic, shocking experience to truly see oneself and realize what you have done.*
> — J.A.M., Newark, NJ

Another abuser wrote,

> *I am the abuser. I cannot believe what I have done to my wife. Learning of verbal abuse woke me up. My wife has not been able to make me see my-self. I feel like an alcoholic that cannot quit but I feel I can learn to control myself. Can you rewrite your book to include information and a list of books which would show men like me how to change?*

The best way to change is to become aware of the effects of your behavior by reading all about women's experiences of verbal abuse. Get into a men's group. Stop controlling. Start feeling your pain. The primary sources of help for men who are verbally abusive are the men's programs established to help men work though their control is-sues, which are often expressed in battering behavior, including verbal battering (verbal abuse). When verbal abuse occurs in a relationship, it is a form of "domestic violence." Men's programs can be found through referrals from state coalitions on domestic violence and through referrals from women's shelter programs.

A survivor tells us how she has set limits and asked for change.

> *This is real, it's not my imagination! I had seriously begun to question my sanity and wondered what was wrong with me. What had I done to deserve this? In private I have been depressed and sometimes feel un-able to get up and get going, however, after this weekend I began to feel alive. In fact, when I looked in the mirror tonight I felt I saw a light in my*

eyes instead of depression. I had written my husband a letter outlining his behavior and setting some guidelines—how powerful I felt.
— A.N., MEDFORD, OR

Verbal abuse can be overt and even apologized for. However, if the abuser does not resolve his need to control, he will, like the physical batter, verbally batter, apologize, then verbally batter again. Hope for change in this kind of relationship is remote unless the abuser seeks to change *more than he seeks anything else.*

Some Abusers Won't Change

A survivor wrote describing the severe verbal abuse that she suffered.

. . . married over twenty years to my abuser. At one time he told me "If I can't physically abuse you, then I have to verbally abuse you." Another recent comment he has made is "It's not that I don't love you, it's just that you're a woman."
— A.H., PITTSBURGH, PA

This abuser is of the most extreme kind. He not only abuses, he believes he is justified because he is a man. Of course he is incapable of empathetically experiencing the pain he inflicts upon his mate. Without empathy and with a deep prejudice against his mate, he cannot love her.

The Motivation for Change

Remember, there is nothing you can do and no way you can be to get him to change. All you can do is remind him of what he is doing and set limits. He may, in time, want to change.

Here is a story about motivation.

There once was a couple who realized that their relationship was in real trouble. The abuser didn't want a divorce, but wasn't ready to get help either. He and his wife were in a real dilemma. Then one day his wife had an idea. She talked it over with her husband and he agreed. This is what came about.

She had some faith in prayer and he had some faith in positive affirmations and visualization (techniques used by athletes, for example, to improve their game).

They came to an agreement. She would pray for what he wanted and he would visualize her getting what she wanted. The only way they could do this was for each to make a list to give the other. They each put five wants on their lists.

In a quiet place in two separate parts of the house they each took the list that the other had prepared. Here is what they wrote.

His List	*Her List*
Have more fun together	Not be criticized for doing things wrong
Not feel so tense	Not to be yelled at
Feel like she wants me	Not feel like crying all the time
No more anxiety	Find a way to talk so he'll hear me
Not hear her explanations	Not be blamed for anything

As the abuser began to visualize his partner's wants, he began to realize that she really didn't make all the mistakes he accused her of, that she often talked, he hadn't bothered to listen, and that nothing that happened to him, not even getting a flat tire or seeing his team lose, was really her fault. He'd paid no attention to her, but as he *visualized* her happy, he realized he hadn't actually *seen* her happy in a while.

As the partner viewed her mate's list, she prayed that he would find some happiness, fun, and relaxation, that she would be able to enjoy him, and that he would have freedom from anxiety and not have to hear her explain anything.

They met the next day to talk about this mutual project. The abuser said he'd been in shock since he read her list. He felt he'd never really seen himself before. He realized that he'd been given an answer, that if he let go of control, they could both have the prayers and wishes on their list answered.

An abuser is most motivated to change when he realizes the effects of his behavior. By learning about verbal abuse and its effects, many have become aware and been motivated to change. Some men's programs teach men how women experience verbal abuse, in order to bring awareness to participants. Some abusers have told me that they would probably have lost their partners if they had not worked through the underlying forces that compelled them to abuse. They know that if they had not done so, they might at some point find themselves saying what so many other abusers are saying: "I really messed up my life."

Sometimes a verbal abuser will remain oblivious to the painful impact of his abuse until he hears about it from someone other than his mate. That is why learning about women's experiences of verbal abuse is helpful. In the following anecdote we meet a man who is oblivious to his behavior. If he or others of a similar bent were to read this scenario, they might see themselves from a different perspective altogether.

A man called in on a radio talk show in San Francisco and said he was having some problems with his relationship. And why? "After all," he said, "I allow her to have quite a few of her opinions."

It is alarming to think that a person would believe he had a right to "allow" or "disallow" another person's opinions. Every human being has the right to her or his own opinions. In countries where dictatorial governments preside, people take a great personal risk in expressing their opinions, but to find this kind of thinking in a democracy is truly appalling. Yet many women have lived in fear and intimidation and have even had to confront rages because they held an opinion or belief different from that of their mate. One man said that he felt *attacked* if his wife had a different opinion from him. Doesn't this sound like the very same totalitarian governments whose policies we, as a nation, have claimed to set ourselves in opposition to?

Many men who are in relationships and do not want them to end are highly motivated to change. From time to time I talk with a man in his second or third marriage who now knows that if he doesn't change in this relationship he will simply go through the same tragedy and the same struggle again. He knows that if his relationship did end, he would become abusive in the next, and so on.

One man wrote,

> *I have just learned about verbal abuse. I am a verbal abuser and it is still very hard for me to admit it. Two long marriages ended by my being told I was verbally abusive. I now believe that I was.*
>
> — M.B., CINCINNATI, OH

This is not to say that all men or women in their second or third marriage or relationship are verbally abusive. It may simply be that they do not know yet how to choose a compatible mate, or that they are learning faster than their spouse, who prefers to stay fixed.

The conversations are strikingly similar.

Every month several men who have read my work contact me through my publisher. A man might say something like, "I just found out about this verbal abuse thing. My wife did too. I know I'm doing it, and, yeah, I don't even realize it till she says something like, 'You just blamed me,' and you know something? She's right. I just did."

I tell him, "Yes, I don't doubt it. Tell me, did she tell you all this, about what you were doing, many, many times before?"

"I guess."

"But you *couldn't* hear her, could you?"

"Never. Not her, not my first wife; and . . ."

"And do you find that, even when you're trying not to do it, you're doing it?"

"That's it. How'd you know?"

"Because so many men say the same thing. The best thing is that you've come a long way because you're willing to look at it."

At this point, he usually says something like, "I need help. Boy! All I need is to come home and find she's taken the cat and left." He'll laugh a little, as if to keep the panic at bay.

I tell him, "I don't know anyone in your part of the country. But I could tell you a little about what I know about this problem, about what might be going on with you maybe. You should know, though, that it might be something that you might be really shocked to hear."

I'll hear him take a deep breath; then, "Okay, shoot."

"This is all about dominance and control—putting her down, sneering, snapping, blasting, bullying. An abuser does it to control his mate. Both physical and verbal abuse originate with the intention of controlling your mate. So if you want help, call your nearest shelter and get a referral to a program for men who batter."

"Are you sure?"

"Here is a question for you. Between verbal battering and physical battering, which one do you think takes longer to heal from?"

"I'll call," he says.

Initiating Change

> *Changes are coming! Even at this old age! Even if I must leave!*
> — A.C., COLUMBUS, OH

The following letter is from a survivor who wants to see change in her relationship but finds that her mate does not take her seriously and actually enjoys inflicting the abuse.

> *How can I really make an impact? When I say "Stop it," he laughs and says something meaner.*
> — C.I., PATTERSON, NJ

Her question brings to mind a comment from a man who was working on his own control issues. He said,

"If my mother had thrown a bucket of ice water on my father, I think he would have pulled back and stopped. But only for a while."

"Have you thought about your wife feeling as oppressed as your mother was?"

"No, it never occurred to me."

In assessing the possibilities for change in a relationship, it is sometimes helpful to ask the question, "What is he communicating? "

In the case of the abuser who laughs and says something meaner, he is communicating that he doesn't want to stop.

If you are dealing with this kind of relationship, I suggest you acknowledge that he doesn't want to stop. Ask him, at a time when he is not being abusive, whether he is willing to work on the issue of verbal abuse with you and to accept being reminded of what he is doing when you feel verbally abused.

For example, "I recognize that you do not want to stop the abuse when you are doing it. However, would you be willing to work on trying to stop the abuse if I remind you of it when I hear it?" If you would rather, write this in a note and give it to him, or mail it for more impact.

If he says *yes*, then:

1. Tell him in what way you will remind him. For example, "When I feel abused, I'll say, 'Stop it' or 'That hurts' or 'I'm not feeling respected.'"

2. Ask him whether he would be willing to read about verbal abuse.

3. Ask him whether he would be willing to attend a men's group to get help in stopping the verbal abuse. (Women's agencies in the appendix are an excellent source of referrals for men's groups.)

If he is cooperative and is showing evidence of really wanting to change, even though, in the moment of being abusive, he isn't *now* able to stop, you might with hard work and open communication see some changes. As one couple I know pointed out, it's often three steps forward, one step back—and it absolutely, unequivocally takes two people. *He has to want to change very much.*

If he shows no signs of wanting to cooperate, to change, to stop his abusive ways, decide whether you want to hear "meaner and meaner things" said to you. Decide how much pain you want to bear. Decide whether the relationship is nourishing to your spirit. There is an old adage: "A wise woman makes her bed in feathers. A sad woman makes her bed in cactus."

Negotiating Change with a Cooperative Mate

Ask your mate for a time to talk about your relationship. When you do sit down to talk, ask him whether he would be willing to work with you on one area where you request change, and ask him whether there is any area where he would like to see change. You might begin with whatever is most important to you. For example, you may want to discuss your resources, such as your time, space, or money, or an area of verbal abuse. Following are two examples of areas where change can be discussed. One is about a resource, and the other is about a specific area of verbal abuse.

Example 1.

Time together and time apart can be discussed and planned. Both the partner and her mate may spend time away, either on business, visiting friends, going fishing, taking a retreat, or in some other way nourishing themselves. You may even need to discuss what you will be doing when he is watching TV or doing something else, so that he will not expect you to be doing what he is doing.

You may want to talk about planning short or long trips, vacations, or Saturday activities. Being able to plan together and to negotiate differences is a sign of a healthy relationship.

If you and your mate need time to yourselves, plan for that time so that you know when he will be "off fishing" and he knows when you will be "off visiting." Then take it. If, for some reason, your mate "won't let you," or threatens you, then you are in the position of being controlled like a prisoner. Your fears may be very real, very concrete, and you will need the support of a shelter program or support group to ensure your spiritual and possibly your physical survival (see chapter 15, "The Support Group").

Example 2.

A verbal abuse issue, such as criticism, can be discussed. You will need to tell your mate that you don't want to hear criticism and that you realize he may not be aware of criticizing you. You might say something like, "When I hear criticism, I will make an effort to tell you right away. If you want to tell me something about what I am doing or how, would you be willing to leave a note with any suggestions?" He may ask you to agree to the same thing. Which is fine. If he says, "You're critical," respond with, "No name calling, please." Then, if you hear criticism, remind him by saying, "Please write that down." Eventually he may realize how often he is critical and stop.

When people do not see other people as separate from themselves, they are prone to be abusive. If you are dealing with a spouse, parent, caretaker, or boss by saying, "I don't want to hear that kind of talk," or "I'm feeling criticized," the abuser may recognize that you are a separate person. You must determine what is appropriate at the time.

By reminding her mate of the abuse every time she hears it, the partner in an abusive relationship may establish herself as a separate person. She is setting a boundary, reminding the abuser, *"This is where you leave off and I begin."*

In some relationships, when the partner sets limits (says "Stop it") to protect herself from a violation of her boundaries, her mate realizes that he has gone too far. He will consider that he has possibly acted out some feeling that has nothing to do with her, has forgotten, for example, that as a separate person she has a right to her own views. Realizing this, he is quick to communicate that realization. He will correct himself, apologize, and talk over the problem.

In other relationships, when the partner of the abuser says, "Stop it," she may be further intimidated by an even more aggressive boundary violation. This could indicate that she is with a confirmed abuser and that he may be a danger to her.

Speaking up and asking for change is worth the effort. Sometimes it takes several tries. A man wrote expressing the distress he felt over recognizing that he had been acting abusively while not realizing the impact of his behavior.

> *I am a very verbally abusive person, and until my wife courageously brought that fact to light, I would have never suspected it. I fit the bill of nearly every case of verbal abuse. I am a classic example of an anger addict.*
>
> — C.T., ANN ARBOR, MI

Another survivor, who wrote that her husband learned of verbal abuse and decided to seek therapy said, "I believe he will succeed." There is a good possibility that he will, because he has actively sought change. The best possibility of change comes when the abuser seeks help *for himself.*

Making Changes

> *He goes for days and doesn't speak to me. He discounts most of what I say in the Power Over mode. I have tried and tried to make changes, accept the blame, stay calm, etc. But nothing, of course, is working. This I am finally admitting and am now getting the support I need.*
>
> *My life isn't too great yet. But I am beginning to stand up and say STOP. He, of course, is denying and telling me to leave if I think I'm being abused. So I have for the time being. I am setting limits. My spirit feels weak at times, but my spirit has been spoken to and I am feeling some confidence in what I'm doing.*
>
> — J.P., SAN JOSE, CA

> *When he said "You this or you that, you think you know it all," I used to say "That's not true!" Then he'd answer with something worse. I'd*

sit there thinking, How can he think that? How can I show him I don't think "I know it all?" Now all I have to do is say, "Stop, Stop, Stop. I don't ever, ever, ever want to hear you tell me what I think again." No more will I allow him to tell me what I think!
— B.W., NEW YORK, NY

Hope's an insidious thing. But once you direct it toward the possible for yourself, it's powerful medicine. Optimism balances my grief.
— A.B., PHILADELPHIA, PA

I'm learning to say, "Stop it," and to set firm boundaries. My husband's father was very verbally abusive to his mother so why should I be surprised that I'm in the same kind of relationship?
— M.H., SAN FRANCISCO, CA

I love my abuser enough to help him to get help. If it were me I would want my partner to do the same.
— W.K., AMHERST, MA

Getting Help

Could you tell me, what kind of questions I should ask a counselor-psychologist to be sure they have experience in verbally abusive relationships? Do those counselors who understand physical abuse also understand the verbal abuse?
— J.P., HARTLAND, MI

I would like to know more about therapy that works for the abuser.
— N.B., STOCKTON, CA

What therapy is effective for the abuser?
— M.W., DAYTON, OH

One of the best therapies for a verbal abuser is to go through a men's group program for men who are physically as well as verbally abusive. If you seek counseling, I recommend that you and your spouse go separately. There isn't much that makes a verbal abuser angrier than hearing someone else tell about what he has done.

If you are in counseling you will need to bring up what you experienced, and you may not feel free to do this in front of your mate. Counselors who work with physical abusers are usually excellent at working with verbal abusers in groups. Both kinds of abusers are abusing for exactly the same reason: to control you and their own feelings, and to make you responsible for everything—to make you the scapegoat.

Whatever you decide, please, no matter what, know that you can interview as many therapists as you feel are necessary and that you can leave if you feel your needs are not being met or the therapy isn't right for you. A survivor writes,

> There are no witnesses and so many times you are made to look the "bad guy", even to trained therapists.
>
> — H.J., PITTSBURGH, PA

Working Together

> I would like to know more about mustering the confidence to recognize the abuse while it is happening and not to just let it happen as though I wasn't even feeling abused.
>
> — A.G., FORT SMITH, AR

When a couple is working on change, the abuser needs to be reminded when he is acting out—and he needs to be reminded at the moment of abuse, not later in the day. Being aware and "mobilized" in the present to respond to verbal abuse is extraordinarily difficult for most partners of abusers. They may feel confused by what they are hearing, and by the time they sort it out, the time to speak up has probably passed.

One way to facilitate a quicker response to verbal abuse is to focus on your mate's delivery. If you are working on change with your mate, stay aware of what you are seeing. For example, does he look angry, aloof, tense, etc.? Be aware, too, of what are you hearing. What does his voice sound like? Is it sarcastic, angry, intimidating, loud, bored to death? Then respond to the look and the sound. This way the abusive words, which are always irrational, will not throw you. Saying, "Don't talk to me like that," or "I don't want to hear that" is an appropriate response to most verbal abuse and will give you time to think.

Another way to stay aware is to practice paying attention to your own feeling of surprise, shock or pain when you hear abuse. Become used to saying, "Stop it," when you feel shock, pain, or confusion.

> He has "admitted" that he has been picking on me way too much and that he doesn't want to "be like" his father. I hope this is his "cry" for help and we can both get the relationship we need.
>
> — A.H., ONTARIO, CA

Change for the Better

> For the past two years, our relationship had slowly turned into a verbally abusive relationship. We are in our twenties. I lost all of my self-

*esteem, confidence and self-respect and became depressed. When my
boyfriend realized he was being abusive our relationship changed dramatically. He has been respectful and courteous and I am beginning to
feel good about myself.*

— R.S., FOLSOM, CA

*After so much effort and four hard years of work on himself (mostly in
a men's group), my husband healed. He isn't the bully he was, always
trying to be a big shot by putting me down. This wasn't easy. I am his
fourth major relationship and we did separate for a while. I'm sure
finding our relationship going down woke him up to his abusive behavior. He went through a dark time. Now he is consistently warm, kind,
definitely alive and real. We talk things over.*

— B.P., FREMONT, CA

If your mate is willing to work with you to build a better relationship, you must both be willing to do the hard work of staying
aware and conscious every day and *he must be willing to stop and feel his
pain when he wants to bury it in anger and act out*. The keys to success are
total commitment and great determination.

The Power of Mutuality and the Context for Change

The power of a really mutual relationship is awesome. When two people are emotionally supportive of each other, and can live their own
lives, they empower each other to grow and to flourish. This kind of
nurturing relationship has extraordinary benefits. It is truly a world
apart from the toxicity of one person covertly and insidiously diminishing and destroying the integrity of the other.

Change can be effected if you and your mate are willing to relate
to each other within the context of mutuality. Furthermore, you have
the opportunity of enjoying a Reality II relationship in which each
one's development is encouraged by the other. *Both* must be willing to
communicate and to listen, or there will be no mutuality.

It usually takes an abuser several years of intense work on himself,
including participation in a men's group for controlling personalities, to
show significant change. It also takes great dedication to remain conscious and aware in the relationship. Finally, the abuser must work
through the pain of his own childhood abuse if he is to become the
whole, kind person many abusers appear to be to people outside of
their relationship.

If you and your mate have agreed to work on your relationship,
one of your objectives might be to create the context within which you
agree to view your relationship. Making changes in the relationship,

reorganizing its components so that it is more satisfying and supportive to the partner, can be accomplished only if both parties are willing and seek the same end. The basics that can be discussed are equality, partnership, mutuality, good will, intimacy, and validation.

Equality

The beliefs, feelings, opinions, interests, perceptions, likes, and dislikes of each are equally real, valid, and sacred, and so are respected.

When one takes a stance of superiority, equality is negated. For example, a woman once told me that she asked her husband not to reveal certain personal events about her family to his family. She wanted the prerogative to explain them in her own way. He agreed. However, when the husband saw his family, he failed to respond appropriately to their questions. He might have replied, "That's something my wife wants to tell you herself." Instead, he broke his agreement with her and told all. Why? Because he decided he should. This husband betrayed his wife and revealed her personal business. He felt justified in doing so because he believed that he knew best. "Knowing best" is his stance of superiority. Without equality, a relationship is not healthy.

Different wants can be negotiated between two people who are acting within the context of mutuality and equality.

Partnership

If the partner and her mate are actively engaged in improving the relationship, then they are acting as partners in supporting each other's awareness. One calls the other on an abuse when it is heard; for example: "Hold it, I don't like hearing orders. " The abuser, in recognizing and changing his behavior, responds, "Oh, I'm sorry. Would you be willing to . . . when you have time?" Then both are acting as partners in improving the relationship. The partner's self-esteem increases as she establishes her boundaries and sets limits, and her mate's awareness of her as being a separate person entitled to respect increases.

In a partnership, each individual shares the tasks inherent to the relationship and discusses any action that affects the other in a material or spiritual way.

Two separate people in a relationship have their own lives, interests, and occupations, as well as their life together. Anyone dominating the other, that is, abusing the other, ends the partnership in the relationship. Partners have equal say and equal value and discuss differing wants.

Some abusers, over time, eventually do learn that their mates are free persons living in a free country. One man said that when his wife reentered college to complete her degree, she refused his *help* with studies, and when she became pregnant she would not let him *supervise* her eating. He could not understand her behavior. Although she achieved superior grades and gave birth to a healthy child he thought that her refusal to be directed was verbally abusive.

Actually, his partner's ability to set limits was healthy behavior. It was his own oppressive behavior he did not recognize. He wanted to make her dependent and more easily dominated. Since he saw his wife as an extension of himself, he could not imagine that she might, as a separate person, handle new situations herself. He believed he had the right to control her, to tell her how to study and how to eat. This was his idea of partnership!

Mutual Benefit

When two people are in a relationship and want to make changes that will improve their relationship, they may naturally wish to discuss what changes would be mutually beneficial to the relationship, including those behaviors either one feels are not beneficial to her or to him.

When there is mutuality in a relationship, both parties are equally considerate of the other. One does not automatically expect the other to take care of his or her physical needs, cooking, cleaning, and washing. The work is divided through negotiation.

Verbal abuse does not generally occur in the context of mutuality. Sometimes one party in the relationship has totally different expectations than the other. If both parties in the relationship each make a list of their expectations and then discuss these expectations, there is more possibility of developing a mutually satisfying relationship. Ideally, men and women will learn to do this before entering into long-term commitments.

Good Will

If both parties can discuss the relationship, including such issues as personal, social, business, and economic plans, and can compromise, negotiate, and come to agreements, and if both can listen to each other's thoughts and feelings, there is good will in the relationship.

If you and your mate are working together to improve the communication in your relationship, good will on the part of both parties is essential. One way to introduce an issue of abuse is to say, for example, "When I hear orders I feel that equality, mutuality, and partnership are no longer present in our relationship. I will bring it to your attention if I hear you ordering me." Your mate may then say, "Okay, sometimes I don't realize it when it happens."

Validation

All verbal abuse is invalidating of another's personhood. Validation is most easily achieved through common courtesy and respect for the other's individuality. A criteria of validation is that your feelings, thoughts, ideas, interests, likes, and dislikes are acknowledged by your mate.

If you are working on improving your relationship, an effective beginning goal is that both parties treat each other politely and respectfully. A very obvious and common form of invalidation is described by a survivor in the extract that follows. The abusive behavior she describes invalidated her existence as a separate person. It takes the form of withholding by means of a physical demonstration of invalidation; the abuser simply pretends that his mate does not exist.

> *I sat down to watch my favorite TV show. It's only on once a week and I never watch TV much. Joe came in—all of a sudden the restaurant scene changed into a newscast. I thought it was for a commercial. Then there was a city, then a building and the inside of an office. I was trying to figure out what was happening. Then there was Joe changing channels, not saying anything—as if I wasn't there! When I asked him to stop he never said a single word.* — F.P., RIVERSIDE, CA

Intimacy

If all the qualities listed above—equality, partnership, mutuality, and good will—are in your relationship, intimacy will be established. Intimacy depends on emotional rapport and empathy. If neither party has other issues that affect the relationship, sexual intimacy will usually flow from the emotional intimacy.

If He Won't Change . . .

> *I always wondered what I could do to make him see that his behavior toward me and the children was destructive.*

> *I would like to know how the abuser can realize his abusiveness.*

> *I want to know more about what happens to these people if they don't seek help.*

> *I would like to know more about getting the abuser to realize his insidious and destructive behavior is real and his fault.*

> *I felt so powerless trying to get him to understand he was abusing me.*

One cannot necessarily get a verbal abuser to recognize his behavior, much less realize its destructiveness. However, he *may* admit to doing it if you are able to be very clear in the way you respond to his behavior. If you respond clearly by setting boundaries, telling him what you will and will not accept, he *may* be willing to change. On the other hand, *he may never be willing to change*. It's all up to him, and it all depends on how tightly his identity is tied up with his being in control, always right, superior, and overtly or covertly in charge.

Abusers who don't change bring their behavior with them to the next relationship. Usually they will gradually begin their abusive behavior after the courting period, and it will slowly escalate until the partner leaves. One man told me that he had been very verbally abusive and for eighteen years had denied that he was. After four major relationships ended, he began to get the message.

If the partner of an abuser leaves the relationship and then comes back thinking he's changed, the abuser will almost always intensify the abusive behavior. Why? Because from his standpoint, if he'd really had enough control the first time, she wouldn't have gotten away.

Interview with an Abuser and His Partner

Abuser: By doing this over here [abusing] I get out of myself, and out of my pain and out of my frustration and my fear, anger, anxiety, what have you. And now I can focus over here on her and now I don't have to deal with *it* [his feelings].

Partner: If I never called you on it over the past few years, would you *ever* have looked at it yourself? Would you have *ever* thought about how you treated me?

Abuser: No. I didn't want to deal with it. I wanted to avoid it. I was going to have to deal with it or get a divorce. I didn't want to get a divorce.

I think initially, I probably tried to act as if she was completely off base, as if the whole thing was ridiculous and she was being just overly sensitive, and when that didn't work, I probably would have nagged her and just tried to buffalo her into backing down if I got angry enough and said, Look, it's the way I am. If you don't like it then you just take a hike! And then that didn't work either, so I just had to deal with it.

It was the pain that got me. There were these times I swear to God, I was hearing this roaring in my ears. I was so angry that I couldn't control this and I couldn't shut her up; that I would just hear this roaring in my ears. It was like, Oh, Jesus, I've either got to deal with this or I've got to get a divorce. One of the two. And I haven't really given this a shot, so I better give this a shot before I get a divorce.

At first, the abuser does not recognize the consequences of the pain he inflicts with the abuse because his goal is not to feel. ("... and now I don't have to deal with *it*.") You don't stick a needle in someone and then think you can get them to "back down" as if the cry of pain was an attack. This man is unable to feel for his partner because he is unwilling to feel his own pain. The anger covers it up and vents it but never really ends it. His own feeling self is what he has locked away. Wouldn't you be angry if you were locked away in a tomb you could not open? No wonder people often say, "Put a lid on it!" when they hear anger vented.

Generally, if the abuser doesn't get help and doesn't want to change, he gets worse, according to survivors. Ninety-three percent of those who were in verbally abusive relationships were able to recognize that the abuser's behavior grew *worse* over time—more abusive, and angrier. If one relationship ends, he takes up his abusive ways once he is in another committed relationship. When he realizes how destructive his behavior is, he may feel as the writer below feels.

It is indeed a very traumatic, shocking experience to truly see one's self and realize what you have done—I had never cried until now. I feel so strongly committed to changing myself and repairing a beautiful marriage.

— V. L., ROCHESTER, NY

Chapter 13

Healing and Recovery

I am on a difficult journey to a "light at the end of the tunnel." I know it will not be easy.

— B.I., WOODBRIDGE, VA

Recovering all of yourself would bring you to perfection and wholeness—that state of clarity, meaning, purpose, joy, wonder, and spontaneity that comes with full Personal Power. In the meantime, in the process of recovery that is the process of life, we are presented with many opportunities to recover ourselves. The flow of life brings forth our own unfolding, and our sense of self is strengthened by our own participation. Our doing is the weaving of our lives on the loom of days: doing meditatively means *making* meaning, starting out and trying and seeing what happens—and allowing that it may be better, not worse, than we ever imagined. Finding one's true self means finding a balance, finding what nourishes, staying with our purpose, knowing that even the tiniest talent, the slightest inclination, deserves our full attention. We must try it out, check it out, see whether, like a tiny stream in an empty landscape, it opens up to an underground river.

The flow of life through time actualizes itself in experience and records itself in forms. At any moment, change is possible. All that we might have been, and are not, is potential unrealized. All that is, in the present moment, rests upon all that was. Everything that went before brings us to now and the moment of choice. What *might* be lies behind a gate where all that was has passed. We stand at eternity's gate, able to beckon, to choose, to imagine, and to bring forth our own experience.

We make our own lives in patterns with beginnings and endings and spaces in between, like a hand-made carpet with the self woven in. I once stood silent before a display of ancient hand-made carpets and sensed the selves of the weavers, like centers of knowing, radiating in and through each work. So it is for those of us who choose to make our life a focused work. If you stand silent and still before your day, you will find the weaver.

Personal Power fills us as we make our lives whole and as we experience the nourishing flow of our own creativity, bringing something new, unsung, and unknown, newly born into the world.

Recovery is about time and caring and attending to ourselves. This chapter on recovery is developed and synthesized from survivors' suggestions and women's wisdom. The survivors of verbal abuse have contributed ways and means by which they support themselves in the process of recovery, which, it turns out, is nothing less than the process of life itself.

Although therapy may be very beneficial, there is much that survivors of verbally abusive relationships can do to support themselves in recovering self-esteem, clarity, spontaneity, meaning, purpose, and joy in life without therapy. If you have experienced abuse, there is much that you can do to facilitate the process of healing, and of integrating, of growing strong, confident, and assured.

Begin with Yourself

I would like to know more about sorting it all out and self-confidence.
— J.M., BOISE, ID

One way in which a woman can become aware of her great value and her deep connection to the Creative Force that feeds the spirit of life at her center is always to act in accordance with her own best interests. Practicing this art instills confidence, because the practitioner comes to know that she can take care of herself as a precious and valuable person.

Acting on your own behalf, whether or not you are in a relationship, requires that you do four things:

1. Protect yourself and your own inner child in order that the spirit of life within you may flourish.

2. Develop your talents with dedication and discipline, taking them seriously as the gifts that they are.

3. Determine your needs and make plans to meet them yourself, taking action every day.

4. Build structure into your days and your life. Your inner child feels more secure, for example, when you know you are going

for a walk or off to work every morning than if you aren't sure of what is happening next.

As you meet your needs, you rebuild the connection between yourself and the Creative Force that impels your becoming. In other words, what is outside you, what you manifest, becomes congruent with what is on the inside: your feelings, thoughts, and inclinations.

For example, the symphony writer produces symphonies that others hear. There is a correspondence between what was within (the musical talent) what developed out of it (the symphony) and the end result (a symphony performance). Some survivors have spent so much time dealing with abuse, waiting till "later" to get on with their own lives, and having their abilities diminished and their integrity assaulted, that they have seen their spirit, their purpose, and their meaning fade into a fog of uncertainty.

To recover what has faded into the fog, we must act. Waiting for the right "anything" will never do. We begin as when we wake up in the morning: first, we stand. In our new-found resolve we take a stand and so connect to our purpose and our meaning. We may resolve to do anything at all that we feel is good. With a connection to our purpose and our meaning, we are connected to the great resources of our deeper greater origins.

Standing allows us to see more than we would see when sitting, and is thus a metaphor for recovery. Our awareness increases. Standing is an anticipation or readiness to take a step. And this step is something that had been put off, set aside, not "that important," kind of scary, a bit challenging or out of the ordinary. We might begin with little risks, as though taking shots at a basketball hoop—first ten feet away, then twenty feet—each day becoming more able to know what can be done. Knowing what can be done and counting on oneself builds self-esteem.

Step follows step, and the next step announces itself, ready or not. Whether to take a walk, take a class, take a job, take a risk, or simply take off, with awareness and a connection to the earth, standing firm, we act and at the same time we attend to our feelings. This means that we let ourselves feel what we feel without becoming lost within the feeling. We are in a place that both feels what we are feeling and attends to the feeling. When the body wakes, we do not become the painful tingling of the foot that had gone to sleep. We are not the foot. We feel the pain, attend to it, and know that we are both feeling it *and* observing it. And a part of us is waking up.

When we wake up a part of ourselves, we have taken a stand and have become aware that we are not what we've been told and do not need to act as we have been told. This waking, though wonderful, may also be painful.

But if we do not act, we cannot know ourselves. We take our stand in order to get the circulation going, the energy flowing, the creative juices stirring—to see better, to have a change of view. And when we are able to take a step, to begin to do what we must do, where do we step out to, or up to, or into, or out of? Why, in whatever direction, from our own view, our own best interests lie.

Reweaving

We act on our own behalf and meet our needs according to our nature. We heal, and according to our nature we rebuild the connection, the integration between ourselves and our world. When the correspondence between inner and outer, the thread of connection, is assaulted through verbal abuse, it becomes frayed, unraveled, almost disintegrated. *Our task becomes to reweave it, and stronger than ever before.*

If we choose to live in accordance with the natural universe, which is expansive, changing, creative, and mutually supportive, we also chose to live in harmony with our own nature. To live in harmony with our nature affirms our integrity. The natural everyday universe that we experience has perfect integrity. The universe is true. Living with integrity is empowering because there is a correspondence between ourselves and the world around us. There *is* a correspondence between what we do and the results we get. This state of integrity is empowering—and is just what we need to flourish.

In an abusive relationship this correspondence is assaulted with every abuse, every diminishment, and every denial.

Plants, birds, and animals do not have to stop to think in order to act on their own behalf. They automatically put themselves in the most suitable environment. Plants automatically seek the sun. Birds automatically build their nests to meet their needs. The beaver places itself out of harm's way in the middle of the river.

We are often drawn to be in natural surroundings, to go to the mountain or the river, to be by the sea, in the forest or under the oak, because this is where we are at one, whole and integrated. We are balanced by the vastness, the intensity, the color, the rhythms, the ineffable texture, the simplicity, and the complexity. *The inner and outer are in correspondence.*

The apple appears on the apple tree, not on the birch. No part of nature is pretending to be what it is not. Everything is of one piece. Everything fits. If we choose to live with this integrity, then we choose that which is in accord with our own nature, that which fits, is harmonious, enhancing, mirroring, life-giving, nurturing, reflecting, and pleasing to us.

We live with integrity if, for example, when we love details and numbers, we don't seek a job in public relations. And if we love tradition and chintz, we don't choose to live in a modern artist's loft.

Thus, the more we live with integrity, the more we choose what suits us and what is suitable to us. *We create a life that supports us,* and the more the people and the environment we choose support us, the more satisfying, creative, and purposeful our life becomes.

If you build integrity through aware choice, within the context of mutuality and from a position of Personal Power, the action taken and the final result will benefit you and all concerned. For example, if you say, "Stop it," when you hear abuse, you act to protect yourself and, at the same time, remind another person who has crossed a boundary that doing so is not acceptable to you. You give the abuser the opportunity of evaluating his behavior and (possibly) facing his feelings rather than acting them out in an irrational and childish way.

Meeting Your Needs

Any suggestions on what to do from here? I would like to know more about dealing with the depression from an abusive relationship, meeting people and making friends.

— C.G., LUBBOCK, TX

Recovery is the process of taking back, of bringing back to life the self within us that has shrunk like a wilted plant. By meeting our needs and taking care of ourselves, we are brought "back to life."

Throughout the days, weeks, and years, our needs will change. Sometimes one is not sure what one needs. Survivors have suggested many ways of determining their needs. I have compiled the following checklist from their comments. This list is by no means complete, but is enough to begin reweaving the thread of connection so often unraveled by verbal abuse.

Do I need

❑ more supportive people around me?

❑ more education?

❑ more money?

❑ a good book?

❑ a different physical environment?

❑ a different routine?

❑ more organization?

❑ a more specific goal?

❑ a creative outlet?

❑ something accomplished?

❑ something begun?

❑ a hobby?

❑ a different career?

❑ a vacation?

❑ more time to myself?

Often, once a person has written down her needs, she can think of something she can do to begin to meet those needs, one step at a time. If you have a need and you do not see a way even to begin to meet it at the present time, writing it down brings a positive acknowledgment of that need and validates your feelings. If a little time goes by and you still see no way to meet the need you have written down, ask three or four friends or your support group for creative ideas. You may find that articulating needs and meeting them is a good confidence-building kind of exercise.

As you build your conscious awareness of the Creative Force, this increased connection will bring you increased congruence between your inner self—your thoughts, feelings, talents, etc.—and your outer world—your actions and your environment. What is on the outside will reflect what is on the inside. Here are some examples.

If you like to be around conservative people, then you'll make friends who are conservative.

If you like to be around artists, then some of your friends will be artists.

If you like to wear bright colors, you will wear them.

If you like details, you will work with details.

If you dislike details, you will work where someone else handles them.

Your home, work, friends, colors, interests, routines, style, exercise, and wardrobe will all reflect you, and as you change, they will change.

Healing and the Inner Child
There is much talk these days about the child within. This is the "part" of ourselves that keeps the feelings of magic and mystery, of spontaneity and wonder we had as children, the part that really likes to play a

lot. This child also keeps memories of our own early childhood, and definitely feels the wounds of abuse and the fears of change.

C.G. Jung wrote a great deal about the importance of developing dialogue—establishing a relationship—with the unrecognized aspects of ourselves. Alice Miller brought us her great work in wonderful everyday language about childhood and the inner child. Much healing work today is influenced by their works.

Many women in crisis feel that they "become" their own "wounded child." If you are overwhelmed with sadness, you may for a time feel that you *are* your inner child. Your sadness may be so pervasive that the capable, resourceful, talented, unique woman feels that she has, in a way, disappeared.

If a woman has been invalidated, "put down," criticized, or in any other way disparaged, her feelings of rejection and (if the relationship ends) loss may be quite overwhelming. Therefore, as she begins the process of healing from any emotional wounds, she must, it seems, resolve to care for and nurture her own inner child—that feeling part of her that suffered the abuse. Her determination to care for that child within will bring her into relationship not only to her inner child but also her inner parents.

The inner child speaks out "I don't like that!"—and so calls forth the inner mother and father who care for and attend to the inner child. The inner mother recognizes your feelings, your thinking, your needs. The inner father stands behind you, supporting you in what you want to do.

Recovering and healing involves the process of recognition of ourselves, the three in one, the mother, the father, and the child within. For example, if you are facing change in your relationship and are feeling uncertain of your future, your own inner child may be feeling very frightened. Your inner mother/father can assure your child within as if to say,

I'll make sure you are safe.

I'll make sure you are comfortable.

I'll make sure you have plenty of healthy food.

Once you assure your inner child of something, it is best to follow through with some action to show her that you mean what you say.

Begin recovery with the awareness that you are involved in your own mothering, your own fathering and your own loving of that inner child. Sometimes it is easier to be in dialogue with your inner child when you pay particular attention to your feelings and your body's messages.

Can you talk to your child? Act for your child? If your inner child is ignored too long, you may feel her depression and not be sure why she feels so badly. As you validate your inner child's feelings, being loving in a motherly/fatherly way to your inner child, you will feel more secure and more nourished. You will feel the you that is a part of, and apart from, these feelings within. This will make it less difficult to recognize and accept all aspects of yourself, including your hidden talents. Following are some ways you might act on behalf of your inner child.

Yes, you feel bored; I'll find something good to read or do.

Yes, you feel frightened; I'll take care of you.

Yes, you feel lonely; I'll pay attention to you.

Yes, you feel restless; I'll commit to something.

Yes, you feel sad; It's okay to cry, then let's do something enjoyable.

By acknowledging your feelings and acting in accordance with what your feelings tell you, you are strengthening your connection to the Creative Force that feeds the spirit of life at your center.

You might relate to your inner child by saying, for example, "I see how sad you are, how badly you feel. What would you like? What do you need?" When you relate to your inner child this way, you accept and recognize your own feelings, and through this self-acceptance and recognition you gain self-esteem. At the same time, as you attend to your feelings in a motherly way and act with determination in a fatherly way you recover more of yourself and your Personal Power. Who is it that is relating to the inner child and is drawing upon the motherly/fatherly aspects of nurturance and action? It is you, who hold all three within yourself.

The Process of Healing and Recovery from Abuse

1. *Healing and recovery take time.* Although we would like to put all the pain in a little package of, say, one hour a week, preferably with someone there to support us, the feelings and insights that accompany the process of recovery may arise unexpectedly and periodically over a period of time.

2. *The process of healing can be helped along, but it cannot be rushed.* Many techniques can give us greater awareness and understanding, but our feelings work their way out in their own time. One can't say, "Okay, that's it. That is the last time I'm going to feel sad about that." The psyche won't take orders.

3. *Healing and recovery are processes, so one doesn't see a lot of hard*

physical evidence that one is recovering. Survivors say, "I've changed, I'm different on the inside." Inside is where it counts. Later there may be changes on the outside. For example, one may be rid of various physical complaints—appear to be more energetic, alive, and enthusiastic.

4. *Increased awareness is a result of healing and recovery.* Once one realizes what is "happening" within and without, the circuits are activated, so to speak. One is able to identify as abusive or aberrant, behavior that had previously seemed to blend with the atmosphere.

5. *Healing and recovery lead one to the truth.* Everyone has her own path, and as we heal and recover, the truth of our own path becomes clear.

6. *In recovery, one's feelings inform one.* One has more than an intellectual understanding of what was, or is, going on. One knows one is not crazy.

7. *Healing means increasing self-esteem and awareness.* A survivor said, "My spirit is working its way up, little by little."

Healing and Growth

1. *Growth is a constant in the universe.* Everything in the world seems to grow in some way. The universe itself is thought by many scientists to be expanding. We grow too. After we grow up physically, we continue to grow in awareness. We do, that is, if we don't become rigid or "closed-minded."

2. *The universe is true.* The central fact about the universe is that it is true. We don't see apples on orange trees. We don't wake in the morning and see one piece missing in the sky, like a puzzle with the last piece lost. On the contrary, everything fits together. *Everything* fits together, and *everything* about the universe is true. You can count on it. It is congruent. It has integrity. When you look away from the sun, it doesn't disappear. It fulfills its purpose of being in the sky. No matter how fast you spin back around to look at it, you can't catch it forgetting to come back to where you just saw it. It is dependable. It has its place. And so do you.

It is especially reassuring to people in recovery from verbal abuse to find the universe reliable and true, because they have been around people who were in some ways so unreliable in their behavior and so untrue to their human nature that they were incongruent with the world around them. The truth and congruence of nature is healing.

3. *Everything in nature has a place and acts in freedom to meet its own needs.*

It is very important to keep this in mind, because in an abusive relationship, everything is done by the abuser to thwart or control the free actions of the partner—sometimes extremely covertly. When one is verbally abused, one is hearing the opposite of the truth.

If nature is growing, is true, and acts freely, there is an overwhelming incongruence between nature and the abuser. The abuser seems to try not to grow, denies truth, and attempts to act in exact opposition to the dynamics of the universe.

If we are to act in accordance with the universe, we must align our actions with the universe. This eventually brings us to the all-consuming question, "What should I do?"

4. *Doing what is best for you is acting in accordance with the Truth.* In other words, when you act in accordance with the truth, you are acting in accordance with the universe, or in accordance with universal truth. What this means is that the dynamics of the universe, which move toward order, diversity, complexity, and growth and are true, do support you. So congratulations! That is a lot of energy, or lucky coincidences, or synchronicities, or good fortunes, or being in the right place at the right time, working for you.

5. *No one but you knows what is true for you.* No one has the right to tell you what you "should" or "should not" do, nor what you "should" or "should not" have done, nor what is best for you, nor what you feel, nor what your motivations are.

The Healing Environment

To avoid being verbally abused, anyone whose orientation is toward mutuality needs to be aware of the manner and means by which those who do not share their orientation may act destructively toward them. To avoid being verbally abused, one must also become the choice maker, the seeker, the discriminator, the action taker, the doer, and the purposeful one.

Anyone healing from abuse must first be free of the abuse. To be free from verbal abuse you must have your limits respected—whether by getting cooperation, going away for a while, or separating from any who would try to control you.

To heal, a survivor needs to protect herself emotionally and spiritually. She needs to discover whether her abuser is able and willing to change. She needs to decide whether the relationship is nourishing to her.

An abuser begins to recover himself when he asks, "How can I change to be happy for my wife as she becomes her own person?" A survivor begins to heal herself when she determines, "I must act on my own behalf today." *To connect becomes his goal. To act becomes her goal.*

Healing from Loss
The process of healing begins with the recognition of what has occurred, of what you have suffered, of how you have been deprived and of how you have been abused.

> *The thing that I miss the most in this relationship is that I may never have a chance to feel loved and wanted, which is what I have always wanted.*
>
> — S.E., WILLITS, CA

With that awareness you may experience much loss, the loss of "what might have been," and the loss that is felt when a need is not met. This woman wrote that the loss she felt was that of never being loved. Other losses may be,

enthusiasm lost to self-doubt
confidence lost to the fear of "doing something wrong"
clear thinking lost to confusion
the loss of hope that he will one day understand
the loss of trust, in self and in others

Even though you know that you are not in any way responsible for the abuser's behavior, your own healing comes from accepting that he may never realize his behavior is insidious and destructive— and if he does realize it, he may not be able or willing to change.

Recovery, Values, and Choices
If you have the feeling that there is too much pressing upon you in a difficult time, stop everything and think over your values. Then you can determine your priorities.

As we heal, we recover more of ourselves and our awareness increases. Increased awareness gives us an increased ability to see differences and, therefore, to make choices. We are then more able to take a chance on ourselves, stick to our goals, value our talents, establish our values, and take our interests and our work very, very seriously. Awareness is increased by paying attention to our intuition. The more aware we are of ourselves, our values, our intuition, and the world around us, the better the choices we make.

We can't decide anything or think clearly if we do not know our values. We can best determine our values when we realize that we have a right to our own resources: time, space, energy, intelligence, creativity, and so forth; and we have an obligation to ourselves to use these resources for ourselves in our own best interest and the interests of our dependent children.

When we know our values, we can set our priorities. When we know our priorities, we can gather information, both inner and outer. When we know how to interpret that information, we can make good choices. When we make good choices, life works better for us.

Following is an exercise that demonstrates in a concrete way how life lived in this manner works. Think of a few difficulties you have had in your life and write them down. Some might be:

Missing something important
An unhappy love relationship
A bad job situation
A loss on an investment
Being taken advantage of by someone
Being conned by someone

As you write them down, ask yourself what your values and your priorities were when you made your choices, and which choices you made that contributed to your being in this difficulty. Are there are any similarities between the choices? This exercise may bring insight into how you may not have chosen in your own best interest.

Since how and what we choose for ourselves is of utmost importance, consider your values carefully when you have a choice to make. At one time we may place security as a very high value, especially when there are others who are relying on that security with us. At other times we may value freedom or new adventures, like self-employment. If you value peace and serenity and are considering a new relationship, then you might ask yourself whether you are feeling peace and serenity when you are with your new relationship.

It may be beneficial to make a "Values List" with your highest values at the top—first on the list. See if you can come up with thirty or more values. Then determine to use your resources, including your time and energy, wisely according to your values.

Self-Validation and Self-Discovery
What we recover in recovery is who we were meant to be.

I didn't know I was being lied to. I was always trying to understand the logic in what I was hearing. Nobody ever told me that what I was hearing had no logic. Now I know that if I think things out and make a decision I can be pretty sure of the results because I am a logical thinker.

— H.J., SPRINGFIELD, MO

I thought that whatever I had to say, the way I saw things, sensed things, anticipated things, was wrong, wrong, wrong, because I couldn't "prove it." All I ever heard was "That's not so. You can' t prove it." But I have this wonderful mind—didn't get A's in school by accident. I just didn't know it anymore because my whole world said, "What you think is worth nothing."

— W.B., NEW YORK, NY

I would like to know more about not having other people's approval to validate my feelings and decisions.

— J.L., LAS VEGAS, NV

I would like to know how to get enough self-esteem to validate my own experiences by myself.

— T.N., OMAHA, NE

Could the current popularity of positive thinking and visualization be our own culturally acceptable means of counteracting the effects of verbal abuse? It certainly seems to work that way. For example, the expression "Go for it!" counteracts the expression "What makes you think you can do it?" or "You think you're so smart."

All verbal abuse is invalidating. I believe that if there were no verbal abuse (or physical or sexual abuse), we might not be able to find anyone with low self-esteem. Of course all abusers have low self-esteem, or they wouldn't need to control, put down, and bully others. You are invalidated when you are told that what you feel is the "wrong feeling," or that you are "too sensitive," or that what you heard wasn't spoken, or that what you saw didn't happen.

If you are recovering from verbal abuse, it is very healing to validate yourself often. Self-validation and validation from others builds trust in yourself and your own perceptions. Look for people who validate you. Emotional support validates your

ideas	feelings
views	hopes
needs	dreams
efforts	talents
achievements	opinions

Following is a list of statements made by survivors of verbal abuse who are beginning the process of recovery. This is a very small sampling, representative of hundreds of women who come from all walks of life, from corporate president to retiree, from certified therapist to college student. If you are healing from a verbally abusive relationship, as you read these statements you may take heart in knowing that you are with many others who in some way share with you your own experience. You are not alone.

I feel like I am just coming out of a psycho ward.

I accept full responsibility for never allowing my spirit and soul to be taken by another person again.

No matter how my relationship ends up, I know now, I am not at fault for the abuse.

Did a tremendous amount of crying, not for him but for me. I finally stopped beating myself up.

I don't know if my future will include my husband. But if it doesn't, I know it will be for the better—for me.

I am starting to see the type of men with this behavior and I am staying clear away.

Just acknowledging the terrific losses of self and spirit helps start the process of healing and rebuilding a self—I am enough, adequate, worthy.

I try never to be abused verbally by anyone again. I see how the erosion of spirit and self occurs and why I once felt so crazy and confused.

I have much more hope for a better life, whether it be with or without my husband.

I left. I now understand what I had dealt with for more than twenty years. I'm so happy to be free from the verbal abuse.

It was so confusing. I started making tapes and listening to the abuse. This helped. Also I used journal writing as a catharsis.

As the relationship has progressed, it seems my tolerance level has been lowered. [Lowered tolerance is a sign of returning health.]

I never thought I would find myself in this type of marriage. I am very disappointed in myself for getting into this type of marriage and, since I do love my husband, I hope we can work to improve our marriage.
— E.N., CHARLOTTE, NC

I am now trying to pick up the pieces of my life. He calls me and abuses me over the phone, telling me I'm jeopardizing his sobriety—I am getting support from a friend and am looking for a new job in a different state—trying to get the pieces of my life back together and my self-esteem back. I have met people that treat me like a person, not a doormat. I hope I have learned from this relationship and wanted other women to know that verbal abuse is a hidden disease and you are not crazy.

— N.B., Patterson, NJ

I was married to a noted attorney and a friend is married to a doctor. We both think that being married to powerful professionals, highly respected in the community, makes the partners more prone to this kind of "one-down" abuse."

— W.K., Leavittown, NY

The next chapter offers guidelines for holistic healing and explores methods for building self-esteem.

Chapter 14

The Sixty-Minute Me and Self-Esteem

I was fifty years old when I returned to college to get my Masters. At the same time, I learned that I am intelligent, have a sense of humor and people like and respect me—I am grieving my losses and am happier than I have ever been. Now I have a name for my pain!

— R.P., Long Island, NY

The *Sixty-Minute Me* is a method designed to support you in remembering to attend to yourself for at least one hour a day. It is a holistic approach to self-recovery and discovery—a twelve-part program touching on Spirit, Feelings, Mind, and Body. Since it is essential that we take care of our needs, acknowledge our feelings, act in our own best interests, and nourish ourselves, the chart on the following page is provided to serve as a reminder of the balanced way in which we need to nurture ourselves all of our lives.

This is not meant to be a rigid schedule or plan but simply a reminder. It helps me to remember to take a deep breath, relax, visualize a personal symbol, take a break, or take a walk. There are additional details and instructions on how to use the chart on the following pages.

The Sixty-Minute Me

The chart shown can be used as a guide to spending time meeting your needs. It is a synthesis of ideas from many survivors.

In the center section, the numbers indicate minutes, ranging from one to twenty, to give you an idea of how much time you might spend on each practice. By attending to these four aspects of yourself, your body, mind, spirit, and emotions, you assist yourself in growth and recovery. Only you can decide whether this method is helpful to you.

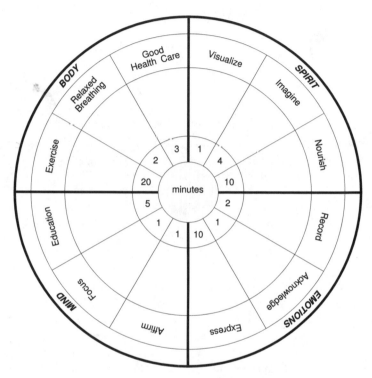

Following is an explanation of how to use the chart. As you will see, some activities can be done in the middle of your busy day. Others, such as twenty minutes of exercise, require a little time to yourself. There are three different activities for each of the four aspects, encouraging a balanced approach to self-awareness and self-development.

The minutes at the center of the circle add up to sixty. If you devote one hour of your day to caring for yourself, you will benefit with increased self-esteem and well-being. The circle itself is an archetypal symbol of wholeness called a *mandala*. If you wish, modify this plan in any way to suit your own needs. The plan may serve as a focus or as a quick reminder of your intentions. You may also wish to make a copy of it to keep at hand.

Following are suggested practices for each of the four categories, beginning at the 1:00 position. The chart below can be changed any way you like. For example, in the exercise section, you may wish to add a particular goal, such as distance walked. If you prefer to use this section of the book with or instead of the circular diagram, I suggest you make a copy of it also.

What follows is only a reminder; it is important that you do not use it as an "I should."

SPIRIT

Visualize *1* *Minute*	Visualize any symbol (for example, a star, a rose, a butterfly) that in your own mind stands for health, happiness, wholeness, or any other quality you wish to increase in your life. This can be done throughout the day, even if just for a few seconds at a time.
Imagine *4* *Minutes*	Imagine a beautiful and nurturing place to be. Make it any way you want. Imagine talking with a wise person there to help you. Imagine successfully achieving your goals and receiving congratulations. Do this for a couple of minutes, twice a day.
Nourish *10* *Minutes*	Nourish your spirit with music, art, or a call to a friend, or use this time to plan activities that nourish you.

EMOTIONS (Feelings)

Record *2* *Minutes*	First thing in the morning, briefly record any dream with the feelings and emotions that went with it and any message it has given you.
Acknowledge *1* *Minute*	Throughout the day, frequently ask yourself, "What am I feeling now?" then acknowledge your feelings to yourself. Also notice whether your feelings indicate any action you need to take. Give yourself permission to feel whatever you feel.
Express *10* *Minutes*	Express your emotions and feelings by drawing or painting them, writing them down, sharing them with someone else, and doing what they indicate; laugh, cry, or pound a pillow.

MIND

Affirm
1
Minute

It only takes a few seconds to repeat an affirmation to yourself. Chose one or two affirmations from chapter 16 and repeat them throughout the day.

Focus
1
Minute

You can focus when you feel distracted by bringing your attention to the present and directing it toward completing any task that is a priority in the present. Stay in the present in order to be responsive to your own needs.

Education
5
Minutes

Beyond formal education, take a few moments to realize what life has taught you today. Reading a little each day can keep you learning and intellectually stimulated.

BODY

Exercise
20
Minutes

Rapid walking is one of the best exercises for overall well-being and fitness. Stretching is good any time. Do chose any exercise activity you enjoy, then enjoy it regularly.

Relaxed
Breathing
2
Minutes

Breathe into the abdomen, letting your shoulders drop as you inhale. Let out tension as you let out your breath and your abdomen flattens. Remind yourself to breath this natural way frequently throughout the day.

Health
3
Minutes

Take a few minutes each day to remember your health resolutions. Select the most nutritious foods. Take care of medical and dental needs. Don't put off health concerns.

The sixty-minute plan is designed to keep you in touch with your own body, mind, spirit and feelings.

The symbol of the mandala mentioned earlier reminds us at deep levels of our own wholeness. Our dreams are created out of symbols. Symbols are the language of the psyche and sometimes "get the message across" much faster than words. For this reason we may desire something for its symbolic value; for example, a teacher may be attracted to a business suit because it is a symbol of the business career really desired. Status objects are symbols that may be used to make up for low self-esteem. We can use symbols (like mandalas) to communicate with our deeper selves.

To find your own symbol for something, for example, peace, simply close your eyes and ask yourself, "What is my symbol for peace?" Then accept the first image that comes to mind. This is your symbol. By visualizing your symbol you are more able to bring the actual experience into your life.

Words, such as the language of affirmations, can help us to change our beliefs about ourselves. If we learned to believe we were not worthy of, for example, courtesy, respect, or access to our own money, a change in "programming" or self-talk will help us to change that belief.

By paying attention to our feelings, by learning, by nurturing ourselves and our spirit, we are better able to know ourselves, to meet our needs and to cope in the highly technological and fast-paced world in which we live. This is why practicing the exercises suggested in the sixty-minute program can help you develop greater self-awareness, integration, and clarity. You may even wish to spend more than sixty minutes. You may discover, for instance, that you wish to spend more time on exercise, or in dream work, or on inspirational reading. Whatever you decide, remember that balance is important.

When you are relaxed and have nurtured yourself, you feel stronger and better able to deal with life's challenges. If you have children, you will be more relaxed and confident in caring for them than if you felt physically and spiritually deprived or tense and overly demanding.

Again, none of the exercises are to be taken as "shoulds." There may be times in your life when there doesn't seem to be even an hour available. Then just remembering to breathe and relax may be all you can handle.

Low Self-esteem Comes from Verbal Abuse

I believe that low self-esteem is the result of not being treated with the respect and dignity one's human nature demands. When you are not treated with respect and dignity, you are suffering abuse. Most of us have been treated disrespectfully by someone and have treated someone else with disrespect. If the modus operandi, the style of behaving, the attitude one has toward another is one of disrespect rather than respect, then one's way of relating to that person cannot but be disrespectful, that is to say, abusive. If you have been in a relationship lacking in the dignity and respect your humanity deserves, you may have low self-esteem—sometimes without quite realizing it.

The following questions are about self-esteem.

Do you criticize and question your appearance or place a great deal of importance on how you look? If so, try to recall when in your life and from whom you heard your looks criticized or put down—or overly emphasized, as if how you look is anyone's concern before your own! Some visual media, such as TV and magazines, encourage completely unrealistic expectations of how we "should" look.

If you find that you criticize yourself, congratulate yourself on the fact that you recognize your own self-criticism. Once you realize that it was someone outside yourself who *taught* you this criticism, you can more easily break the pattern of self-criticism.

Do you criticize and question your actions? Do you recall anyone telling you that what you did wasn't good enough or that your motives were wrong, or that you "did it wrong," or that you shouldn't have done what you did?

Now do you find that you worry about how well you'll do, what you "should" do, whether what you do will be "any good," whether what you do will be misunderstood, or whether what you do is what you *ought* to be doing? All these concerns can be the result of experiencing abusive anger, which leaves one feeling as if nothing she does is right or enough.

Do you feel defensive when you are blamed or criticized? It is certainly a universal response to defend oneself when one is blamed or criticized. However, a defense, taking the form of an *explanation,* is usually employed to convince the blamer or critic that what they have said is not true. This desire to convince the other implies that the abuse has some validity—and what a marvelous power trip for the critic or blamer to find that you consider the abuse to be worthy of explanation. Better to protect yourself from criticism and blaming or any other verbal abuse by saying, Stop it! Enough! Chill out! Relax! Give me a break! Hold it! or any combination of similar responses.

Do you question your feelings? Do you recall anyone telling you that, "You're making a mountain out of a mole hill," or that "You're blowing everything out of proportion," or that "You're too sensitive," or that "You like to complain," or that "You shouldn't feel that way?"

Now, do you sometimes hear yourself say, "I shouldn't feel this way," "I'm probably exaggerating things," or "I must expect too much"? All of this self-criticism and self-doubt is the result of having had your feelings discounted. To grow, it is essential that you accept your feelings, even and especially if no one else in the world ever did.

Many women say that the greatest step to self-esteem and self-recovery is self-acceptance. If a woman accepts herself and her pain, she will come to accept her feelings, her gifts, her talents, and ultimately her increasing awareness of her great value.

Do you find it easier to give to others than to give to yourself? Do you recall hearing "You spent too much on that," "Don't make yourself important," "Who do you think you are?" "Don't be frivolous," "Don't be silly," or "You can make do without it"?

Do you sometimes feel it's better to take care of others' needs before you take care of your own? And do you put off spending money on yourself because there is always someone who seems to have a greater need? Do you recall hearing, "Put the other person first," "Don't be selfish," "Be a good 'help mate,'" and so forth?

One way to build your self-esteem is to reaffirm to yourself that each person's challenges are his or her own and that growth comes from meeting one's own needs—not from your meeting them. Except in the case of your children. Until they can do things for themselves, you are "there" to meet their needs. In that regard it is important to be realistic. Usually ten-year-old girls and boys can run the washer, pick up their things, make their sandwiches, and choose their friends.

Do you worry about your choices or fear starting a project because you don't know how it will turn out? Do you recall having your ideas and thoughts constantly countered? "You don't know what you're talking about." "You can't prove it." "What did you go and do that for?" "You're just trying to be a 'know-it-all.'" "You can't do anything right." "You couldn't find your head if it wasn't attached." "Who are you trying to impress?" "Who cares!"

Now do you find yourself procrastinating or doing so many things at once that you feel scattered? One way to build your self-esteem is to *affirm* to yourself, "Whatever I do is worth doing and completing. By doing my best and working consistently on one thing at a time, I will find more of what I can do well and I will learn by managing each challenge that arises."

In this age of recovery, self-esteem is a high priority. Possibly this is because high self-esteem allows us to undo the damage done by verbal abuse.

If you are feeling trapped in a relationship, the experience of "making your dreams come true" in small ways can grow into the confidence to take on larger challenges. We grow when we successfully meet life's challenges.

Taking action for yourself every day can include some down-to-earth, practical steps. Survivors have had one or more of the following items on their wish lists. You can make a wish list similar to the needs list discussed in the previous chapter.

Wish List

- ❏ An uninterrupted hour
- ❏ A stimulating class
- ❏ A new friend
- ❏ A visit out of town
- ❏ A walk in the country

Using every spare minute to make your wishes come true increases self-esteem.

When people approach the problem of low self-esteem, they often focus on two important areas: changing their behavior, for example by giving themselves more treats, and changing their self-talk with affirmations like, "I am doing a good job." "I deserve all the nice things I can give myself."

These two approaches are very important. However, a third approach is usually missing. That is *avoiding people who put you down* or who disturb you by putting other people down; or if they cannot be avoided, developing the habit of saying "Stop it."

Survivors of verbal abuse have been told that what they said was "untrue and unprovable," that what they did was "not good enough," and that what they felt was "wrong." Could anyone experience the rejection of withholding or the denigration of criticism and not lose self-esteem? Survivors write:

According to him I'm always doing something wrong or forgetting something I should have remembered.

More was always expected of me.

No matter what I did it was not enough.

I was not worth his company or conversation.

Getting Help

I want to know more about how to get help.

I would like to know how to find a counselor that is well informed about verbal abuse.

How can I identify a supportive, knowledgeable therapist who won't make me feel as if I haven't tried hard enough?

Take your time. Interview your therapist. If you feel that you are being told to try harder, which translates into "you are to blame," leave. No explanations are necessary. It is enough to say, "Thank you for your time. This isn't working for me."

In every state there are organizations for women who want help. A representative listing of these services is in the Appendix. You do not have to have been physically battered to get support from agencies set up to help abused women. Verbal battering involves exactly the same motivations, the same dynamics, the same reasons, the same issues of Power Over and control, as physical battering. Most of these agencies work with therapists who are trained in these issues and can give referrals. Women can gain a great deal of support from someone who clearly understands the issues of abuse. Beyond individual, one-on-one support from a therapist, belonging to a women's support group is generally a tremendous support for women. The support group is discussed in full in the chapter that follows.

Chapter 15

The Support Group

I am seventy-two years old. I cannot believe that for fifty-two years I have put up with this abuse. When my husband abused me I accepted it thinking that I should. Now I know better. I've only told one person about this abuse. I must find a support group to give me my confidence back.

— I.K., OAKDALE, PA

A support group gives one strength, validation, and information, and may serve as a valuable support system over a long period of time. It is particularly validating to anyone who has just recently recognized that she has been experiencing verbal abuse. The group allows one to get "reality checks," to find out whether what one is experiencing is "normal," that is, healthy, or whether one is being treated abusively. Sometimes it is difficult to know. For example, "We're leaving right now!" (ordering) and "You're trying to start something" (accusation) may be heard so frequently they seem "normal." In the long run, being ordered, blamed, criticized or in any other way abused will wear down the highest self-esteem and confidence.

A woman who was abused for much of her life and who has been healing over a number of years contributed the following.

It's my belief that women can perhaps be best helped in a group (with a trained facilitator in abuse), because I didn't know what to tell the counselor. It seems as if I needed to hear others telling their stories to raise my consciousness about my own marriage.

I still struggle with feeling responsible for what happened. Most

therapists I've talked to tell us women we participated in maintaining
the relationship. That there's no villain. That it's a "family problem."
— F.I., SEDALIA, MO

When partners of abusers hear "therapy talk" such as "there's no
villain," or "it's a family problem," they usually believe that they are
doing something to cause the unhappiness in the relationship. Nothing could be farther from the truth. In fact, the problem is that they are
with an abuser. A survivor shares her thinking on support groups.

I used to think support was whining and complaining. He'd say,
"You're just bitching. All you and your friends do is gossip. You just
love to gossip," like it's trivial. I began to think, "I shouldn't burden oth-
ers. What can they do anyway?" like it was a waste of time to tell any-
one of my problems. I was told it was chatter. I realize I believed him.

Remember the coffee klatches? They were really support groups.
They weren't based on competition. They were about sharing informa-
tion. About reality. Support was what it was. It was about life. I won-
der if women in their thirties now know what a support system like
that was. Support gives you reality checks and the courage to go on.
— S.W., LOS ANGELES, CA

I recommend a women's support group for women who are now
in a verbally abusive relationship or who were in the past and want to
increase their understanding and self-esteem. Support groups can assist the partner of the abuser in coming to terms with the realities of
the relationship, in identifying verbal abuse, in getting reality checks,
responses, encouragement, and validation, in making new friends,
and in finding community resources and interest groups.

A survivor who was constantly blamed for her spouse's behavior
wrote about her confusion. She had believed the blaming. She was being made the scapegoat, and she had no support group in which to
"check it out." She wrote,

My husband is "successful" and he is a church leader. He never says
"no" to anyone (except me), and is always ready and willing to do any-
thing for anybody. Sadly, that's not how he treats me. He is extremely
controlling and manipulative. I'm an intelligent person and can't be-
lieve that I was so stupid not to realize what he was doing to me. If I
would have had a support group, he never would have convinced me
that I was the one with all the personality problems.
— A.H., CHARLOTTESVILLE, VA

I receive a constant stream of letters requesting information on support groups. Women want to get out of their isolation and to achieve validation and clarity. They write,

I want to know more about support groups and getting support.

I want to know how to find them.

Can you recommend a support group in my area?

How can I start a support group?

Survivors of verbally abusive relationships *can* find each other and gain mutual validation. Being seen through another's eyes, hearing others respond to your story, and finding out how others cope can be of great benefit whether you are dealing with verbal abuse now or are recovering from having been in a verbally abusive relationship.

Getting support is an indication of self-esteem. It's your message to yourself that you want the best for yourself. (Again, a listing of support organizations nationwide appears in the Appendix.)

Validation

Women sometimes forget that it's "*Shame on you* if you abuse me" and end up feeling shamed *by* abuse. Many believe that verbal, physical, or sexual abuse can only happen to someone else. Yet abuse affects the lives of celebrities, of public figures, of rich women and poor women, of sophisticated younger women and sophisticated older women, of naive, trusting women, loving women, careful women, smart women, brilliant women, down-to-earth women, and most of all, of women who can hardly imagine it happening to them.

When women find each other and receive the validation a group can give them, their recovery is enhanced tremendously. It stands to reason that if you were told that the abuse that was happening to you *wasn't* happening, or if you were told that if the abuse did happen, then it happened because of the way you were, you would need to recover from the lie, to understand how you had been "brainwashed" and invalidated. The support group can give you this validation.

Support groups bring clarity and validation and comfort to those who have survived abuse. A support group of women who have shared similar experiences works best. It is not surprising then, that hundreds of women are looking for support groups.

Some survivors have received good support from twelve-step programs, particularly from meeting and making friends in them. Others, however, have found them unhelpful for a number of reasons:

1. The no-cross-talk rule left no room for validation, which is essential to those who are victimized by very crazy-making verbal abusers, "masters," so to speak. Some groups' "no-response" style was felt as withholding and crazy-making to the participants, who truly require reality checks, validation, and normalcy. In fact, the abnormalcy of withholding response to personal pain can generate flashbacks in the participant. After all, her abuser didn't feel for her either. A woman wrote,

> It is so important to know that you can be angry about the abuse even when the abuser doesn't seem to understand what he's doing wrong. You can be angry about the injustice. Injustice is a good thing to be angry about. Anger gives us the energy to act.
>
> — H.M., TRENTON, PA

2. Survivors did not receive the information they needed to learn how to respond to verbal abuse, how to protect themselves, or how others coped with abuse.

3. Many felt directed to look *inward* for the culprit who is actually *out there*.

4. No forum was available for identifying abusive behavior.

Following is information on how to form your own support group as well as how to use resources already available.

Community Resources

One of the simplest ways of starting a group and connecting with women who have similar needs, insights, experiences, and wisdom is through family and women's support and shelter agencies. Many of these agencies conduct ongoing support groups for women with particular needs. One way that you can start or join a group is to contact your local agency (see the Appendix) and ask for information.

If you cannot locate an agency near you, you might find a church or other community center that would allow you to start a support group, or you might find a licensed counselor willing to facilitate a support group. Following are some steps you might take to use agencies already in place.

1. Check the Appendix for the agency that is closest to you. Other women in your area will probably be calling the agency as well. If the agency listed nearest to you is not in your immediate area, ask for a referral to one that is.

2. Tell the agency that you are interested in attending a support group to deal with verbal abuse.

3. Find out whether there is such a group or whether anyone in the agency will facilitate a group dedicated to helping women who experience or have experienced verbal abuse. Perhaps the agency might enable you to start one after a training program. Many agencies offer training in facilitating support groups.

4. If there is no agency within a reasonable distance, or if your local agency isn't equipped to operate a support group and doesn't have the means to start one, look into other resources. Try a local hospital community outreach or health department, a therapist referred by a women's shelter program who might be able to begin your group, a community center or church, or a YWCA facility.

5. Once you have a location, you can start an informal group by putting up a few notices in churches, libraries, clinics, etc. Use a voice mail number for contacts so that you can screen your calls.

It is usually possible for one individual to start a support group and to find other women who have had similar experiences. The group should meet on a weekly basis and offer support without criticism, preferably with a facilitator trained in group dynamics. The primary purpose should be to hear and validate each other and to share information, as well as a sense of community. As soon as women realize that someone understands and has had similar experiences, they usually feel much saner and clearer about what is happening to them.

The benefit of starting a group through an already functioning agency is that any woman in your community who wants to be part of the support group can find the group quickly through a call to the nearest women's shelter. When I was doing research to locate the agencies listed in the Appendix, I found that there are more than 1,500 women's shelters and crisis centers in the United States. Although I have not spoken with the directors of every one of these agencies, those I have talked to offer support for women dealing with past or present verbally abusive relationships. Of course you'll have to take into account that these agencies are generally underfunded and rely heavily on volunteers.

Women who attend support groups are in different stages of awareness. I have outlined below some basic stages women in these settings describe.

Stages

In and Out of the Verbally Abusive Relationship
The survivors of verbal abuse have written about how they thought and felt as they entered into relationships with their mates; how they felt when they first experienced the abuse; how they managed and how they finally realized that the behavior was abusive; how they felt as they sought change; and finally, if change was not forthcoming, how they felt as they moved out of the relationship.

Dating and Courting Stage

At first when we met I kind of idolized him or looked up to him. In some ways I thought he was somewhat exceptional. Other people did too.

I thought I was lucky he loved me and that he felt lucky also. It seemed as though he really admired me and appreciated who I was. After all, he called all the time.

I never doubted that he was really interested in my thoughts and ideas and that he cared about my interests, even if they were different from his. He was so courteous I believed he respected me and my individuality so I "knew" he saw me as his equal and his partner.

I wanted to be really worthy of his admiration. That's why I wanted to do the best possible job I could, no matter what it was I was doing. It seemed like we were beginning a great life together. Of everybody, he was the one that said he cared most.

The following survivors were so committed to making their relationships work, they unwittingly put up with their mate's abusive behavior.

Commitment Stage

I'd feel a lot of pain over something he'd say. I didn't want to upset him. I thought if I hinted about some of his behaviors that bothered me, his feelings wouldn't be hurt and he would understand right away.

I thought that I should defer to his wishes if it wasn't extremely important to me. That this in itself was an act of love.

I found it more and more difficult to deal with his behavior. I thought I should try even harder.

I thought maybe I should change somehow what I felt because he seemed to think I was crazy.

I thought I should be more like other people he got along with.

Pain and Confusion Stage

I began to feel that I just couldn't cope with this.

I began to feel unsure of myself. I realized I didn't have the confidence I used to have.

I thought the criticism was because he cared and that after all he was really trying to help me or when he took over I thought it was because he was trying to protect me, take some burden off me.

Especially I got confused by religious beliefs. I blamed myself and felt guilty and thought there was something I should do.

My friends would remember some awful incident that I had already started blocking out.

Why was this happening?

Sometimes he'd seem nice so he was also an image of comfort.

I spent a lot of time crying.

There was a lot of anxiety.

It was so confusing. I'd feel totally disintegrated.

I got so numb I didn't care about anything.

Isolation, no one understanding, no one to turn to is critical.

Depression can set in. You can't do or say anything right. I was afraid I was crazy.

The doubts split me apart.

I began to see repeating patterns. If they knew how typical they are— that all these patterns are the same don't you think they'd be appalled?

Coping Stage

With support finally you find some empathy. Empathy has to be experienced.

Once I found out it was happening because he was trying to control me, I started to realize it wasn't anything to do with me.

I started feeling reconnected not disintegrated but a whole lot of pain and sadness about it.

Things are clear.

I'm feeling so much more whole and so much more sad.

Reaching out Stage

Outside support became essential. It is essential.

Getting validation was essential.

I realized I wasn't alone.

At this stage in the relationship some abusers have become conscious of and willing to admit to their abusive behavior and are willing to work on the relationship. Some partners stay and work with their mates, some do not want to stay and chance many years of effort and hurt.

Change Stage

The main difficulty I had trying to leave the abusive relationship was that I wanted to hold onto something concrete. Right when I wanted to let go I wanted to hold on even tighter.

Knowing I could have an address and phone number through a women's service and could make a few calls made all the difference in the world. I didn't know I could get that kind of support; I had never been hit.

We were driving one time and he said, "I ought to knock you out of here" (from the car). At first I felt outraged, then really afraid. Then I knew things had to change.

What I want to say is sometimes it was so bizarre I just couldn't hear it, or I'd hear it, but then I couldn't remember it. If you saw ET right this second and no one else did and then a second later you didn't, your mind might tell you it just didn't happen.

A survivor who had been married twenty-two years wrote to say that after she recognized she was in a verbally abusive relationship, she spent several more years in the relationship staying aware and putting forth even more effort to be understanding and supportive of her husband, wanting to give the relationship every chance and hoping that he really would respect her limits.

She said that it had been so hard to realize that someone who was an extremely successful and respected member of the community, and quite intelligent, could not really be hearing her or understanding what he was doing. She did not realize that denial was a part of his abusive behavior. Affluence added to the illusion that it wasn't "that bad," she said. Everything looked so good on the outside that even she thought it must not be as bad as it felt. However, after finding out that it was as bad as it felt, she said,

If it weren't for a support group I might not have realized that what counts—what helps us most is what we cannot see. We cannot see,

love	*creativity*
friendship	*knowledge*
feelings	*truth*
emotional support	*warmth*
concern	*companionship*
acceptance	*appreciation*
intuition	*kindness*

All the other things we can see are not what help us most. I'm not saying they're not nice to have and use, but they don't help us to grow.
— J.A., Topeka, KS

Ending verbal abuse in our culture will not come about by going after verbal abusers. It will be achieved by seeing that our children are validated and never abused, and by recognizing it when it happens, calling it to the attention of the abuser, and at the same time taking a stand: making a statement, declaring the truth, setting limits, acknowledging the violation, and, whenever necessary moving out of range of the abuser.

It will happen when all our children are treated with dignity, respect, warmth and encouragement, when our sons are taught to feel and our daughters, fully valued and recognized, are taught to stand strong and equal to all.

Chapter 16

Affirmations

In order to deal with verbal abuse now I need to reaf firm myself and my own worth—on a daily basis.

— E.N., Westfield, MA

Affirmations are an effective and powerful tool for building self-esteem, confidence and a sense of wonder about the world and oneself. Affirmations help us to realize that there is always new terrain to travel as we participate in our own unfolding—more to learn of ourselves, more to learn of potentials undeveloped and possibilities unexplored.

We know that there is a built-in timetable for our physical development. Everyone expects a child of five, for instance, to have different physical, mental, and emotional characteristics from a child of ten. It is the same with our psychological unfolding. Like the unfolding of an adult from an infant, a flower from a bud, or a tree from a seed, we become more ourselves through time. This is our potential. We can affirm our potential and empower ourselves when we act within the context of an affirmation. It is never too late to flower.

No one can tell you what is best for you. There may be times in one's life when an affirmation a day keeps discouragement away, and there may be other times when other activities take precedence. If you chose to work with affirmations, I suggest that you pick one each day that resonates with you, one that you are attracted to, and meditate for a few minutes on how it applies to you and whether you can begin to believe in it for yourself. After you have chosen an affirmation for the day, I suggest that you

1. Repeat it to yourself several times.

2. Visualize it in some way.

3. Act on it when appropriate.

4. Keep a journal just for your affirmations or use a section of a journal you already have. Your journal can be as simple as a notebook or a loose-leaf binder. Write down the affirmation you have chosen in your journal.

5. Repeat the affirmation to yourself frequently throughout the day.

6. Notice how you feel after working with the affirmation for a day or so. At the end of the day, write in your journal about how you feel and how the affirmation affected you. Following are just some of the feelings you might consider.

FEELINGS

abandoned	able	abused
accepted	acknowledged	adequate
agitated	alive	angry
anxious	apprehensive	assured
authentic	certain	cheerful
cherished	clear	comfortable
competent	confident	confused
content	determined	disinterested
distracted	distressed	enthusiastic
fearful	frightened	frustrated
furious	good	grief stricken
guilty	happy	held back
helpless	inadequate	incensed
indifferent	inferior	insignificant
invalidated	irate	lonely
loved	motivated	numb
optimistic	overwhelmed	panicky
positive	powerful	powerless
protected	remorseful	resolved
restricted	sad	satisfied
secure	selfish	shy
stuck	sure	thwarted
timid	trapped	unable

An example of how the affirmation affirms our potential and empowers us to act on our own behalf follows each affirmation listed.

I can do something special for myself today.

Whether it is to soak in a hot tub, sign up for a painting class, take a long walk, or do something else, it will be what I feel like doing.

The Creative Force supports me in discovering new things about myself.

I will ask myself what I may have discovered about myself today or this week because I know that my potentials and characteristics are always unfolding. I am growing.

My intentions are in accord with my greatest good.

No one will confuse me by telling me what my intentions are or by telling me that they are negative or questionable.

What others say and do has nothing to do with me.

I know that nothing others say and do against me is justified in any way. My knowing why others say and do what they say and do will not change them. However, my understanding of other's motivations helps me to be wary and to protect myself. I cannot change others, nor can I "help" them to realize what they are doing.

I remember to say "Stop it" to all abuse.

Since there is no reason to try to figure out why the abuse is occurring, I don't spend a second thinking or wondering about it.

The moment I hear anything hurtful I speak up quickly and very firmly.

Noticing the tone of voice and speaking up if it sounds sarcastic or rude helps me to respond appropriately.

I am growing more and more able to say no and yes to what I don't want and what I do want.

Rather than "make do" with what is only partly what I want, I wait to choose that which feels right for me, puts a smile on my face, and makes my inner child feel secure and sure.

When I act in accordance with what is true, the universe, which is always true, supports me.

Since we all came from the one first starburst, we are all a part of the whole and belong.

I do not let fear and doubt stop or dissuade me.

Feeling doubtful doesn't mean that I can't do what I choose to do.

I protect myself from dangerous and toxic people and situations by avoiding them.
My unfolding requires a nourishing atmosphere.

I listen carefully to my gut feelings, my intuition, my consciousness, which tells me who and what to trust and not to trust.
My intuition is always with me, so I can count on it.

I am more and more aware of myself.
By trying new things I learn more of what I like and don't like.

I bring like-minded people around me.
There are people who value what I value and who are good to be with.

I make better and better choices every day.
With every choice I see results and so can tell how I'm doing.

I have the courage and strength to actualize my intentions.
There is always something I can do toward my goals.

I stop and remember myself many times a day—breathe deeply, stand tall, and appreciate the great miracle of my existence.
I am glad that I haven't forgotten myself.

No matter how badly I feel, I can act to improve my situation.
Once I know I can act, I usually think of an action to take.

Today I let go of the past and focus my thoughts on a creative project or uplifting idea.
Fortunately, I am in charge of my mind and can focus my thoughts.

Watered by tears and fed with truth, my spirit revives.
My spirit thrives when my pain is released.

My good choices in the present make my "good luck" in the future.
When I am on my path, doors open where never expected.

My awareness of what I want and don't want, and what I like and don't like, increases daily.
Every day I make better choices as every day I know myself better.

I know that what is for my highest good is also good for those around me, because the highest good is not exclusionary.
When I do the best for me, it is the best for everyone.

I have talents that, like gifts, may be opened and used.
Even when I don't know them, my talents will surface as I follow my interests.

I am more valuable than diamonds or gold, so I protect myself accordingly.
The spirit of life at my center thrives in the shelter of my courage.

I do not have to explain myself to anyone.
No one is in charge of me.

Neither pride nor shame prevent me from seeking support and wise counsel.
When I feel validated and affirmed, I gain strength.

I take a stand and speak out on injustice to increase awareness, because injustice disempowers the human race.
When I speak up for what I feel is right, I am empowered.

I know that in the eyes of my Creator I am born of equal value to any being who has ever, or will ever, live on this planet.
Knowing my value helps me to act on my own behalf.

Wherever I have missed the mark, I forgive myself.
To sin is to miss the mark, to take a step off my path. It helps me learn that my path is a little to the left or a little to the right, and thus rediscover my direction.

Personal Power comes from within. I feel it as a Creative Force.
New ideas, new solutions, and new directions remind me of my personal power.

I touch the Creative Force when I discover creative solutions to my problems.
It is a very good thing that my creativity can never run out.

I touch my own center when I express myself in creative endeavors.
Nothing feels more like me than that which I originate.

I affirm my connection to the Creative Force when I acknowledge my own feelings.
Every acknowledgment increases self-acceptance.

I do more each day to meet my own needs.
My confidence grows as I gain satisfaction.

I take risks and have adventures, especially when I feel immobilized.
There is something new and interesting, maybe outrageous, to do.

I know that I can ask for assistance.
Other people often have solutions I haven't thought of.

I take myself seriously and pursue my interests.
My interests bring me satisfaction and are of more importance to me than to anyone else.

I bring balance into the structure of my days.
All of my needs are important. Income is important, but not at the expense of my health and well-being.

I refuse to let self-doubt stop me.
In order to thrive, I need to feel great faith in myself and then proceed as if I know the results will be beneficial. I won't know until I try.

I protect myself from all that brings harm.
I stay wary and aware with people I don't know well and walk away from any situation I'm not comfortable with.

I face the unknown with confidence.
As long as I can handle the next hour, I'm sure I can handle life.

I know that I can live with uncertainty, because change is the constant of the universe.
Sometimes I'd really like to know how certain things will turn out, but reality demands that I stay alert and appropriately responsive to whatever comes up at the moment.

I am connected to the Creative Force within.
I wouldn't be here if I weren't.

I am choosing for my happiness and tranquility.
The best combination for my soul right now seem to be happiness and tranquillity, so I will think about these qualities each time I make a decision.

I feel the abundance of my heart, and it is radiating out to the world around me.
Wherever I am I trust in the abundance of the universe, and I act as well to bring what I need to myself.

I see a clear, still pool within where I am reflected back, smiling and relaxed. I see a winner in that smile. I see knowing in that smile.
This vision fills me with trust in myself and brings me relaxation.

I feel a warm and protective blanket wrapped entirely around my heart.
Seeing myself so protected calms me and reminds me always to choose for myself not against myself.

I see a gracious world around me, filled with respect and dignity.
Before a thing can be, it must be known that it can be.

I am standing solid as a rock on my two feet in a secure place, and I hear laughter that is my own.
My personal symbols of security and strength bring me fortitude and courage.

I envision my state of being as secure, warm, full.
Wherever I am I bring my personal strength and creative resources. These are my security, my comfort, and my abundance.

I have great respect for myself and the work of my soul.
I honor every feeling felt and every insight garnered as the most important work I've done.

I surround myself with people who radiate positive energy and are secure, calm and strong.
Being wise to the ways of the world, I am very selective about what or who to trust or not to trust.

Affirmations can be about setting limits. Survivors can find out whether their mates are willing to respect them by affirming themselves and voicing the protection they seek. Following are some affirmations that declare boundaries by setting limits.

My mind is my sacred and inviolate space. No one may enter that space and tell me what I am thinking, feeling, or perceiving. If anyone presumes to tell me what I am thinking, or to tell me that I am not feeling what I am feeling, or to tell me what I am going to do or not do, they will have violated me in an unconscionable way.

My conscience is my sacred and inviolate space. No one may violate my conscience by presuming to be it, telling me what is right and wrong or good and bad for me. I am more and more aware. When I hear, "You should" this, or "You should" that, I refuse to accept it and I say so.

The tranquility of my home is my sacred and inviolate space. There will be no displays of rage, sarcasm, sneering, criticism, physical violations of any nature, kicking of the pets, firearms displays, tripping, tickling tortures, indecent exposures, threats, or breaking of property by anyone in my home. Any such violation of my sacred and inviolate space will be met with every legal remedy necessary to insure that my home remains tranquil and nourishing to the spirit of life at my center.

My path is sacred and inviolate. I will follow my path of increasing awareness, wholeness, and integration through the development of my creativity, talents, and resources. Any violation of my work through disparagement, trivializing, and ridicule shall be taken as a desecration of my being.

My motives are sacred and inviolate to me. I trust my intentions and will not accept anyone else's version of them.

We have been on a long journey with the Survivors. They have spoken their truth with strength and determination, and in so doing they have given us a vision of freedom. And even now, as this book ends, a new journey begins. This journey is a movement toward awareness, meaning, and purpose; it is founded upon the infinite value of the human spirit. To join in this journey, all we must do is speak our truth with courage and strength. Truth is what dispels the prejudice, shatters the illusions, and breaks the bonds of verbal abuse.

Bibliography

Letters Cited

All letters and related works quoted were contributed by women who have survived verbally abusive relationships, with the exception of Mira, age 8. All names and identifying circumstances have been changed, and any resemblance to persons living or deceased is purely coincidental.

For Further Reading

Bradshaw, John. *Homecoming: Reclaiming and Championing Your Inner Child*. New York: Bantam Books, 1990. This book will give you the tools to heal from the wounds of the past. A culmination of Bradshaw's works that gives you permission to care for and nurture yourself even as you grieve your losses.

Este's, Clarissa Pincola Ph.D. *Women who run with the Wolves*. New York: Ballantine Books , 1992. Women's wisdom was coded into stories over centuries. The author decodes these messages as she retells the stories for modern women. This work is energizing and inspiring.

Evans, Patricia. *The Verbally Abusive Relationship: How to Recognize It and How to Respond*. Holbrook, MA: Bob Adams, Inc., 1992. This book describes what is abusive and why. It takes the reader on a journey of recognition from the first clues of confusing feelings to the recognition of patterns in the verbally abusive relationship.

Flores, Bettina. *Chiquita's Cocoon*. Granite Bay, CA: Pepper Vine, 1990. Survivors of verbally abusive relationships recommend this book. It is directed toward supporting women in freeing themselves from abuse.

Jeffers, Susan. *Feel The Fear and Do It Anyway*. New York: Ballantine Books, 1987. If you take the steps Susan Jeffers recommends, you are sure to grow in confidence and self-esteem. If you want to take action in your life, this book is a must.

Keirsey, David, and Marilyn Bates. *Please Understand Me: Character and Temperament Types*. Del Mar, CA: Prometheus Nemesis Book Co., 1984. Surprisingly, after you score your answer sheet in this book, you will find your temperament and can read all about yourself.

Lindbergh, Anne Morrow. *Gift from the Sea*. New York: Vintage Books, 1978. A little book of wisdom about finding your center and understanding yourself.

Miller, Alice. *The Untouched Key*. New York: Random House, 1990. In this book we discover a key reason for the difference between the empathetic person and the abusive person. A fine introduction to Alice Miller's work.

Nicarthy, Jenny. *Getting Free*. Seattle: Pepper Vine, 1986. If you are looking for ways to take charge of your own life as well as information on emotional abuse, this book may provide some answers.

Sinetar, Marsha. *Do What You Love, the Money Will Follow: Discovering Your Right Livelihood*. New Jersey: Paulist Press, 1987. This book reveals the inner rewards (high self-esteem) and outer rewards (money) of integrating who we are with our life's work. This book is an excellent guide to authentic living.

— *Elegant Choices, Healing Choices*. New Jersey: Paulist Press, 1988. A nurturing and inspiring book that presents a way of recognizing the many choices we have in our everyday life to create the best for ourselves. I highly recommend this book.

Tieger, Paul D. and Barbara Barron-Tieger. *Do What You Are*. Boston: Little Brown & Co., 1992. If you aren't quite sure whether you should follow a particular career or make a change, or if there is something you never thought of that is really you, this book will lead you rapidly and pleasantly to the answers.

Appendix

The agencies in the following list may serve as a resource for support group programs and training programs for support group facilitation. Many agencies offer referrals to therapists who understand the control issue underlying verbal abuse.

These agencies are suggested because the causes of physical and verbal abuse are the same. *Even if you have not been physically abused*, you may contact these organizations.

This list has been derived from more extensive listings in the National Directory of Domestic Violence Programs: A Guide to Community Shelters, Safe Homes, and Service Programs. Compiled by the National Coalition Against Domestic Violence.

The list below offers two or more agencies in each state. Each, if not convenient, may refer the inquirer to a closer agency. The agencies are listed alphabetically by state. If you cannot find a program or service agency in your area, contact the national office of the National Coalition Against Domestic Violence.

The National Coalition Against Domestic Violence
P.O. Box 18749
Denver, CO 80218-0749
(303) 839-1852

The National Coalition Against Domestic Violence, the author of this book, and the publisher cannot be responsible for any claims of services made by programs listed, nor for the quality of services provided.

ALABAMA
Hope Place Inc.
Business (205) 534-4052
Hotline (205) 539-1000
P.O. Box 687
Huntsville, AL 35804

Montgomery Area Family Violence Program
Business (205) 263-0677
Hotline (205) 263-0218
Kiwanis Domestic Abuse Shelter
P.O. Box 4752
Montgomery, AL 36101

Sabrah House Black Belt Regional Domestic Violence Program
Business (205) 874-8711
Hotline (205) 874-8711
2104 Franklin Street
Selma, AL 36701

Spouse Abuse Network
Business (205) 758-0808
Hotline (205) 758-0808
P.O. Box 1165
Tuscaloosa, AL 35403

ALASKA
Kodiak Woman's Resource and Crisis Center
Business (907) 486-6171
Hotline (907) 486-3625
P.O. Box 2122
Kodiak, AK 99615

LeeShore/Women's Resource and Crisis Center
Business (907) 283-9479
Hotline (907) 283-7257
325 South Spruce
Kenai, AK 99611

ARIZONA
My Sister's Place
Business (602) 821-1024
Hotline (602) 821-1024
961 West Ray Road #4
Chandler, AZ 85224

Chrysalis Shelter
Business (602) 944-4999
Hotline (602) 944-4999
P.O. Box 9956
Phoenix, AZ 85068

Brewster Center for Victims of Family Violence
Business (602) 623-0951
Hotline (602) 622-6347
P.O. Box 3425
Tucson, AZ 85722

ARKANSAS
Abused Women & Children, Inc.
Business (501) 246 3122
Hotline (501) 246-2587
P.O. Box 934
Arkadelphia, AR 71923

Family Violence Prevention, Inc.
Business (501) 793-4011
Hotline (501) 793-8111
P.O. Box 2943
Batesville, AR 72503

Advocates for Battered Women
Business (501) 376-3219
Hotline (800) 332-4443
P.O. Box 1954
Little Rock, AR 72203

CALIFORNIA
Battered Women's Alternatives
Business (510) 676-2845
Hotline (510) 930-8300
P.O. Box 6406
Concord, CA 94524

Tri-Valley Haven for Women
Business (510) 449-5845
Hotline (510) 449-5842
P.O. Box 2190
Livermore, CA 94551

A Woman's Place
Business (219) 834-2232
Hotline (209) 722-HELP
P.O. Box 822
Merced, CA 95341

Mid-Peninsula Support Network for Battered Women
Business (415) 940-7850
Hotline (415) 940-7855
200 Blossom Lane, 3rd Floor
Mountain View, CA 94041

Haven House, Inc.
Business (808) 564-8880
Hotline (213) 681-2626
P.O. Box 50007
Pasadena, CA 91105-0007

Calavares Women's Crisis Line
Business (209) 754-3114
Hotline (209) 736-4011
Box 623
San Andreas, CA 95249

Option House, Inc.
Business (714) 381-3471
Hotline(714) 381-3471
P.O. Box 970
San Bernardino, CA 92402

Marin Abused Women's Services
Business (415) 457-2464
Hotline (415) 924-3456
1717 5th Avenue
San Rafael, CA 94901

Shelter Services for Women Inc.
Business (805) 964-0500
Hotline (805) 964-5245
P.O. Box 3782
Santa Barbara, CA 93130

Family Services of Tulare Co.
Business (209) 732-2514
Hotline (209) 732-5941
915 West Oak
Visalia, CA 93291

COLORADO
Boulder County Safehouse
Business (303) 449-8623
Hotline (303) 449-8623
P.O. Box 4157
Boulder, CO 80306

Safehouse for Battered Women
Business (303) 830-6800
Hotline (303) 830-6800
P.O. Box 18014
Denver, CO 80218

Volunteers of America Southwest Safehouse
Business (303) 259-5443
Hotline (303) 259-5443
P.O. Box 2107
Durango, CO 81302

The Resource Center's Domestic Violence Program
Business (303) 243-0190
Hotline (303) 241-6704
1129 Colorado Ave.
Grand Junction, CO 81501

CONNECTICUT
Battered Women Services
Business (203) 794-1624
Hotline (203) 748-5903
265 Main Street
Danbury, CT 06810

Women's Center of Southeastern Connecticut, Inc.
Business (203) 447-0366
Hotline (203) 447-0366
P.O. Box 572
New London, CT 06320

Stamford Domestic Violence Service, Inc.
Business (203) 965-0049
Hotline (203) 357-8162
65 High Ridge Road Suite 378
Stamford, CT 06905

Women's Crisis Center, Inc.
Business (203) 853-0418
Hotline (203) 852-1980
5 Eversley Avenue
Norwalk, CT 06851

DELAWARE
CHILD, Inc./Family Violence Program
Business (302) 762-6111
Hotline (302) 762-6110
11th & Washington Street
Wilmington, DE 19801

Families in Transition Center/People's Place II, Inc.
Business (302) 422-8058
Hotline (302) 422-8058
219 South E Walnut Street
Milford, DE 19963

DISTRICT OF COLUMBIA
D.C. Hotline
Business (202) 223-0020
Hotline (202) 223-2255
P.O. Box 57194
Washington, DC 20037

House of Ruth—"Herspace"
Business (202) 347-0737
Hotline (202) 347-2777
651 10th Street, N.E.
Washington, DC 20002

FLORIDA
Women in Distress of Broward County Inc.
Business (305) 760-9800
Hotline (305) 761-1133
P.O. Box 676
Fort Lauderdale, FL 33302

Spouse Abuse, Inc.
Business (407) 886-2856
Hotline (800) 892-2849
P.O. Box 680748
Orlando, FL 32868-0748

CASA
Business (813) 895-4912
Hotline (813) 898-3671
P.O. Box 414
St. Petersburg, FL 33731-0414

Harmony House Of Palm Beach County
Business (407) 655-6106
Hotline (407) 655-6106
c/o 901 S. Olive Avenue
West Palm Beach, FL 33401-6593

GEORGIA
Liberty House of Albany, Inc.
Business (912) 439-7065
Hotline (912) 439-7094
P.O. Box 273
Albany, GA 31702

Council on Battered Women
Business (404) 873-1766
Hotline (404) 873-1766
P.O. Box 54737
Atlanta, GA 30308

Safe Homes of Augusta, Inc.
Business (404) 736-2499
Hotline (404) 736-2499
P.O. Box 3187
Augusta, GA 30914-3187

Gateway House, Inc.
Business (404) 536-5860
Hotline (404) 536-5860
P.O. Box 2962
Gainesville, GA 30503

HAWAII
The Family Crisis Shelter, Inc.
Business (808) 959-5825
Hotline (808) 959-8400
P.O. Box 612
Hilo, HI 96720

Women Helping Women
Business (808) 579-8474
Hotline (808) 579-9581
P.O. Box 760
Paia, HI 96779

IDAHO
Women Against Domestic Violence
Business (209) 529-4352
Hotline (208) 525-1820
P.O. 323
545 Shoup Ave.
Idaho Falls, ID 83401/2

Mercy House
Business (208) 467-4130
Hotline (208) 465-5011
P.O. Box 558
Nampa, ID 83651

ILLINOIS
Mutual Ground, Inc.
Business (312) 897-0084
Hotline (312) 897-0080
P.O. Box 843
Aurora, IL 60507

Evanston Shelter
Business (312) 864-8445
Hotline (312) 864-8780
P.O. Box 5164
Evanston, IL 60204

P.H.A.S.E./W.A.V.E.
Business (815) 962-0871
Hotline (815) 962-6102
319 S. Church Street
Rockford, IL 61101

A Safe Place
Business (312) 249-5147
Hotline (312) 249-4450
P.O. Box 1067
Waukegan, IL 60079

INDIANA
The Caring Place, Inc.
Business (219) 942-8027
Hotline (219) 464-2128 or (800)
933-0466
426 1/2 Center Street
Hobart, IN 46342-4432

Sojourner/Julian Center
Business (317) 635-4674
Hotline (317) 635-7575
P.O. Box 88062
Indianapolis, IN 46208

Family Services Society, Inc.
Business (317) 662-9971
Hotline (317) 664-0701
Women's Services Division
428 So. Washington, Suite 327
Marian, IN 46953

A Better Way
Business (317) 747-9107
Hotline (317) 747-9107
P.O. Box 734
Muncie, IN 47308

Council on Domestic Abuse
Business (812) 232-0870
Hotline (812) 232-1736
P.O. Box 392
Terre Haute, IN 47808

IOWA
Family Violence Center
Business (515) 243-6147
Hotline (800) 942-0333
1111 University Avenue
Des Moines, IA

Council for the Prevention of Domestic Violence
Business (712) 362-4612
Hotline (712) 362-4612
P.O. Box 151
Estherville, IA 51334

Tri-State Coalition Against Family Violence
Business ((319) 524-8490
Hotline (319) 524-4445
P.O. Box 494
Keokuk, IA 52632

Council on Sexual Assault & Domestic Violence
Business (712) 258-7233
Hotline (712) 258-7233
P.O. Box 1565
Sioux City, IA 51102

KANSAS

Hope Unlimited
Business (316) 365-7566
Hotline (316) 365-3144
Box 12
Iola, KS 66749

Alliance Against Family Violence
Business (913) 682-1752
Hotline (913) 682-9131
P.O. Box 465
Leavenworth, KS 66048

SAFEHOUSE, INC..
Business (316) 231-8692
Hotline (316) 231-8251
101 East 4th St. Suite 214
Pittsburg, KS 66762

Cowley County Safe Homes, Inc.
Business (316) 221-7300
Hotline (316) 221-4357
P.O. Box 181
Winfield, KS 67156

KENTUCKY

YWCA Spouse Abuse Center
Business (606) 233-9927
Hotline (606) 255-9808 or (800)
544-2022
P.O. Box 8028
Lexington, KY 40533-8028

Women's Crisis Center
Business (606) 491-3335
Hotline (606) 491-3335
3221 York Street
Newport, KY 41071

Bethany House
Business (606) 679-1553
Hotline (606) 679-8852
P.O. Box 864
Somerset, KY 42502

LOUISIANA

Family Counseling Agency
Business (318) 445-2022
Hotline (800) 960-9436
P.O. Box 1908
Alexandria, LA 71301

Faith House
Business (318) 232-8954
Hotline (318) 232-8954
P.O. Box 93145
Lafayette, LA 70509

**Safety Net for Abused Persons
(SNAP)**
Business (318) 367-7627
Hotline (318) 367-7627
P.O. Box 10207
New Iberia, LA 70561

MAINE

WomanKind, Inc.
Business (207) 255-4785
Hotline (800) 432-7303
P.O. Box 493
Machias, ME 04654

**Caring Unlimited: York County
Domestic Violence Center**
Business (207) 490-3900
Hotline (207) 324-1802
P.O. Box 590
Sanford, ME 04073

MARYLAND

Abused Persons Program
Business (301) 986-5885
Hotline (301) 654-1881
Montgomery Co. DAVMH Services
4910 Auburn Avenue
Bethesda, MD 20814

**Citizens Against Spousal Assault
of Howard County MD, Inc.**
Business (301) 997-0304
Hotline (301) 997-2272
8950 Gorman Plaza Rte 108
Suite 116
Columbia, MD 21045

MASSACHUSETTS

Transition House
Business (617) 354-2676
Hotline (617) 661-7203
(Harvard)
P.O. Box 530
Cambridge, MA 02138

Help for Abused Women and their Children (HAWC)
Business (508) 744-8552
Hotline (508) 744-6841
27 Congress Street
Salem, MA 01970

Respond, Inc.
Business (617) 623-8370
Hotline (617) 623-5900
P.O. Box 555
Somerville, MA 02143

Daybreak Resources for Women and Children, Inc.
Business (508) 755-5371
Hotline (508) 755-9030
945 Main Street
Box 925
Worcester, MA 01610

MICHIGAN

Domestic Violence Project/S.A.F.E. House
Business (313) 973-0242
Hotline (313) 995-5444
P.O. Box 7052
Ann Arbor, MI 48107

Interim House
Business Hotline (313) 861-5300
P.O. Box 21904
Detroit, MI 48221

Domestic Harmony
Business (517) 439-1454
Hotline (517) 439-1454
P.O. Box 231
Hillsdale, MI 49242

CHOICES (Manistee Co. Domestic Violence Prevention Program)
Business (616) 723-6004
Hotline (616) 723-6004
P.O. Box 604
Manistee, MI 49660

Underground Railroad, Inc
Business (517) 755-0411
Hotline(517) 755-0411
P.O. Box 565
Saginaw, MI 48606-0565

Women's Resource Center
Business (616) 941-1210
Hotline (616) 941-1210
Traverse City
1017 Hannah
Traverse City, MI 49684

MINNESOTA

Women's Center of Mid-Minnesota
Business (218) 828-1216
Hotline (218) 828-1216
P.O. Box 602
Brainerd, MN 56401

Women's Coalition
Business (218) 728-6481
Hotline (218) 728-6481
P.O. Box 3558
Duluth, MN 55803

Women's Crisis Center
Business (218) 739-3359
Hotline (218) 739-3359
P.O. Box 815
Fergus Falls, MN 56538-0815

Harriet Tubman Women's Shelter
Business (612) 827-6105
Hotline (612) 827-2841
P.O. Box 7026
Minneapolis, MN 55407

MISSISSIPPI

Care Lodge
Business (601) 483-8436
Hotline (601) 693-4673
P.O. Box 5331
Meridian, MS 38655

Domestic Violence Project, Inc.
Business (601) 234-5085
Hotline (601) 234-7521
P.O. Box 286
Oxford, MS 38655

The Family Shelter
Business (601) 638-0555
Hotline (602) 638-0555
P.O. Box 57
Vicksburg, MS 39181-0057

MISSOURI

The Shelter/Comprehensive Human Services, Inc.
Business (314) 875-1369
Hotline (314) 875-1370 or (800) 548-2480
P.O. Box 1367
Columbia, MO 65205

Rose Brooks Center Inc.
Business (816) 861-3460
Hotline (816) 861-6100
P.O. Box 27067
Kansas City, MO 64110-7607

Family Violence Center, Inc.
Business (417) 865-0373
Hotline (417) 865-1728 or (800) 831-6863
P.O. Box 5972
Springfield, MO 65801

Survival Center for Abused Adults
Business (816) 429-2847
Hotline (816) 429-2847
P.O. Box 344
Warrensburg, MO 64093

MONTANA

Bozeman Area Battered Women's Network
Business (406) 586-1263
Hotline (406) 586-4111
P.O. Box 752
Bozeman, MT 59715

Safe Space
Business (406) 782-2111
Hotline (406) 782-8511
P.O. Box 594
Butte, MT 59701-0594

Lincoln County Women's Help Line
Business (406) 293-9141
Hotline (406) 293-9141
P.O. Box 2
Libby, MT 59923

NEBRASKA

Friendship Home
Business (402) 474-4720
Hotline (402) 475-7279
P.O. Box 30268
Lincoln, NE 68509

The Shelter
Business (402) 558-5700
Hotline (402) 558-5700
P.O. Box 45346
Omaha, NE 68104

NEVADA

Committee Against Domestic Violence
Business (702) 738-6524
Hotline (702) 738-9454
P.O. Box 2531
Elko, NV 89801

Temporary Assistance for Domestic Crisis Shelter
Business (702) 646-4981
Hotline (702) 646-4981
P.O. Box 43264
Las Vegas, NV 89116

NEW HAMPSHIRE

Carroll County Against Domestic Violence and Rape
Business (603) 356-7993
Hotline (800) 336-3795
P.O. Box 1972
Conway, NH 03818-1972

A Safe Place
Business (603) 436-7924
Hotline (800) 852-3388
P.O. Box 674
Portsmouth, NH 03801

NEW JERSEY

Providence House
Business (609) 871-2003
Hotline (609) 871-7551
P.O. Box 496
Willingboro, NJ 08046

Jersey Battered Women's Services
Business (201) 455-1256
Hotline (201) 267-4763
P.O. Box 363
Morris Plains, NJ 07950

NEW MEXICO

The Albuquerque Shelter for Victims of Domestic Violence
Business (505) 247-4219
Hotline (505) 247-4219
Box 25363
Albuquerque, NM 87125

Battered Women's Project
Business (505) 758-8082
Hotline (505)758-9888
P.O. Box 169
Taos, NM 87571

NEW YORK

Center for the Elimination of Violence in the Family
Business (718) 439-4612
Hotline (718) 439-1000
P.O. Box 279
Brooklyn, NY 11220

Long Island Women's Coalition, Inc.
Business (516) 666-7181
Hotline (516) 777-8833
P.O. Box 183
Islip Terrace, NY 11752

New York Asian Women's Center
Business (212) 732-5230
Hotline (212) 732-5230
39 Bowery, Box 375
New York, NY 10002

Victim Services
Business (212) 577-7700
Hotline (212) 577-7777
2 Lafayette Street
New York, NY 10007

Stop Domestic Violence
Business (518) 563-6904
Hotline (518) 563-6904
159 Margaret Street
Plattsburgh, NY 12901

Grace Smith House
Business (914) 452-7155
Hotline (914) 471-3033
P.O. Box 5205
Poughkeepsie, NY 12602

Alternatives for Battered Women, Inc.
Business (716) 232-3753
Hotline (716) 232-3753
P.O. Box 39601
Rochester, NY 14604

Rockland Family Shelter
Business (914) 425-0112
Hotline (914) 425-0112
300 North Main St. #301
Spring Valley, NY 10977

Vera House
Business (315) 425-0818
Hotline (315) 468-3260
P.O. Box 365
Syracuse, NY 13209

Jefferson County Women's Center
Business (315) 782-1823
Hotline (315) 782-1855
131 Franklin Street
Watertown, NY 13601

NORTH CAROLINA
United Family Services
Business (704) 332-2513
Hotline (704) 332-2513
P.O. Box 220312
Charlotte, NC 28222

Albermarle Hopeline
Business (909) 338-5338
Hotline (919) 338-3011
P.O. Box 2064
Elizabeth City, NC 27906-2064

Care Center Domestic Violence Program
Business (919) 323-4187
Hotline (919) 323-4187
1103 Hay Street
Fayetteville, NC 28305

S.A.F.E.
Business (919) 667-7656
Hotline (919) 838-7233
P.O. Box 445
Wilkesboro, NC 28697

Domestic Violence Shelter & Services
Business (919) 343-0703
Hotline (919) 343-0703
P.O. Box 1555
Wilmington, NC 28402

NORTH DAKOTA
Domestic Violence Crisis Center
Business (701) 852-2258
Hotline (701) 857-2000
P.O. Box 881
Minot, ND 58701

Family Crisis Shelter, Inc.
Business (701) 572-0757
Hotline (701) 572-9111
P.O. Box 1893
Williston, ND 58801

OHIO
Domestic Violence Project Inc.
Business (216) 452-8303
Hotline (216) 452-6000
P.O. Box 9432
Canton, OH 44646

Templum House
Business (216) 634-7501
Hotline (216) 631-2275
P.O. Box 5466
Cleveland, OH 44101

CHOICES
Business (614) 224-6080
Hotline (614) 224-4663
P.O. Box 06157
Columbus, OH 43206

First Step
Business (419) 435-7300
Hotline (419) 435-7300
P.O. Box 1103
Fostoria, OH 44830

Project Woman
Business (513) 325-3707
Hotline (800) 634-9893
1316 East High Street
Springfield, OH 45505

OKLAHOMA
New Directions, Inc.
Business (405) 357-6141
Hotline (405) 357-2500
P.O. Box 1684
Lawton, OK 73502

Domestic Violence Intervention Services
Business (918) 585-3163
Hotline (918) 585-3143
1419 East 15th Street
Tulsa, OK 74120

OREGON
Dunn House
Business (503) 779-4357
Hotline (503) 779HELP
P.O. Box 369
Ashland, OR 97520

WOMENSPACE
Business (503) 485-8232
Hotline (503) 485-6513
P.O. Box 5485
Eugene, OR 97405

Bradley-Angle House, Inc.
Business (503) 281-3540
Hotline (503) 281-2442
P.O. Box 14694
Portland, OR 97214

PENNSYLVANIA
Women's Services of Westmoreland County, Inc.
Business (412) 837-9540
Hotline (412) 836-1122
P.O. Box 246
Greensburg, PA 15601-0246

Women's Help Center, Inc.
Business (814) 536-5361
Hotline (814) 536-5361
809 Napoleon Street
Johnstown, PA 15901

Women's Resource Center
Business (717) 346-4671
Hotline (717) 346-4671
P.O. Box 975
Scranton, PA 18501-0975

RHODE ISLAND
Women's Center of Rhode Island, Inc.
Business (401) 861-2760
Hotline (401) 861-2760
45 East Transit Street
Providence, RI 02906

Elizabeth B. Chase House
Business (401) 738-1700
Hotline (401) 738-1700
P.O. Box 9476
Warwick, RI 02889

SOUTH CAROLINA
Sistercare, Inc.
Business (803) 799-5477
Hotline (803) 765-9428
P.O. Box 1029
Columbia, SC 29202

Spartanburg County SAFE Homes Network
Business (803) 583-9803
Hotline (803) 583-9803
163 Union Street
Spartanburg, SC 29302

SOUTH DAKOTA
Missouri Shores Women's Resource Center
Business (605) 224-0256
Hotline (605) 224-7187
104 East Capitol
Hughes Co. Court House
Pierre, SD 57501

Women Against Violence
Business (605) 341-3292
Hotline (605) 341-4808
P.O. Box 3042
Rapid City, SD 57709

TENNESSEE
Family & Children's Services
Business (615) 755-2840
Hotline (615) 755-2700
P.O. Box 6234
Chattanooga, TN 37401-6234

Safe Space/CCADV
Business (615) 623-7734
Hotline (800) 244-5968
P.O. Box 831
Newport, TN 37821

TEXAS

Genesis Women's Shelter
Business (214) 942-2998
Hotline (214) 942-2998
Drawer G
Dallas, TX 75208

Women's Haven of Tarrant County
Business (817) 535-6462
Hotline (817) 535-6464
P.O. Box 156
Ft. Worth, TX 76101

Family Crisis Center
Business (512) 423-9304
Hotline (512) 423-9304
2220 Haine Drive #32
Harlingenm, TX 78550

The Bridge Over Troubled Waters
Business (713) 472-0753
Hotline (713) 473-2801
P.O. Box 3488
Pasadena, TX 77501

Domestic Violence Prevention Inc.
Business (903) 794-4000
Hotline (903) 793-4357
P.O. Box 712
Texarkana, TX 75504

UTAH

YCC of Ogden/North Utah
Business (801) 394-9456
Hotline (801) 392-7273
2261 Adams Avenue
Ogden, UT 84401

Uintah Basin Counseling
Business (801) 781-0743
Hotline (801) 789-5584
559 North 1700 West
Vernal, UT 84078

VERMONT

Women's Crisis Center
Business (802) 257-7364
Hotline (802) 254-6954
Box 933
Brattleboro, VT 05302

Women Helping Battered Women
Business (802) 658-3131
Hotline (802) 658-1996
P.O. Box 1535
Burlington, VT 05401

VIRGINIA

Shelter for Help in Emergency
Business (804) 293-8509
Hotline (804) 293-8509
P.O. Box 3013
Charlottesville, VA 22903

DOVES, Inc.
Business (804) 799-3683
Hotline (804) 791-1400
P.O. Box 2381
Danville, VA 24541

Help and Emergency Response, Inc.
Business (804) 393-7833
Hotline (804) 393-9449
P.O. Box 1515
Portsmouth, VA 23705

Family Resource Center, Inc.
Business (703) 228-7141
Hotline (703) 228-8431
P.O. Box 612
Wytheville, VA 24382

WASHINGTON

YWCA Women's Support Shelter
Business (206) 272-4181
Hotline (206) 383-2593
405 Broadway
Tacoma, WA 98402

WEST VIRGINIA

Women's Resource Center
Business (304) 255-2559
Hotline (304) 255-2559
P.O. Box 1476
Beckley, WV 25802-1476

Family Refuge Center
Business (304) 645-6334
Hotline (304) 645-6334
P.O. Box 249
Lewisburg, WV 24901

WISCONSIN

Haven Inc.
Business (715) 536-9563
Hotline (715) 536-1300
P.O. Box 32
Merrill, WI 54452

**Regional Domestic Abuse
Services, Inc.**
Business (414) 235-5998
Hotline (414) 729-6395
P.O. Box 99
Neenah, WI 54957-0099

Advocates Inc.
Business (414) 375-4034
Hotline (414) 284-6902
P.O. Box 166
Saukville, WI 53080

The Women's Community, Inc.
Business (715) 842-5663
Hotline (715) 842-7323
P.O. Box 6215
329 Fourth Street
Wausau, WI 54402-6215

WYOMING

Crisis Intervention Services
Business (307) 587-3545
Hotline (307) 527-7801
P.O. Box 1324
Cody, WY 82414

**Teton Co. Task Force on Family
Violence & Sexual Assault**
Business (307) 733-3711
Hotline (307) 733-7466
Box 1328
Jackson, WY 83001

Index

Survey

I invite you, the reader, to answer the following questionnaire so that we might know more about verbal abuse in relationships. Your participation in this survey will be of value and is greatly appreciated. You do not in any way need to reveal your identity.

Please check the applicable response and add any additional notes you feel are appropriate. Return to:

Patricia Evans
Evans Interpersonal Communications Institute
P.O. Box 589
Alamo, CA 94507
Phone (925) 934-5972; Fax (925) 933-9636
E-mail EVANSbooks@aol.com
Web site: www.PatriciaEvans.com

Please include a self-addressed stamped envelope if you need a reply by mail. Return calls outside of the 925 and 415 area codes will be placed collect.

I thank you in advance.

I am
- ❏ female   ❏ male
- ❏ single   ❏ married

My relationship is
- ❏ heterosexual   ❏ homosexual

- ❏ I am now in   ❏ I was in a verbally

abusive relationship.

This abusive relationship is/was with:
- ❏ mate   ❏ parent
- ❏ adult child   ❏ employer
- ❏ other _____

I have been/was in the relationship _____ years.

I am _____ years old.

What has helped me most to survive verbal abuse is:

_____

_____

_____

_____

_____

What I need the most now is:

_____

_____

_____

_____

_____

If you are in an abusive relationship now, please answer the following:

I will probably stay in my relationship.
❑ Yes ❑ No ❑ Not sure

I will probably end my relationship in the future.
❑ Yes ❑ No ❑ Not sure

My mate wants to change.
❑ Yes ❑ No
❑ I don't know

Survey responses become the sole property of the publisher. Sorry, but materials cannot be returned.

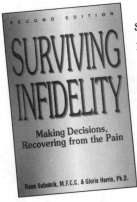

THE VERBALLY ABUSIVE RELATIONSHIP

How to recognize it and how to respond

Expanded second edition

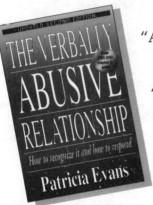

"A groundbreaking book."
—*Newsweek*

"This is a new day for America; the most important thing is to realize that you don't deserve to be treated that way."
—*Oprah Winfrey*

The Verbally Abusive Relationship helps a victim recognize manipulation and abuse at any level. It begins with a self-evaluative questionnaire and a description of the primary patterns of abuse. It then covers the categories of verbal abuse, such as accusation and trivializing, and explores the underlying dynamics of a verbally abusive relationship.

This book helps the victim establish limits and boundaries, and shows how to respond effectively to verbal abuse. There are also guidelines for recovery and healing, and steps for enhancing self-esteem.

The new edition covers the most recent developments in dealing with verbal abuse, as well as the latest information on:

- Working with therapists—how victims of verbal abuse can get the help they need

- Protecting children—how to deal with the impact of verbal abuse on families

- Answers to the questions readers ask most frequently about verbal abuse

Readers respond to *The Verbally Abusive Relationship*:

"This is the first time I have read a book about myself. It is so clearly defined—I believe this book has saved my life."

—*J. M., Danville, NH*

"Thank you for writing [this book] for me and thousands of women everywhere who suffer in abusive relation-ships."

—*B. L., Clayton, CA*

" I can't tell you how refreshing it is to finally read a book on this subject . . . Reading your book has con-firmed everything I have been feeling."

—*J. M., Pittsburgh, PA*

Trade paperback, 5¹/₂" x 8¹/₂", 224 pages, $10.95

About the Author

Patricia Evans has worked extensively in counseling and recovery settings with battered women. After her first book, *The Verbally Abusive Relationship*, was published, she received hundreds of letters from verbal abuse survivors around the world. Those letters form the basis of this book.